D0249143

"This very helpful book focuses on the two essential themes for anyone hoping to seriously witness to the gospel: personal dedication to Christ and effective techniques of communication with those experiencing the call of grace—in the language of our times.

"Catholic and Orthodox Christians will welcome this edition; anyone seeking to respond to the Holy Spirit will feel at home with it."

FR. BENEDICT J. GROESCHEL, CFR
Director of Spiritual Development
Archdiocese of New York; author of Spiritual Passages

"Becky Pippert breathes fresh life into the word *evangelism*, scrapes off all the barnacle-cliches and recruits us to join her in this glad work.

"The timing is strategic. At this moment in our history when popular spiritualities are eroding everything distinctive and unique about Jesus and following Jesus, Becky Pippert does it again— gives fresh impetus and clarity to the great privilege and urgent task of evangelism."

EUGENE H. PETERSON
Professor Emeritus of Spiritual Theology
Regent College, Vancouver, B.C., Canada

"This encouraging and helpful 'classic' is now even better with its penetrating observations and practical illustrations and instructions for sharing the gospel with people around us confidently and effectively. I especially appreciate the passion and wisdom that Becky shares from personal experience."

ROBERTA HESTENES
Senior Pastor, Solona Beach Presbyterian Church
Solona Beach, California

Rebecca Manley Pippert

Out *of the*
SALT
SHAKER
& into the World

Evangelism as a Way of Life

20th Anniversary Edition
Revised & Expanded

InterVarsity Press
Downers Grove, Illinois

InterVarsity Press
P.O. Box 1400, Downers Grove, IL 60515
World Wide Web: www.ivpress.com
E-mail: mail@ivpress.com

1st Edition: ©1979 by InterVarsity Christian Fellowship/USA

2nd Edition: ©1999 by Rebecca Manley Pippert

InterVarsity Press® is the book-publishing division of InterVarsity Christian Fellowship/USA®, a student movement active on campus at hundreds of universities, colleges and schools of nursing in the United States of America, and a member movement of the International Fellowship of Evangelical Students. For information about local and regional activities, write Public Relations Dept., InterVarsity Christian Fellowship/USA, 6400 Schroeder Rd., P.O. Box 7895, Madison, WI 53707-7895.

"The Bridge" in appendix 1 is based on Knowing God Personally, *by Sonlife Ministries, and is used by permission.*

Appendix 3 by Andrew T. Le Peau.

ISBN 0-8308-2220-8 (pbk.)

ISBN 0-8308-2233-X (cl.)

Printed in the United States of America ∞

Library of Congress Cataloging-in-Publication Data

Pippert, Rebecca Manley.
    *Out of the saltshaker & into the world : evangelism as a way of
life / Rebecca Manley Pippert. —2nd ed.*
        p.   cm.
    "Twentieth anniversary edition."
    Includes bibliographical references.
    *ISBN 0-8308-2233-X (cloth : alk. paper). — ISBN 0-8308-2220-8
(pbk. : alk. paper)*
    *1. Evangelistic work.   2. Witness bearing (Christianity)
3. Communication—Religious aspects—Christianity.   I. Title.
II. Title: Out of the saltshaker and into the world.*
    BV3790.P54   1999
    269'.2—dc21
                                                                              99-30885
                                                                              CIP

20   19   18   17   16   15   14   13   12   11   10   9   8

16   15   14   13   12   11   10   09   08   07   06   05   04   03

To Jim and Ruth Nyquist
For your exuberant love for God
and his people
and the way you have touched so many
with the beauty of God's grace—
I dedicate this book to you.

Contents

Introduction ——————————————————— 9

1 Sleepless in Spain —————————————— 15

2 Jesus—the Most Human of Us All ————————— 29

3 Jesus—the Lord of All ——————————————— 40

4 A Question of Love: *Being Radically Identified
   with the World* —————————————————— 55

5 A Question of Holiness: *Being Radically Different
   from the World* ————————————————— 71

6 A Question of Obedience: *Another Way of Knowing
   God* ——————————————————————— 83

7 Christ with Us ————————————————— 94

8 Practicing the Presence of Christ ————————— 102

9 Developing Conversational Skills————————— 117

10 Three Ways to Witness ———————————— 129

11 Cultivating the Soil —————————————— 138

12 Planting the Seed ———————————————— 155

13 Reaping the Harvest in God's Truth & Love ———————— *174*

14 Reaping the Harvest in God's Power ———————— *186*

15 Revealing Truth Through Reason———————— *197*

16 Revealing Truth Through Stories ———————— *212*

17 Revealing Truth Through the Power of the Spirit———— *222*

18 The Witness of Community ———————— *233*

19 Without a Vision the People Will Perish———————— *246*

Appendix 1: *Gospel Outlines* ———————— *261*

Appendix 2: *Books for Evangelism*———————— *270*

Appendix 3: *Study Guide for Individuals or Groups* ———— *273*

Notes ———————————————————— *285*

Introduction

Twenty years ago, when this book was first published, I thought I knew who my readers would be—my parents and grandparents were good for two copies; certainly Christian collegiates, since I was involved in campus ministry work at the time and I knew that world best; a smattering of American Protestants (considering that was my own point of reference); and those who had a special interest in the area of evangelism. Knowing that the word *evangelism* carried a negative connotation for many believers, I assumed the general readership would be small.

But now I am delighted that *Out of the Saltshaker* has reached a wider and more diverse audience than I had ever thought possible. Because of the book I have been invited to teach Catholic nuns, priests and laity; Orthodox Christians; Protestant clergy and churches of every denominational stripe; Christians from around the world; and those who struggle to be a witness where they are placed, be they Fortune 500 businesspeople, prison inmates, college faculty or even LPGA golf pros!

Why has a book about evangelism written from an American Protestant perspective reached such a wide audience? I hope it is partly because this book offers an understanding of evangelism that respects seekers and desires to have authentic relationships with them, and that encourages a style of witnessing that is true to one's own being. But I think there is a more basic explanation: regardless of our tradition or nationality, fear permeates most of our attitudes about evangelism.

Fear, not ignorance, is the real enemy of evangelism. We fear that our friends will reject or marginalize us if we speak about our faith; we fear that what we don't know will be exposed; we fear that our beliefs will be challenged. Back then, as well as today, we resisted shallow techniques for communicating truth to complex human beings. If nothing else, sheer frustration compelled many to explore fresh approaches to the subject of evangelism.

When Andy Le Peau from InterVarsity Press called and asked me to do a revision for the twentieth anniversary of *Out of the Saltshaker,* we talked about what would be involved. Freshen up the language, take out dated examples, add new stories where appropriate, and write one or perhaps two new chapters. Nothing to it. But then Andy proceeded to ask me several compelling questions: What have you learned in these past twenty years about evangelism that you didn't know when you wrote the book? Has the fact that we live in a very different culture from when you wrote it (after all, "New Age" wasn't even an identifiable category back then!) changed your approach to evangelism? Has your understanding of evangelism been altered, having now taught Catholics, mainline and evangelical Protestants, and Christians from many other countries?

As I pondered those questions, I began to realize this would not be a revision—this would almost be a new book! I want to thank Andy for the penetrating questions and even more for not panicking when I turned in so many new chapters! This proved to be one of the most wonderful writing experiences I have ever had.

So while the first half of the book updates and expands on what I wrote earlier about Jesus' life, values and lifestyle, on practicing the presence of Jesus and on the practical issues of conversational skills, what else is *different* about this version? Well, for one, I am. When I wrote *Out of the Saltshaker,* my work had been almost exclusively tied to campus work. But in these past twenty years God has given me extraordinary opportunities to teach and dialogue with believers from many different traditions and walks of life. That has enlarged and enriched my thinking enormously. And like most everyone else, during the past twenty years I have read more, thought more, prayed more and suffered more.

But the times are different too. And different times demand a rethinking and reevaluating of how best to communicate the gospel. We do so not to create a gospel that matches itself up to current trends, but we pay attention to our cultural context so that we may rediscover and proclaim the gospel with fresh power and clarity for "such a time as this."

Another difference comes from lessons learned from doing evangelism training these past twenty years. For example, one question I always ask people at an evangelism conference is, "Where do you get stuck in sharing your faith?" and the answers never vary. Whether I'm in Paris or Peoria, with Methodists or Mennonites, their answers always fall into three categories: 1 percent say it's their fear of being asked questions they can't answer; 1 percent say they are uncertain about the mechanics of evangelism such as how to lead a person to Christ; the other 98 percent say they feel their communication skills are inadequate. For example, this last group wants to know how to bring up the subject of God without seeming awkward, or they are worried about offending someone. Just that feedback alone tells us how important it is to provide not merely the content training of the gospel but the communications skills as well.

So chapters eleven through thirteen deal with such questions as these: What is the role of truth and how can we speak in the power of God's truth? How can we practice the presence of Jesus and mediate his love as we share the gospel?

At one conference, however, a woman raised her hand and said, "If evangelism is essentially a spiritual activity that is predicated on the supernatural power of God, then how do I tap into the Spirit's power? What is the role of prayer and fasting in evangelism? What are the spiritual tools I need to deal with spiritual deception or hard heartedness?"

What stunned me about her comment was that it was the first time anyone had ever raised this issue in all the years I've done training. Why is this? I think in part it is because we live in a culture so saturated with self, in which humans have placed themselves in the center for so long, that our natural tendency, even as Christians, is to focus on the human aspects of evangelism and not the divine. Yet it is God who takes the initiative to pursue seekers; it is his Spirit that converts; it is his gospel that saves. Evangelism is God's business from start to finish.

So I have included in this new edition, especially in chapters fourteen and seventeen, the role of the Holy Spirit in evangelism and what we can do to both depend on and demonstrate the power of God's Spirit.

What else has changed? In the original version the chapter on apologetics was geared more to answering the "modern" skeptic who shared a common understanding of truth. And I still deal with those types of questions in chapter fifteen. But today the "postmodern" person often approaches truth in a very different way. Therefore chapter sixteen offers an apologetic for the postmodern person who often cares more about whether something is experientially "real" than whether it is true.

Furthermore, we live in an age that is more conversion prone than we did in the 1970s. It's in vogue to consider oneself "spiritual" today. However, in the paradoxical "absolute relativism" climate in which we live, we quickly discover that spirituality is more akin to a "flavor-of-the-month club." When I wrote in 1979, the alternate forms of spirituality were hardly a blip on the screen. Today they are commonplace. So chapter seventeen includes new material on how to witness to those involved in New Age and other alternative forms of spirituality.

Last, when I wrote *Out of the Saltshaker,* my experience had been almost entirely with parachurch ministry. But the past twenty years have been rich in church ministry. Therefore the discussion of evangelism and the local church, in chapters eighteen and nineteen, has been expanded dramatically.

Out of the Saltshaker had its beginnings before I became a Christian. Even then I had definite thoughts about the way people communicated what was most important to them. I remember once encountering a zealous Christian. His brow was furrowed, he seemed anxious and impatient, and he sounded angry. Then he told me God loved me. I couldn't help noticing the difference between his message and his style. His message was arresting (me, a sinner?) but ultimately appealing (there is a God who loves me deeply). But his style put me off. I recall thinking, *If God is so good and loving, then why is this guy so uptight?* Surely the way we communicate a message of good news should be as marvelous as the message itself. This book is about getting our message and our style together.

Jesus tells us in the Sermon on the Mount that we are the salt of the earth. And he challenges us not to lose our savor—our saltiness. This means—among other things—that we are to be active in the world as his representatives. We are to get out of the saltshaker and into life itself—not to be trodden down but to be zestful witnesses to Jesus as Lord and Savior, as the one who alone gives life and meaning to a dying world.

I owe debts to many people for their contribution to this book. My mother Sue and my recently deceased father Bob, my brother Bobby and my sister Cathy gave me a joy and zest for life that were perhaps the greatest foundation I could have ever received for reaching out to others. They taught me how to celebrate.

It was Mrs. Ethel Renwick who first introduced me to Christ by reflecting both the love of God and the truth of the gospel. In March 1999, at eight-nine years of age, she went to be with the Lord. Her life illustrated at its best what this book is all about.

My experiences as an undergraduate student in Spain were also critical to my growth and understanding of evangelism. There I met Ruth Siemens. She demonstrated Christ's love to me and to all of my friends whom I would drag over for a meal. But it was the way she lived that taught me more than anything else about lifestyle evangelism. I respect her profoundly.

In the mid-1970s and early 1980s I worked with the collegiate ministry of InterVarsity Christian Fellowship. I am so grateful for their quality of leadership, their commitment to the integration of faith and thought, and the substantial and stimulating teaching I absorbed in those years, not to mention the fun of batting around ideas with fellow staff. That experience shaped and molded my life in significant ways. I am also grateful that I never had the slightest restraint put upon me because I am a woman. Rather, I was constantly encouraged to use and develop my gifts.

I am also thankful for the churches where I have been privileged to teach and train over the past twenty years. One great source of encouragement to me over the years has been meeting so many faithful and committed Christians, be they pastors, church staff or laity. Thank you for allowing me to be a part of your church families.

My thanks go as well to dear friends for their help and prayers as I prepared this new manuscript: Jim and Ruth Nyquist, to whom this book is dedicated, Fred and Elizabeth Catherwood, Bob and Martha Molenhouse, Doug and Adele Calhoon, Nancy Bergner, Kay York, Leanne Payne, Susan Yates, Sally Nevius, Jody McCain, Char Sandberg, Margaret Philbrick, David and Felicity Bentley-Taylor, and David and Pam Bock. I also appreciated the stimulating conversations I had on evangelism with InterVarsity Christian Fellowship staff Rick Richardson, Debbie Abbs, Mark Ashton, Jim Sire and Doug Schaupp.

Most of all, I thank my husband, Dick, for his love, his enthusiastic encouragement and his sacrificial assistance that really made it possible for me to write. I thank God for you every day. And my thanks go out as well to my wonderful children, Elizabeth and David, for your support, your love and your prayers.

A note about other people whose names appear in the book is also in order. Except for Mary (in chapter one), Stephanie (in chapter one) and Pat (in chapter eleven), the names of all of those whom I mention by only a first name have been changed to preserve their privacy.

What I wrote in 1979 still holds true today. I have a deep-seated conviction that much of our evangelism is ineffective because we depend too much on technique and strategy. Evangelism has slipped into the sales department. I am convinced that we must look at Jesus, and the quality of life he calls us to, as a model for what to believe and how to reach out to others. This basic assumption underlies both the content and the structure of this book.

It is my hope and prayer that those who read this book will indeed be freed to live as salt and light, that they will be Christ's agents of healing and hope in a broken world.

1

Sleepless
in Spain

....

Christians and non-Christians have something in common: we're both uptight about evangelism. Our fear as Christians seems to be *How many people did I offend this week?* We think that we must be a little obnoxious in order to be good evangelists. A tension builds inside: *Should I be sensitive to people and forget about evangelism, or should I blast them with the gospel and forget about their dignity as human beings?* Many Christians choose to be aware of the person but then feel defensive and guilty for not evangelizing.

A Year Abroad

I certainly felt that way during my junior year abroad at the University of Barcelona, Spain. Of course I wanted my friends to know God, but every time I got up courage to be vocal about Jesus, an image leaped into my mind of an aggressive Christian buttonholing an unwitting victim. As a nonbeliever I had thought many Christians were weird, spreading leaflets on street corners and nabbing strangers. I was terrified that if I said anything at all about Christ, my friends would consider me just as strange. And I would agree with them.

There was a part of me that secretly felt evangelism was something you shouldn't do to your dog, let alone a friend.

To evangelize, it seemed, required insensitivity and an inclination to blurt out a memorized gospel outline, without inhaling, to every stranger you met. It never occurred to me that my pre-Christian, unredeemed, almost common sense understanding about how to relate warmly to people might be valid. For instance, I knew how offended I had been as an agnostic when someone tried to push religion on me without even bothering to discover who I was or what I believed. That was a proper response, I see now, for I should be offended when I'm being treated as someone's evangelistic project instead of as a person.

Yet when I became a Christian I thought I was supposed to toss in my common sense perceptions in order to be spiritual. I thought I was called to "offend for Jesus' sake." How I thought I was supposed to share my faith went against my very grain. But, I thought with a somewhat twisted logic, *Is it really so much to ask that I turn people off as soon as I meet them, when you think of all that Christ has done for me?*

Still, I knew Christians were called on to do hard things. And because it was so hard to do, I thought such evangelism had to be spiritual. The result was that I would put off witnessing as long as possible. Whenever the guilt became too great to bear, I would overpower the nearest unsuspecting skeptic with a nonstop running monologue and then dash away thinking, *Whew! Well, I did it. It's spring and hopefully the guilt won't overcome me again till Christmas.* (And I'm sure my skeptic friends hoped the same!)

I witnessed like a Pavlovian dog. The bell would ring; I would get ready, activated, juices running; and then—*BAM!*—I'd spit it out.

Paradoxically, I also knew that unless I really cared for my friends, they would never be interested in the gospel. I was deeply moved by the way Jesus demonstrated compassion to the people he met. I wanted to do the same, although it didn't occur to me that this had much to do with evangelism. So I tried to reach out and care for the people God had placed around me. But I felt guilty for not giving a gospel outline to every nonbeliever I met.

It wasn't that I never spoke about my faith; in retrospect, however, I was far too paranoid about people's responses to me and consequently too silent.

But one thing hindered me from speaking: I felt that unless I gave a person the whole ball of wax, all at one time, then I wasn't "evangelizing." So when my friends at the University of Barcelona said they were curious about my faith and began asking questions, I thought, *Isn't that amazing! And I wasn't even evangelizing!*

So I approached my year abroad in Spain seeking to establish caring relationships with students and asking God to touch their lives. I also asked him to teach me how to share my faith and to free me from fear.

During this time I lived with Ruth Siemens, who was working for a collegiate ministry called the International Fellowship of Evangelical Students. She is a remarkable woman, abounding in gifts, intelligence, zest and vision. Every time we talked about my desire for ministry, she suggested I start a Bible discussion for my friends who were seekers. I acted as though it was an interesting idea, but to myself I thought, *Well, that's what happens when you've been in the Spanish sun for too long. You sort of lose touch with reality.*

But Ruth was persistent, and at last I decided to do it even though I thought it was ridiculous. She helped by coaching me on what to say as I asked my friends to a study on the life of Christ. Assuming I was having a conversation that related to spiritual things, I could say, "How would you like to come to a study on the biographies of Jesus Christ?" or "Wouldn't it be fascinating to examine the primary source documents to see for ourselves what Jesus has to say and who he claims to be?" or "Why don't we see for ourselves how Jesus views the role of women?"

When the actual moment arrived, my fear was so great that it reduced me to a rather catatonic state, and I mumbled, "You don't want to come to a Bible discussion, do you?" To my amazement and alarm, they all said that it was a great idea and that they were eager to come. The study was to begin the following Wednesday evening at my apartment.

One of the surprises was the kind of people who wanted to come. Without realizing it I had formed a mental picture of the people God would lead me to. I expected it to be the "likely" ones: those who seemed a bit passive or lonely or vulnerable. But it wasn't at all the anemic types that God brought into my life. They all seemed terribly normal. They were vital, opinionated, interesting people who had strong questions about the existence of God as well as about everything else. They were stimulating to be around, but I would never have thought of them as being open to spiritual things.

Then I met Mary. She was a young Irishwoman taking a year's study in Spain. She was bright and funny, with a ready quip for everything. I invited her over for a meal to meet my roommates. I wondered if she would be interested in coming to the Bible discussion. Suddenly, not knowing yet that I was a Christian, she said, "This has been the best month I've had all year! Do you know that I've talked three people out of being Christians this month!"

I gulped and thought, *Thank goodness I didn't ask her to the Bible discussion! I would die if someone like that ever came.*

The next day I ran into her after class and she smirked. "See you next Wednesday at seven. What a lark that will be! I wouldn't miss it for the world!"

I smiled blankly and said it would be great, but nothing registered in my mind. What was I doing next Wednesday? Wednesday! Oh, no—it wasn't possible. How did she find out? Who told her? Nothing could possibly be worse than Mary coming to the Bible discussion.

I raced to my apartment to tell Ruth and my other roommate, Kathy Lang, the terrible news. Then I noticed a sly expression on their faces. "OK," I demanded, "which one of you did it? Who betrayed me?"

They laughed but refused to confess. They said simply that God was answering my prayer by bringing spiritually open students to the Bible discussion. I moaned and wondered who else God would bring that would be as open and receptive as Mary.

One thing was clear: God and I had drastically different opinions about who was spiritually open. He seemed to have a special attraction to hard-core cases. And I felt he wanted to give them all to me.

I had Christians all over Barcelona praying. It was almost my first experience in leading a Bible discussion, and to do it with a group made up mostly of nonbelievers terrified me. Then Wednesday came. The study was to begin at 7:00. It was 7:15 when the doorbell finally rang. I opened the door, expecting to see the crowd, but there stood Mary, alone. She sauntered in, took a quick look around and said, "My, looks like you're really packing them in tonight."

"Ah, well, you know how busy everyone is, and it's early yet. Listen, make yourself at home and I'll be right back," I said as I dashed to the bathroom, closed the door and burst into tears. I felt so ridiculous. Everyone was praying for me and would ask how the Bible discussion went. And then of all people to show up, it had to be Mary.

I returned and decided to make polite conversation, thinking she would leave soon. Instead, she abruptly asked, "Why are you a Christian? How can you be a thinking person and reject your mind? It's intellectual suicide to believe something without any evidence to support it."

"Mary," I said with unexpected courage, "I couldn't agree with you more. I've always been amazed by people who can accept Christ blindly. But you know what else mystifies me? How anyone can reject Christianity blindly without bothering to investigate the evidence." And so began a two-hour conversation. We discussed such issues as the historicity of the New Testament documents, the uniqueness of Jesus and the evidence for the resurrection. It seemed largely an intellectual exercise to me.

Then as she was leaving I popped John Stott's book *Basic Christianity* into her hands. "Read it sometime in the next couple of years," I said as she walked out the door. No one could have ever accused me of using pressure tactics.

The next day the others who were supposed to come to the study apologized and said they had completely forgotten. But they promised they would be there next Wednesday. And next Wednesday came. I felt reassured. God wouldn't let me go through another experience like that. And once more I asked several Christians in Barcelona to pray.

So 7:00 came. Then 7:10, 7:15, 7:20, and finally the doorbell rang. I rushed to the door, eager to see my friends. I threw open the door, but only one person was standing there—Mary.

Once more she took a quick look around and said, "This Bible discussion is really dynamite, isn't it? Never seen such crowds."

That did it. This was the closest thing to martyrdom I'd ever experienced. "Mary, would you excuse me for a minute. I'll be right back," I said and rushed into the bathroom again. I couldn't believe it. This was the second week I had prepared the same passage. I had prayed every day. And the only "faithful" member was Mary!

I didn't understand, but I returned to Mary, hoping she would leave quickly so I could cry later. Instead, she said, "I read that book you gave me. I came to that chapter on sin and I wanted to hide under the bed."

It never occurred to me as she spoke that the Holy Spirit was convicting her of sin. I merely thought it was a strange but interesting response. She plied me with questions and told me a great deal about her life and her family. I began to glimpse for the first time who she was—a sensitive young woman who covered her questions and wounds effectively. I was moved as she shared her life, and I genuinely cared for her.

Still, her initial disdain and negativity toward Christianity intimidated me. I thought that perhaps God was seeking her. What I didn't see was that her badgering me with questions, her coming to the study, even her hostility and anger were signs that she was grappling with God.

Then came the bomb. She suddenly looked straight at me and said, "I feel like God is over there," as she gestured with her hand, "and I am over here. I've really wanted to know God all of my life. But how do I bridge the gap? What would I do if I wanted to become a Christian?"

I stared at her in disbelief. No one had ever asked me that question. I felt not only inept but terrified that at this crucial moment God wouldn't come through. I had wondered what I would do if this ever happened, but the same scenario had always plagued me: The person would ask me to become a Christian. I would say, "Fine. Let's just pray together and ask God to come into your life." We would pray and then she would say, "Uh, Becky, I hate to say this, but . . . um . . . I don't feel any different. I mean I feel just exactly the way I did before we prayed." I would secretly think, *Oh, how embarrassing!* but I would say, "Well, listen. Why don't we just try it again." We would pray again, but then she would tell me she still felt the same. Then I would say, "Well, look, it's Saturday. Maybe weekends are a busy time. Let's try it again next week." And I would escape as fast as I could.

Just the thought of facing such an episode made me quake. And here was Mary, asking me to help her, immediately, directly and now.

"Well, what should I do?" Mary asked me.

"Uhhhh, well, I guess you could, um, pray," I answered weakly.

"I don't know how. What should I say?" she persisted.

"Well, uh, you could tell God what you told me," I stammered.

"OK. When should I tell him?" she asked.

For the first time I brightened. "You can tell him the minute you get home," I replied, leaping from my chair and ushering her quickly out of the room. "As soon as you get home, just tell him everything," I said as I pushed her through the front door. "And read the last chapter of Stott's book on how to become a Christian," I shouted as she walked down the steps looking a bit bewildered.

I felt miserable. God wasn't asking John Stott to lead Mary to faith; he was asking me. And I felt I had failed. I had been ashamed and embarrassed. I felt inadequate and unqualified to help Mary. But most of all, I lacked the faith and the guts to believe that God actually would come through and that he could use me. So I tried to forget the entire incident. After all, maybe Mary had just had a bad day. She was probably feeling emotional and would have been terribly embarrassed later if I had done anything anyway.

The next day Ruth returned from a trip. As I recounted my experience with Mary to her, she became more and more excited. Before I could even finish, she interrupted, her eyes shining, and she said, "Oh, Becky, then you led her to Christ, right?"

And I answered, a bit subdued, "No, actually I led her out the door."

It was the only time I ever saw Ruth unable to cover her disappointment. "Becky! Why not? You've led other friends to Christ, haven't you?"

"Uh, well, let's see now. It's kind of hard to remember. I guess, uh, actually, uh, no."

Mary returned to my apartment a few days later. I was amazed to hear her account of what happened after she left me and amused by how she described it. She told Ruth in a somewhat exasperated tone, "Well, I asked Becky what to do and she told me to go home. But at least she said to read the last chapter of that book. Now listen, I really do believe this stuff and I prayed that prayer at the end of the book. Does that mean I'm 'in'?"

Ruth assured her that she was indeed a child of God. But I remained somewhat skeptical and waited to see the results. The results, by the way, were that Mary grew steadily and is a Christian to this day. It was apparent that God had been working on her a long time before I ever met her.

Being Yourself

Two feelings came from this experience. One was a feeling of failure. I think we could safely say that, by most standards, I had failed. I felt sadness over my lack of faith and courage—but not despair. In fact, my other feeling was hope. That experience made me realize that when God is seeking a person, he will not allow my fear, my feeling of intimidation or my lack of knowledge or experience to prevent that person from finding him. With all the mistakes, I still had seen the power of God at work overcoming my clumsiness and helping me speak to Mary.

The more I reflected, the more I realized that I couldn't have done it worse. And yet Mary had survived me! Even with all my mistakes, God had used me. Granted, I wasn't much more than a warm body sitting in front of her. But I had guided her to the right book. At least I had tried to answer her questions, and I genuinely cared for her.

This experience forced me to reflect seriously about my problems in evangelism. I had thought that only with a slick presentation, a polished formula and memorized verses could anyone be successful in evangelism. But I discovered that God was indeed glorified in my weakness.

If anyone had told me then that I would eventually be writing a book on evangelism, I would have laughed uproariously. The incongruity simply would have been too great. It has been a long pilgrimage with many failures from my experience with Mary to where I am today. And even now, when I speak on the subject of evangelism, I often sense people are breathlessly waiting for the same thing that I was: a new argument-proof, jelled approach, the magic formula that works on one and all or your money back. But even if I had such a formula to sell, it still wouldn't work.

Our problem in evangelism is not that we don't have enough information—it is that we don't know how to be ourselves. We forget we are called to be witnesses to what we have seen and know, not to what we don't know. The key on our part is authenticity and obedience, not a doctorate in theology.

We haven't grasped that it really is OK for us to be who we are when we are with seekers, even if we don't have all the answers to their questions or if our knowledge of Scripture is limited.

But there is a deeper problem here. Our uneasiness with non-Christians reflects our uneasiness with our own humanity. Because we are not certain about what it means to be human (or spiritual, for that matter), we struggle in relating naturally, humanly to the world. For example, many of us avoid evangelism for fear that we will offend someone. Yet how often have we told our skeptical friends that that's why we are hesitating?

At Sproul Plaza on the campus of the University of California, Berkeley, I met a female student one afternoon. Our conversation moved to whether we believed in God. It was an easy, almost casual talk. I began telling her about my faith in Christ, and she seemed interested. But as I became more enthusiastic about what it meant to be a Christian, she seemed to withdraw emotionally. Still, I kept on talking about Jesus—for want of knowing what else to do. But even though my mouth kept moving, I was very aware that I was turning her off. So there I was, having a private conversation with myself, trying to figure out how to stop, while I could hear myself talking to her about Christ.

Suddenly I realized how ridiculous all this was, so I said, "Look, I feel really bad. I am very excited about who God is and what he's done in my life. But I hate it when people push 'religion' on me. So if I'm coming on too strong, will you just tell me?"

She looked at me in disbelief. "I can't believe you just said that. I mean, I cannot believe you honestly said that," she answered.

"Why?" I asked.

"Well, I never knew Christians were aware that we hate being recipients of a running monologue," she answered. (So much for my evangelistic skill.)

"Listen," I responded, "most Christians I know are very hesitant to share their faith *precisely* because they're afraid they'll offend."

"But as long as you let people know that you're aware of where they're coming from, you can say anything you want!" she responded immediately. "And you just tell Christians that I said so."

Her response was perceptive. What she was saying was that when I told her I hated to be someone's evangelistic project, I was also establishing that we had a great deal in common: I didn't want to dump the gospel and she didn't want to be dumped on. That is a natural response, a human response and a shared response. What surprised her was that I was human, too, not some superdisciple whose feet never touch the ground. In fact, I am offended by the same tactics she is. So on the basis of our strong, common human bond, I was freed to communicate my faith.

God has given me increasing freedom to talk about him to others. But my experience with Mary made me realize that, although some of my friends had become open to God through my influence, no one had ever become a Christian in my presence. Even if they wanted to, I wouldn't let them! As I pondered my discomfort about evangelism, I discovered several things about myself.

For one thing, I was so afraid of being identified as a religious fanatic or a Bible banger that I often remained silent when the topic of God came up. How people saw me mattered more than how God saw me. Ironically, most people respect and respond to a person who has definite ideas and who communicates them clearly rather than to someone who seems apologetic and wishy-washy. My experience in Spain confirmed that.

When I was a student in Spain, I was amazed to see how "evangelistic" and bold the Marxists on campus were. Their style wasn't obnoxious, but they were convinced and it showed. They communicated their beliefs articulately and with zeal. As I watched students respond to them, I was surprised to see how open they were and how much respect they had for someone who really believed in something and was willing to stand up for it.

All of my paranoia about how I thought people would respond if I were bold about Christ had made me defensive. If I had gone to a religious retreat, I would stammer when asked, "How was your weekend?" Or I would tend to hide my Bible under other books so my agnostic roommates wouldn't think I was strange. (As if that kind of behavior would keep people from thinking I was strange!)

I was behaving this way, I told myself, in order to be sensitive to seeking friends. But to them I looked weird, and the Marxists seemed confident and convinced. I finally had to agree with the apostle Paul that if we fear God first, then we will try to persuade people (2 Cor 5:11). Whatever you fear (or supremely respect) the most you will serve. Fearing what people thought of me, I served them and it backfired. When I began to fear and respect God the most and then serve him, I felt a new freedom to share my faith, whether I won a popularity contest or not. I didn't feel called to be offensive, just more bold. And the irony was that, since I wasn't trying to please them first but God, people listened and wanted to know more.

I found out something else: I didn't understand other people's genuine desire. Although I saw the needs and emptiness in the lives of my friends, I couldn't imagine that it was Jesus Christ they were really searching for. Jesus was for "religious folk," not for my pagan friends. So because I never really expected them to respond to the gospel, they didn't.

This feeling was associated with my own self-doubt. I feared that Jesus was just "my thing." Wasn't it arrogant to suggest that my view was the only way? But as I grew to understand the nature of Christianity, I saw that our faith stands on historical data as well as subjective experience. Truth was the ultimate issue, not a feeling in my heart. God was asking me to stand not on my own ideas or emotions but rather on the person and work of Jesus Christ. If anyone was guilty of being offensive, it was Jesus—not me. Realizing this freed me from cowering when accused of being narrow. I could answer, "I know, and isn't it amazing that Jesus actually said so many scandalous things? People of his day were as offended by his claims as we are. Wouldn't it be intriguing to study him to discover why he felt justified in saying what he said?"

Still, I was paralyzed by the fear of offending people and forever ruining their chance of entering the kingdom. So I thought, "I'll just be nice and smile and hope they catch on." Well, Girl Scouts smile too, so that can't be all there is to witnessing for Christ. Furthermore, I realized that I was giving myself too much credit. What I was saying was that if I made one mistake or couldn't answer one of their questions, then it was all over. They were doomed. Their eternal destiny rested on my ability to know every answer. God might be eternal and powerful, but he could never again reach the person I had offended or the one whose question I could not answer.

It's odd. If you are sensitive enough to realize that you could offend someone, then offending others is probably not your problem. What I often see is this: sensitive people who run around saying, "I'm just so afraid of being insensitive." So they remain silent when what they need to be is more bold. Or instead of finding creative ways of expressing faith, they spend their time proudly pronouncing what they don't do. "I have never used gimmicks or buttonholed people like those others guys." It's easy to agree about how evangelism is done poorly. But how pleased is God going to be when he asks us what we have done with our lives and we reel off everything that we *didn't* do?

Finally, I saw that I had a problem talking about God naturally. I was fine until the topic of religion came up. Suddenly I felt as if I needed to sound spiritual, and instead of listening I would panic because I couldn't remember any Scripture verses. My hands would get clammy; my eyes would dart from side to side in the hope that no one else was listening; the tone of my voice would change and I would begin to talk "religiously." Then I would wonder why they looked so uncomfortable when we talked about spiritual things.

The truth is, *I* was the one whose tone had changed. My problem was that I didn't think God could be a natural, integrated part of an ongoing discussion about films, raising children, taking classes or gardening. When speaking to skeptics, I kept my discussion of God too compartmentalized and separated from "normal" living.

The Strength of Weakness

These new insights began to free me. Mary's growth and flourishing as a young Christian affected my faith and my ability to witness. But it was the conversion of another atheist friend of mine eight months later that brought fresh discoveries and permanent change into my life. I will tell that story later in chapter ten. But it was what Stephanie told me the night she became a Christian that startled me.

"At first I thought, *Fine, let Becky have her religion—that's her thing,*" she said. *"I'm not the least bit interested, but if that's her thing, then it's all right with me.* Then you invited me to dinner and before we ate you asked if we could thank God for the food. I thought, *Oh, how quaint.* Only you didn't just thank him for the food—you thanked him for me and our friendship. It touched me profoundly and unexpectedly. I'd never heard anyone pray so personally before, much less thanking God for *me*. I never thought you felt our relationship had anything to do with God. But then I caught myself and thought, *That's ridiculous—thanking someone who doesn't exist for me.*

"Then we went to the Bergman film and afterward you said you'd studied the very same concept that was in the film in the Bible that day. I never dreamed an ancient faith would have anything remotely in common with cinema! Another day you invited me to an objective, no-strings-attached study of the person of Jesus in the Bible. Fine. Only the trouble was—I was truly drawn to this figure called Jesus! He seemed so real as we would read about him each week. I found myself wondering what Jesus would say about different situations I'd find myself in during the week.

"But you know what affected me most? All my life I used to think, *How arrogant for someone to call himself a Christian, to think he's that good.* But then I got to know you—and Becky, you are far from perfect, yet you call yourself a Christian. So my first shock was to discover you 'blow it' like I do. But the biggest shock was that you admitted it, where I couldn't. Suddenly I saw that being a Christian didn't mean never failing, but admitting when you've failed. I wanted to keep Christ in a box and let you be religious during Bible studies, but the more you let me inside your life, the more impossible it became to keep the lid on Christianity. Even your admission of weaknesses drove me to him!"

That confession changed my life. What astonished me was that she had seen me in all kinds of circumstances—she had seen the real me—and it gave the gospel more power, not less. I had always thought I should cover up my doubts and problems because if she knew me she wouldn't become a Christian. But the more open and transparent I was (even with my weaknesses), the more real Jesus became to her.

Please get this straight. In saying we must be human with each other, I am not condoning sin. God calls us to obedience. I am not suggesting we share our weaknesses as if we were in a "competitive sinning" match in order to prove we are real. Sin isn't God's desire for humanity; loving obedience to him is. But so is humble confession when we fail. So our goal must be to live within the balance of aiming for full obedience and humble openness. The paradox I constantly experience is that as I allow people inside—to see who I am with the pain and problems as well as the successes—they tell me they see God. It's when I cover up (ironically, for "God's reputation") and try to appear "together," with no problems, that they can see only Becky.

I had to learn from experience what Scripture teaches in 1 Thessalonians 2:8: to share the gospel we must share our life, our very selves. If we don't grasp that Christ has freed us to be authentic, we will see evangelism as a project instead of a lifestyle. And we will tend to see non-Christians more as objects of our evangelistic efforts than as authentic persons.

I once asked a woman if she felt comfortable about evangelism. "Oh, yes!" she responded. "I do it twice a week." (Somehow it sounded more like taking multiple vitamins.) Evangelism isn't just something you "do"—out there— and then get back to normal living. Evangelism involves taking people seriously, getting across to their island of concerns and needs, and then sharing Christ as Lord in the context of our natural living situations.

The problem stems from our great difficulty in believing that God is glorified in our utter humanity rather than in our spiritually programmed responses. Most of us fear that who we are inside just isn't enough. So we cover up our honest questions and doubts, thinking we won't sound spiritual. But in doing this we forfeit our most important asset in evangelism—our real person. Not to accept our humanness means we lose our point of authentic contact with the world. We, of all people, should be offering the world a picture of what it means to be truly human. Yet it is often Christians who fear their humanity more than anyone else. When we get a good look at Jesus, we will see that it is not our humanity we need to fear.

2

Jesus—
the Most Human
of Us All

....

Our humanity is not our problem in evangelism. In fact, if we could learn how to be authentically human as God designed us to be, we would discover that our humanity is not a liability—it's an asset! The most human of all human beings had no difficulty with who he was.

Though Jesus shared God's divine nature, he also came to us as the first whole person since Adam and Eve before the Fall. It is Jesus then who provides for us the model of what it means to be human. By following his lead, we will not only take on more of God's character but also find ourselves becoming more comfortable with our humanity. As God frees us to be authentically human in the way he designed us, we'll discover that evangelism will begin to flow naturally from who we are.

Jesus, One of Us

Jesus told us that as the Father sent him into the world, so he is sending us (Jn 17:18). How then did the Father send him? Essentially Jesus became one of us. The Word became flesh (Jn 1:14). God became human. The implications of the incarnation are vast, but one area that greatly affects evangelism is this: Jesus gives us permission to be human. Yet we struggle to believe that God intends for us to be truly human. We think we must get dressed up in our Sunday best to talk with God. We're afraid that being made of flesh and blood meets with divine disapproval. The fact that we love to laugh, take a walk with a friend, sip tea and read a good book for the sheer pleasure of it is probably regarded from on high, we fear, with a cosmic frown. We forget that it was God's idea, not ours, to make us human. He did not fashion us as angels who operate only in the realm of the spirit, nor did he make us animals without will or reason. God made us *human.* How do we discover what it means to be authentically human? We look to Jesus.

The fact that God became human also affects the style in which we share our faith. God didn't send a telegram or shower evangelistic books from heaven or drop a million bumper stickers from the sky saying, "Smile, Jesus loves you." He sent a man, his Son, to communicate the message. His strategy hasn't changed. He still sends men and women—before he sends tracts and techniques—to change the world. You may think his strategy is risky, but that is God's problem, not yours.

In Jesus, then, we have our model for how to relate to the world, and it is a model of openness and identification. Jesus was a remarkably open man. He didn't think it was unspiritual for him (fully realizing he was the Son of God) to share his physical needs (Jn 4:7). He didn't fear losing his testimony by revealing to his disciples the depths of his emotional stress in the Garden of Gethsemane (Mk 14:32-52). Here is our model for genuine godliness. We see him asking for support and desiring others to minister to him. We must learn, then, to relate transparently and genuinely to others because that is God's style of relating to us.

Jesus commands us to go and then preach, not to preach and then leave. We are not to shout the gospel from a safe and respectable distance and remain detached. We must open our lives enough to let people see that we too laugh and hurt and cry. If Jesus left all of heaven and glory to become one of us, shouldn't we at least be willing to leave our circle of church friends or Bible discussion group to reach out to a friend?

There is also confusion about what it means to be spiritual. We feel it is more spiritual to take our seeker friends to a Bible discussion or to church than to a play or out for pizza. Just as we do not understand our natural points of contact with the world, so we don't understand our natural points of contact with God himself. Again, he made us human. He is therefore interested in every aspect of our humanness. It is the stuff of our humanity—the everyday grit and glory that we all encounter simply by walking out the door each morning—that God uses to shape a holy life within us. We dare not limit him, then, to Bible studies and discussions with Christians. He created life, and he desires to be glorified in the totality of all that adds up to life. And his power and presence will come crashing through to the world as we let him live fully in every aspect of our lives.

How can we relate to people in a way that will change the world? Jesus did it in two ways: by his radical identification with men and women, and by his radical difference. Jesus seemed to respond to people by noticing first what he had in common with them (Jn 4:7). But it was often in the context of their similarities that Jesus' difference came crashing through (v. 10).

As people discovered Jesus' profound humanness, they began to recognize his deity. God's holiness became shattering and penetrating as Jesus confronted people on their own level of humanity. But the point is that it took both his radical identification and his radical difference to change the world. So it will be for us.

Jesus the Delightful

One of the more fascinating aspects I've witnessed in recent years is the emerging phenomenon of white, middle-class, reasonably well-educated adults thirty-five to fifty years old who are returning to the fold or at least are willing to reconsider traditional Christianity. In the past they considered Christianity unenlightened, narrow and a retreat from postmodernism's complex reality. But with mature careers and young children and aging parents, they are slowly, quietly, privately searching for the deeper significance of life and the possibility that faith may offer hope to people like themselves with real lives and real burdens.

If I have learned anything over the past twenty years, it's that besides demonstrating the love of God to seekers, there is nothing more important than drawing them to consider Jesus. People simply don't know who Jesus is or what he is really like. When seekers look beyond their Sunday-school stereotypes and are willing to take a fresh look at Jesus, the scales from their eyes begin to fall. I've never seen a person yet who hasn't been fascinated to encounter the Jesus of the Gospels.

Even we who know him need to be refreshed and reminded. I reread the Gospels a while back out of a desire to "rediscover Jesus." I was a bit alarmed by several attitudes that I sensed increasingly among believers. One was that the Gospels are light reading for the spiritually young whereas the Epistles are the real meat and potatoes for the mature. Another was an attitude that focused only on the Gospels but manipulated Jesus into being the Lord of their particular cause—the environment, women's rights, religious tolerance or the like. These can all be valid causes, but they sometimes revealed more about the person advocating the cause than they did about Jesus.

If a disciple must first master the life of the Master, then we need to grapple in radical, accurate and penetrating ways with the Gospels as they reveal the person of Jesus. As I reread the Gospels, I was struck by how vastly different Jesus is from the common stereotypes that many people have about Christians.

For example, isn't one common stereotype that Christians are dour, with a holier-than-thou attitude toward anyone who doesn't share their beliefs? And we'd be their last choice to invite to a fun party! Yet look at Jesus. He liked to go to parties and to weddings. He was the kind of man people invited for dinner. And he came. He went to where people were.

Jesus was utterly delightful. He enjoyed people. When two men first approached him, they became tongue-tied and unsure of what to say (Jn 1:35-39). When Jesus asked them what they wanted, they responded, "Oh, well . . . we were kind of wondering where your apartment is." Now Jesus knew that how he decorated his apartment was not the burning issue in their hearts. But instead of delivering a sermon, he took them home with him, and they became his disciples. Later some of their relatives were among the first people he healed. But Jesus was more than merely charming; he cared about building a sense of family.

Jesus established intimacy with people quickly. It was partly because he was open but also because he understood people and wanted to establish rapport with them. He let people know that he had a sense of who they were and that he appreciated them. The first thing he did on meeting Simon was to give him a nickname. The first thing he told Nathaniel was that he recognized the basic honesty of his character. Jesus drew people. Some came because Jesus recognized who they were, others because they had glimpsed something of who he was. He was approachable; he wanted people to know it, and they did.

Children loved him. Adults were affected so much by him that some just wanted to touch his clothes. Why? They saw that Jesus loved them. His love was extravagant, almost reckless—never cautious or timid. And he talked of his Father's endless love.

The people of Jesus' day thought holy men were unapproachable. But Jesus' work was in the marketplace. He made people feel welcome and that they had a place. His life was a constant demonstration that there are only two things that really matter in this life: God and people. They are the only things that last forever.

Isn't another stereotype of Christians that we care far more about following the rules and getting converts than we care about people and their pain? Yet Jesus was profoundly compassionate. He cared deeply and was not afraid to show it. He was profoundly committed to setting people free and making them whole. He touched people at the deepest level. He wanted to heal not only blindness and leprosy but also the things that prevented joy and beauty and freedom and justice.

The Stoics may have been proud of concealing their tears, but Jesus never concealed his. He showed them plainly on his open face, whether he was weeping for a city or for a friend's loss. He healed people because he cared about them, not merely so they would follow him. He saw a woman weeping over the loss of her only son (Lk 7:11-17). No one asked him to do anything, probably feeling it was hopeless anyway. Moved with compassion, he took the initiative and brought the boy back to life. In fact, he even touched the bier on which the boy lay. As it was the Jewish practice to use the open bier, Jesus' touching it meant pollution according to ceremonial laws. But Jesus responded to human need first.

Once Jesus was on his way to heal Jairus's daughter, who was at the point of death. A woman who had been hemorrhaging for twelve years and had "endured much under many physicians" (Mk 5:26) suddenly touched his garment and was healed. Jesus had so much concern for her that he stopped long enough to find out who he had healed and to learn of her story. Can you imagine Jairus's anxiety as the long story unfolded? But Jesus listened patiently and lovingly.

On another occasion a leper came to Jesus, no doubt full of shame and wounds (Mk 1:40-45). Timid but desperate he said, "Well, if you want to, I think you could heal me." And Jesus, moved with compassion and looking at him steadily, said, "Oh, I want to," and healed him.

I was also struck by the practical dimension of Jesus' compassion. His feelings were no deeper than his practical concern. He healed Jairus's daughter, and at the moment of this stupendous miracle he simply told them to get her something to eat. His care was consistent. Never flashy, sometimes almost quiet. Even after his death, Jesus demonstrated the very same care. If I had been resurrected, I would have rented the Coliseum and hired the London Philharmonic Choir to sing the "Hallelujah Chorus." But in one postresurrection account we find Jesus making the disciples a little breakfast!

Another mistaken idea is that all Christians are judgmental and have little understanding or sympathy for the complexities of the human condition. Yet Jesus was perceptive. He had an extraordinary ability to see beneath the myriad layers in people and know what they longed for, or really believed, but were afraid of revealing. This is why his answers so frequently did not correspond to the questions he was asked. He sensed their unspoken need or question and responded to it instead.

Jesus could have healed lepers in countless ways. To the leper in Mark 1:40-45 he could have shouted, "Be healed . . . but don't get too close. I just hate the sight of lepers." He did not. Jesus reached over and touched him. Jesus' touch was not necessary for the leper's physical healing, but it was critical for his emotional healing.

Can you imagine what it meant to that man to be touched? A leper was an outcast, quite accustomed to walking down a street and seeing people scatter, shrieking at him, "Unclean, unclean!" Jesus knew that this man had not only a diseased body but an equally diseased self-concept. He needed to be touched to be fully cured. And so Jesus responded as he always did, with total healing for the whole person.

If someone had asked me in my agnostic days to describe what I thought Jesus was like, I would have readily given an answer. I pictured him as a sweet, kind man, his hair parted down the middle with a kind of halo effect. I thought he probably spent most of his time skipping along the shores of Galilee, humming religious tunes with his disciples—the kind of person everyone would love, especially your mother. I sincerely believed this and did not think it was the least irreverent. Granted, my biblical understanding stemmed largely from a Hollywood film director of the 1920s—Cecil B. De Mille—and Hollywood seems to have a knack for making spirituality and severe anemia almost synonymous. But even from the few Christians I knew, I sensed that Jesus was something of a limp wrist, and several of them certainly behaved that way.

Then one day I looked at the New Testament. Instead of a meek, mild Jesus, I found a man of profound passion—an extraordinary being, flinging furniture down the steps of the temple, casting out demons and asking people how they expected to escape the damnation of hell. He said such bland, innocuous things as "I came to bring fire to the earth" (Lk 12:49). G. K. Chesterton points out that even Jesus' literary style reflects his passion: "The diction used about Christ has been, and perhaps wisely, sweet and submissive. But the diction used by Christ is quite curiously gigantesque; it is full of camels leaping through needles and mountains hurled into the sea." Moreover, his style consists of "an almost furious use of the 'a fortiori.' His 'how much more' is piled one upon another like castle upon castle in the clouds."[1] After seeing this shattering personality who fills the Gospels, having gotten even a glimpse of him, I could never, never again say with casual indifference, "Oh, how interesting."

Jesus the Exasperating

How do the Gospels shatter stereotypes that people have about Jesus himself? For example, take the sentimental notion I mentioned above, the one that believes Jesus was always sweet and smiling, abhorred conflict and would never get angry or say anything that would offend. I've had skeptics willing to study the Bible with me just on the promise that there was a biblical story of Jesus getting so angry he threw furniture down the stairs!

For if my first impression of Jesus was that he was delightful, another equally forceful impression was that he was exasperating. Wherever he went, he produced a crisis. He compelled individuals to decide, to make a choice. In fact, he struck me as the most crisis-producing individual I had ever encountered. Eventually nearly everyone clashed with Jesus, whether they loved him or hated him.

A friend of mine has said that he always discovered a lot about a person when he knew who liked the person and who did not. In Jesus' case we have the story of the holiest man who ever lived, and yet it was the prostitutes and lepers and thieves who adored him, and the religious folk who hated his guts.

Why did he cause so much controversy? I will examine this more closely in later chapters. But partly it was his unabashed claims. In his address at the synagogue in Nazareth he read from Isaiah and then, as the congregants looked straight at him, said, "Today this scripture has been fulfilled in your hearing" (Lk 4:21). In other words, "It's become true now because it is fulfilled through me. You are looking at the fulfillment."

Characteristically, the first response was favorable as they "wondered" at his "gracious words." But on reflection they began to think, *Wait a minute. Isn't this Joseph's boy?* Then Jesus mentioned that prophets have always been rejected by the people. And within moments they became so outraged they tried to kill him. They struggled not only with who Jesus said he was but with who he said they were as well. He made them confront both themselves and him.

Or what about the common misunderstanding that Jesus' followers were drawn from the religious of his day? What a surprise when people discover that many religious leaders were profoundly offended by Jesus' understanding of religion and piety. The religious of his day were particularly incensed that he deliberately healed on the sabbath. But what do you do with a man who is supposed to be the holiest man who has ever lived and yet goes around talking with prostitutes and hugging lepers? What do you do with a man who not only mingles with the most unsavory people but actually seems to enjoy them? The religious accused him of being a drunkard, a glutton and having tacky taste in friends. It is a profound irony that the Son of God visited this planet and one of the chief complaints against him was that he was not religious enough. Do you realize, just for that quality alone, the appeal Jesus will have to skeptics? He is irresistible!

The religious of his day were offended because he did not follow their rules and traditions. He was bold and outspoken. He favored extreme change and valued what they felt was insignificant, which was largely the "unlovely." Jesus knew the power and prestige of the Pharisees, a key group of Jewish leaders. And he knew they expected people to show deference to them. But he loved the Pharisees and wanted them to see plainly who they were and how far many of them were from God's kingdom.

What did he say to them? Well, I think Jesus would have been my last choice as a speaker for a fundraising drive. To say he was not the master of subtlety would be to put it mildly. Imagine a scene in which you would gather all the powerful leaders and religious elite so they could hear Jesus give a talk. (Matthew 23 describes such a scene.) When they are seated, Jesus comes out and his opening words are "You bunch of snakes. You smell bad. You remind me of decomposed bodies walking around. You're hypocrites and blind guides. And I want to thank you very much for coming." It was not exactly a speech that endeared Jesus to the Pharisees, which was what the disciples pointed out when they told him with a sudden flash of insight, "We think you might have offended them."

But for those who loved him he was equally exasperating. He constantly kept smashing some of his own followers' expectations of what the Messiah should do. He simply did not fit their mold. He did not try to. They thought the Messiah would come in power and liberate Jerusalem. But the only power that Jesus demonstrated was the power of servanthood. His disciples wanted to know who would be first in terms of prestige. Jesus told them the first would be the greatest servant, for Jesus' own greatness was seen not in the degree to which he was elevated but in the degree to which he came down and identified.

Eventually even John the Baptist struggled with who Jesus was. He did not feel Jesus behaved as the Anointed One. John had taught that the Messiah would bring an age of judgment—but Jesus brought mercy. John felt the Messiah should separate himself from sinners and tax collectors (like the prophets of the past), not invite them for dinner.

Jesus put people into crisis by compelling them to do something. He commanded Peter to lower his nets for a catch of fish after he had caught nothing all night. He told the rich young ruler to sell all his possessions. He told a Samaritan woman, who he knew was living with another man, to go and call her husband. He insisted that John baptize him when doing so would violate John's understanding of the Messiah. He told the Pharisaical lawyer, who was far more interested in debate and discussion than obedience, to do what he understood and not to talk about it.

Last, there is the popular notion that Jesus was tolerant of all religious positions. Some people foist on him the modern view that all roads lead to God. But while some religious leaders might be self-effacing, Jesus was self-advancing. Other religious leaders often required their followers to obey rules or laws or "a way." Jesus said, "I am the way, and the truth, and the life" (Jn 14:6). Based on that we are asked simply to follow him. Jesus was a confident man. He was secure and he knew who he was. Jesus didn't make suggestions; he uttered commands ("come to me," "follow me," "drop your nets"). I think we can safely say that Jesus was hardly the victim of a poor self-image!

He believed he was the Son of God. All these traits—his delightfulness, his compassion, his sensitivity, his passion, his ability to establish rapport as well as to exasperate—sprang from the fundamental fact of his deity. He said he was the bread of life (Jn 6:35), the light of the world (8:12), and the resurrection and the life (11:25). He said, "The Father and I are one" (10:30). He informed people that knowing him was the same as knowing God (8:19), seeing him was the same as seeing God (12:45), believing in him was the same as believing in God (v. 44) and receiving him was the same as receiving God (Mk 9:37).

C. S. Lewis warns in *Mere Christianity* against the claim that Jesus was merely a good teacher but not the Son of God. John Stott also points out that Jesus could hardly have been a good teacher if he was so wrong about the chief subject of his teaching, namely, himself.

Let us suppose that I made the kind of claims that Jesus did and people began to say, "Isn't Becky terrific?! I mean, the way she forgives sins—she really has a style all of her own, doesn't she? And her ethics are so brilliant and impeccable! And what a superb teacher, not to mention her perfect, sinless life. There is one little problem. She does seem to be a little confused about her deity. But other than that, she really has it all together!" Now whom do you think they would lock up first, the people saying this or me? No one is a little confused about his or her own deity and is sane. Yet intelligent, well-meaning people say this about Jesus every day. So let us eliminate the option that Jesus was merely a good teacher. That was never left open to us.

But the continuing question that Jesus faced because of his claims and action was voiced the loudest by the Pharisees. They saw Jesus healing on the sabbath and asked, "Who do you think you are, healing on the sabbath?" And Jesus answered, "The Lord of the sabbath."

Which leads me to my last impression of this towering figure. How did Jesus justify his behavior and claim that seemed to eventually lead everyone into conflict or crisis? I think it could be stated briefly like this: "I do what I do because I am the Lord—and you are not. You follow me; I do not follow you." His answers were most often that simple. He said he was the Lord. He knew it. He lived like it. He acted like it. He wanted people to respond accordingly.

3

Jesus— the Lord of All

....

Once I was invited as part of a team to Stanford University to teach for a week on evangelism. I lived in a dorm with the students, and on the first day I met Lois. She was bright and sensitive—and skeptical about the existence of God. After we had several talks about God, I told her I was having a Bible discussion for the floor to look at the person of Jesus. She could come and examine the primary source material as critically as she would any historical document.

"OK, I'll come. But the Bible won't have anything relevant to say to me," she replied.

You Have No Husband

The next day I discovered Lois was living off campus with her boyfriend, Phil. To my great surprise he came with her to the Bible discussion. Not knowing her background, I had already decided to lead the study on the woman at the well in John 4. I began introducing the chapter to the group, noticed Phil and Lois sitting there, and suddenly remembered the passage dealt with a woman who had sexual problems. I feared Lois would think I had planned this just for her.

With a step of faith I frantically tried to think of how to avoid the crunch of the passage (though I was sure God had gotten me into this mess). Lois and Phil were seated close to my left. Thinking it would be better if Lois did not read the passage aloud, I asked each person to read one paragraph aloud in turn as we went around the circle. I called on Sally, who was immediately to my right, to start, calculating we would finish before it was Lois's turn.

To my dismay, a woman three seats away from Lois started reading. (I discovered later it was Sally's twin sister who happened to be sitting next to me.) Then Lois's turn came and she read the portion that says, "Jesus said to her, 'You are right in saying, "I have no husband"; for . . . the [man] you have now is not your husband.' " It was her first experience of reading Scripture, and her eyes grew as big as saucers while I hid behind my Bible!

"I must say, this is a bit more relevant than I had expected," she commented with considerable understatement. And as she saw with what sensitivity and perception Jesus interacted with the lonely woman, Lois's face showed how moved she was.

The next day Lois and I talked again. In fact, she came every day for the entire week to discuss faith and bring her questions. She was raised in a Japanese home with parents who were prosperous, well educated and morally conservative. She knew her parents would be mortified to know about her living situation. "Even though I think my parents love me, they never have been able to show it," she said.

"What drew me to Phil was my desperate need to be loved. He does love me, yet it feels like sand being poured through a sieve. My heart has this unslaked thirst for love that can't ever seem to be filled," she said sadly.

"Lois," I responded, "romantic love can be real and deep, but only if it is not asked to be what it isn't. It is not within Phil's power to give you a sense of being and purpose. No human can fill every inner crevice of our longings."

"So it's all a sick joke, right?" she replied. "Why do we carry such a hunger when it can never be met? I told him that I thought our love would give ultimate purpose and meaning to my life. I banked all my need for love in him. He's already told me that he feels an unbearable pressure to be all that I need. And it's odd, but even knowing that he loves me, my heart is still restless and unfulfilled. Can this immense wish to be loved ever be gratified?"

"Lois, your longing for love is very valid. But human love, for all its wonders, will never be able to handle the immensity of the task. It can go away or die or fail us at the precise moment we need it most. And if it is to meet our needs and longings, love must have a base."

"But what base is there that is big enough and stable enough to build our lives upon?" she asked.

"The only base we can really count on is God's love. That's what Jesus saw in the Samaritan woman. He recognized a woman who was thirsting for a love that would truly satisfy her and never leave her. So he directed her toward himself. Jesus knew that what the soul longs for is a safe home, a place where we are loved and known perfectly—and that can only be found in God."

Lois sat for a long time, taking in what I had said. Finally I broke the silence and said, "Lois, would you like to come home now? Would you like to ask Christ to come into your life?"

"Yes. But what do I bring to the equation?" she asked.

"All you bring to God is your faith and your willingness to let him be at the center of your life. Can you think of anything that would block Christ's rule in your heart?" I asked.

"No," she said.

"Well, I can think of one," I said. "What will you do about Phil? Loving him is not the problem. But desiring to please him over loving and obeying God first, is." Then we talked about how becoming a Christian isn't merely fire insurance; it's a living relationship that affects every aspect of our lives: values, lifestyle, sexuality.

As we talked, it became clear God had been pursuing her for a long time. There were tears and struggles followed by an utterly sincere prayer asking Christ to come into her life as Lord.

Immediately she said, "Becky, as a young Christian, I've got problems. I'll have to tell Phil and move out; I have no place to go; it's impossible to get a dorm room this late, and now I'll have to pay this month's rent in two places." So we prayed again, and as she left my room, I agonized over how such a young believer could handle so much.

After dinner the students who had attended the Bible discussion stopped me in the hall saying they were fascinated by the study on Jesus. Then we heard a noise and turned to see what it was. Here came Lois, slowly walking down the corridor, carrying several suitcases and smiling with tears streaming down her cheeks. I silently thanked God. I too felt the tears slip down. Seldom have I seen a more graphic picture of what it means to become a Christian. Everyone began asking her why she had left home.

"Oh, no, I haven't left home. I've finally found my home," she replied. "You see, today I became a Christian."

That one decision had far-reaching effects. That same night three women on the floor decided they wanted to become Christians. Another woman who had assumed she was a Christian realized she wanted no part of it if it demanded total commitment. The next day Lois was told she could move into a dorm (unheard of at such a late date), and she discovered her new roommate was a dynamic, mature Christian.

Three months later her boyfriend, Phil, became a Christian, and he too grew rapidly. He had been hostile over her conversion and furious with her for moving out. But after he was converted he told her, "Lois, if you hadn't been willing to obey Christ, even when you saw I was hurt and angry, I would have been forever dependent on you to meet all my needs—just as you had been dependent on me. Your obedience affected my eternal destiny."

Lois's conversion was profound for her friends as well as for her. She recognized that becoming a Christian had tremendous implications. She came to see that if Jesus is Lord, then the only right response to him is surrender and obedience. He is Savior and he is Lord. We cannot separate his demands from his love. We cannot dissect Jesus and relate to only the parts that we like or need. Christ died so that we could be forgiven for managing our own lives. It would be impossible for Lois to thank Christ for dying for her and yet to continue running her own life.

She also saw that submitting her life to Jesus involved a cost. Jesus discouraged enthusiasts from committing themselves to him until they had weighed the implications. "Follow me" was his repeated command. "But there could be no following without a forsaking, a renunciation of competing loyalties, of personal ambition, of material possessions, of family relationships (Lk. 14:25-33)," John Stott writes. "Before a person could follow Jesus, he had to repudiate himself and his right to organize his own life."[1]

Why Jesus Is the Lord God

One may ask, what right does Jesus have to ask for so much? How can he get away with it? The biblical answer is: because he is the Lord. This is what the disciples preached ("We proclaim Jesus Christ as Lord," 2 Cor 4:5) and how they told us to live ("In your hearts sanctify Christ as Lord," 1 Pet 3:15). He is Lord because of who he is: God incarnate, Lord of creation and Lord of life.

First, Jesus is God incarnate. Colossians 1:15 tells us, "He is the image of the invisible God, the firstborn of all creation." Hebrews 1:3 says, "He is the reflection of God's glory and the exact imprint of God's very being." And Colossians 2:9 says, "In him the whole fullness of deity dwells bodily." Commenting on this last text, Dr. Martyn Lloyd-Jones says, "There is nothing beyond that, He is the sum total of all the Divine attributes and power."[2]

C. S. Lewis puts it this way: "Then comes the real shock. Among these Jews there suddenly turns up a man who goes about talking as if He was God. He claims to forgive sin. He says He has always existed. He says He is coming to judge the world at the end of time. . . . And when you have grasped that, you will see that what this man said was, quite simply, the most shocking thing that has ever been uttered by human lips."[3]

But how do we see this shocking God side of Jesus' nature? Certainly the events of his birth are a good place to start: the angel announcing to Mary the virgin birth, or the wise men being guided by the star of Bethlehem, or Simeon and Anna identifying the baby Jesus as the Messiah to his astonished parents in the temple. Or think of Mary and Joseph unobtrusively making their way to Bethlehem without any fanfare. But when Jesus is born, all heaven seems to break loose! The heavens part, and angels burst into paeans of praise right in front of shepherds who were merely minding their own business. They're terrified, and who can blame them (Lk 2:8-14)? We also see the God side of Jesus' nature affirmed at his baptism when a voice from heaven is heard saying, "This is my Son, the Beloved, with whom I am well pleased" (Mt 3:13-17).

Second, Jesus is Lord because of his relationship to the universe. He is the Lord of creation. Colossians 1:16-17 says, "In him all things in heaven and on earth were created, things visible and invisible, whether thrones or dominions or rulers or powers—all things have been created through him and for him. He himself is before all things, and in him all things hold together." And Hebrews 1:3 teaches that by Christ all things consist. The Son is the agent of creation. He upholds "all things by his powerful word."

How do we see Jesus' supremacy in "things visible and invisible"? We see it when Jesus has a pointed one-on-one conversation with Satan himself. Satan tempts Jesus with everything he's got and is roundly defeated (Mt 4:1-11). We see Jesus' supremacy when the demons recognize him instantly and bow to his authority fearfully (Mk 1:23-28). We see it when Jesus takes Peter, James and John up to a mountain and, as he prays, his face begins to shine like the sun, his clothes become as white as the light, and Moses and Elijah appear and begin to speak to Jesus. As they discuss his impending death, a cloud envelops them and a voice from heaven is heard again: "This is my Son, my Chosen; listen to him!" (Lk 9:28-36).

Of course the disciples are terrified. Think of it. Earthlings have just been allowed a peek into that other unseen dimension called eternity. Not only that but they actually eavesdropped on a conversation among Jesus, Moses and Elijah! They were permitted that opportunity because of who Jesus is. What they heard and saw but only realized the full implications of later was that Jesus had existed prior to the prophets, his death had been planned before he ever came to earth, and Jesus was not only the Son of God but was ushering in the kingdom of God!

Third, Jesus revealed his God-nature in his authority over nature. The first miracle Jesus ever performed was at a wedding party. The wine had run out, so he turned the water into wine. What kind of label would you put on wine like that? "Glory!" from the Hallelujah vintage perhaps. Another time the disciples and Jesus were in a boat headed for the shore. Jesus was sound asleep when suddenly an awful storm arose. The wind and waves were so great that the boat began to sink. Experienced fishermen were alarmed. In desperation (and probably irritation at Jesus for sleeping and for suggesting they set out in the boat in the first place) they woke him up and said, "Teacher, do you not care that we are perishing?" And in the midst of this vicious storm, Jesus casually got up, looked at the lake and said, "Peace! Be still!" Then the wind ceased and there was a dead calm. If you think the disciples were feeling overwhelmed by the storm, think how they felt on seeing this! "They were filled with great awe and said to one another, 'Who then is this, that even the wind and the sea obey him?' " (Mk 4:35-41).

Finally, Jesus' deity is revealed in his authority over life itself. He is the Lord of life. "I am the good shepherd. I know my own and my own know me" (Jn 10:14). He created us. He understands human nature. He knows us thoroughly. He loves us and died for us. He is not only competent to direct our lives, but he has the power and authority to be the only true guide.

But how can we be sure that Jesus can be trusted to govern our lives? What would Jesus know, for example, about how to handle a person's hellish bondage to drugs or alcohol? What can Jesus do about the guilt and grief of past sins that haunt us? How can he help the anguish of a mother who aborted her baby years ago and still grieves the loss? What does he know about the complexities of modern relationships? The answer, as it turns out, is plenty.

The Gospels show that Jesus had immense authority over everything that wounds and destroys human beings. Those in deep bondage to evil he delivered; those suffering enormous guilt for their sins he forgave; those suffering illness he healed; and even the dead he raised to life. He did exactly what the text in Isaiah said the Messiah would do: "The Spirit of the Lord is upon me, because he has anointed me to preach good news to the poor. He has sent me to proclaim release to the captives and recovery of sight to the blind, to let the oppressed go free, to proclaim the year of the Lord's favor" (Lk 4:18-19; compare Is 61:1-2).

In the New Testament the lordship of Christ is no mere abstract principle. The Gospel writers illustrate as well as teach the principle. Mark does this through the idea of authority. Jesus began to teach, and the people were astonished, "for he taught them as one having authority, and not as the scribes" (Mk 1:22). Jesus showed authority over the spirit world as he healed a demon-possessed man. And the people were amazed, saying, "He commands even the unclean spirits, and they obey him" (v. 27). Jesus demonstrated authority over the physical body as he healed Peter's mother-in-law (v. 31). And Jesus also revealed his authority over death by restoring the daughter of Jairus to life (5:35-43). Jesus is Lord because of who he is.

Jesus also revealed his authority by forgiving sins (Mk 2:1-12). Here he moved into dangerous territory, for the people correctly realized one thing: "Why does this fellow speak in this way? It is blasphemy! Who can forgive sins but God alone?" Jesus answered, "But so that you may know that the Son of Man has authority on earth to forgive sins, . . . I say to you, stand up, take your mat and go to your home." And the people were all amazed, saying, "We have never seen anything like this!"

Of course, Lois did not realize the full extent to which Jesus is Lord. But she understood enough to know she could not follow him without obeying him. She either had to live under new management or forget about Jesus. I wish I could say that Lois is the norm. All too often, however, people say they believe in Jesus and their lifestyles betray their beliefs. Cathy, for instance.

Go Greyhound

When I did collegiate ministry, I frequently took the bus to visit the campuses where I worked. Once when I boarded the bus for Willamette University in Salem, Oregon, I found myself sitting next to a rather nervous-looking young woman. As it turned out, Cathy was only seventeen. During our conversation she told me she was a Christian from a Christian home. Yet she looked frightened and lost, and as I began probing, I discovered she was running away from home. She had used all of her money to buy a ticket to Salem; from there she planned to hitchhike to California. She had no money, she hadn't eaten for a while, and she was afraid.

We discussed her inability to get along with her parents, among other personal problems. When I asked how her faith in Christ affected her decision to leave home, I was disappointed (though not surprised) by her impoverished understanding of what it meant to be a Christian. At no point did she seem cognizant that following Christ involved letting him be the Lord in her life; she just described her faith in Jesus as a "neat feeling in my heart." As we talked about who Jesus Christ is and how he is Lord as well as Savior, she decided she wasn't willing for him to have that much control, though she fully believed he is God.

After arriving in Salem, I persuaded Cathy to let me buy her lunch, and during the next hour as we talked I silently but fervently prayed while she continued to insist on continuing her trip. I had previously scheduled appointments with students all day, but by merely observing me with her in the student union, they sensed the situation and realized I needed prayer. So the Christian students quietly prayed at several tables while I continued to talk with her.

Suddenly at 12:15 Cathy looked at me in surprise and said, "I can't believe I'm saying this—but I'm going to go home. And not because you want me to, or because I want to, but because I've decided to mean business with God. If Christ is going to be Lord of my life, then he'll have to call the shots and he'll help me work out my family problems." We rejoiced and thanked God together. We even prayed together in the student cafeteria as she committed her life to Christ in a new and total way.

Then I tried to catch up on my appointments while Cathy called her parents. She was certain they wouldn't have seen the farewell note yet. To her disappointment, her mother answered the telephone weeping because they had found the note and were frantic with worry. They had gone immediately to their knees in prayer asking God to protect her and bring her back. (They began praying, I discovered later, five minutes before her decision to return.) Then Cathy told them she had meant to run away from home, but "God put this Christian right next to me on the bus—it was spooky!" I laughed as she described me as "this woman who goes from one university to the next and just talks about God—all day long—and she even gets paid for it!" It was evident that God wanted her parents to read the note in order to bring healing in their relationships not only to God but to each other as well.

I put Cathy on the bus, and with a radiant face she thanked us all. (By now all of the Christians in the union were in on this drama!) I thought that would be the end of this episode, but there is an exciting sequel.

One month later Katey Finney, then an associate of InterVarsity Christian Fellowship in Portland, was sitting on a city bus next to an older woman.

When this woman discovered that Katey worked with InterVarsity, she said, "I love InterVarsity! One of their staff workers sat next to my runaway daughter, and she came back home to us. Consequently we talked and really listened to her, and we just sent her to California for a vacation. But as a result of that crisis, I realized I need to grow more in God. I feel I'm stagnating. Do you think we could meet again?"

The amusing thing is that a Greyhound bus driver who was a Christian heard the story and shared it at the Christian bus drivers' monthly meeting. (I didn't know such a group existed!) Later I was told that it had been an inspiration to them all, and they were grateful that I chose to "go Greyhound." Perhaps I should have asked for a "spiritual discount"!

A Question of Control

Cathy's story ended marvelously because of God's great grace. However, what is distressing to see as we consider Cathy's story is how little her faith actually affected the way she lived her life. The truth is, up until the point she decided to pray, it would be hard to see the difference between Cathy and any secular person. Why is that? How is it possible to say we believe in Jesus and yet see it make so little difference in how we live?

Cathy is a classic example of what we see all too often in the "modern" believer. Her faith operated exclusively in the realm of her personal, subjective, private experience. She said she was a Christian, but the truth is, she behaved like a modernist.[4] For example, she made her decisions essentially as a moral relativist—what was right was dictated by the situation she was in, not from any consideration of whether her behavior violated any absolute truths. She operated as an autonomous individual in assuming all the moral authority she needed in her decision to leave. That decision came from within herself, not from any revealed truth in the Bible. She exhibited a narcissism that focused on her own desires and personal needs, putting her will ahead of understanding what God's will may be. What made her vulnerable to behaving this way? She was unwittingly reflecting the characteristics of what our modern culture believes.

My point is this: if Christians are this influenced by our modern secular culture, then imagine the impact our culture has on those who don't believe in God. One of our great challenges in evangelism is how to convey the truth of the gospel to people who live in a morally relativistic culture. How do we communicate that what we believe must dramatically affect how we behave and the kind of person we become? Especially how do we do this to people who have little or no appreciation of what it means to say that anything is true? The complete loss of belief in any moral absolutes in our world today makes it difficult to understand that truth has any binding consequences. Our impoverished understanding of truth inevitably affects our understanding of what it means to call Jesus Lord.

Lois, the student from Stanford, was perhaps unusual in recognizing quickly the tie between belief in Christ and behavior. But how do we communicate Christ's authority and lordship to those who do not believe as we do, who do not accept Christ's lordship over all of life?

Clearly two things must be avoided. First, we must not be so anxious to get our friends across the goal line that we fail to present a clear and honest picture of Christianity. Unless seekers have as clear as possible an understanding of the gospel, both its costs and privileges, before they commit themselves to God, our harvest will be poor indeed. We must seek to communicate that salvation is tied to a relationship to the living Christ as Lord as well as Savior; it is tied to objective truth that demands a total response. Warm feelings and shivers are not enough; they are not even required.

Second, we must avoid the trap of legalism both in tone and content. It is vital that we help seekers see the connection between belief and behavior. Yet we mustn't communicate God as a distant tsk-tsking God who will have nothing to do with seekers until they get their act together. That leads only to despair.

Neither may we put roadblocks in the way of faith, demanding behavior that is based on our personal views of sanctification. A friend once told me that she felt unable to become a Christian because she loved to swim on Sundays. That, she was told by her parents, was an unforgivable affront to God. Her husband, who came from a less conservative background, said, "Oh, I knew Jesus didn't mind if I swam on Sundays; he just didn't want me to dive!"

How do we talk about Christ's rule over human life in a way that draws the seeker? One way to do this is by showing our friends that God's rule for our lives stems from his love for us and his desire for our best. In fact, following his commands helps us avoid heartache and pain.

Recently a collegiate friend of our family, a young man who is a gifted guitarist and singer, asked my husband and me to come and hear him sing in a coffeehouse. His lyrics reflected much of the sentiments of our age: disenchantment, alienation, disappointment and the deep longing to connect. One song dealt with his anger and pain over a recent breakup with his girlfriend. Some of the lines went something like this: "Someday you'll realize that you need to ask my forgiveness. What you did was so wrong, you'll even have to ask Jesus Christ to forgive you. And even if Jesus never existed, you'd better ask him anyway!" All right, I wouldn't encourage him to quit his night job to become a systematic theologian. But what was striking were his frequent allusions to religious metaphors. Clearly he was seeking to make meaning out of his life.

The next day he came over to our home and thanked us profusely for coming. Then he said, "You know, my mom doesn't like that song about my breakup with my girlfriend. She's into New Age stuff and says I shouldn't be putting out all that negative energy."

"Well," I responded, "you're not going to get anywhere by trying to pretend your anger isn't there. First, you have to own it—and it sure sounded to me like you've done that! But the next step is being sure you don't get stuck there. It's learning how to forgive—that's the hard part."

His eyes lit up and he said, "That's exactly the stage I'm in right now. But, man, it's hard to do! Sometimes I wonder if it's worth the effort."

"You know, Jack," I answered, "Jesus talks a lot about forgiveness. He tells us it's only reasonable for us to forgive others since we need God's forgiveness. But I think Jesus wants us to forgive so *we* won't be carrying around that smoldering anger inside of us. Forgiving others is also for our benefit."

"So Jesus was really arguing hedonism in telling us to forgive?"

"Well, actually, his argument is the exact opposite," I answered. "Hedonism says that if you feel like hating, then go right ahead. Go with your impulses. Jesus says that if we resist doing what we feel like—to seek revenge—and do what he says—to forgive—we'll end up truly free. Hedonism promises freedom and leaves us in bondage. Jesus promises freedom and delivers."

"Whoa! Gotta think about that. That would make an awesome song, though," he said shortly before he left.

What will happen next? I don't know. But what if he really tries to forgive her and then discovers he doesn't have the power to do so? Maybe he'll learn what most serious seekers eventually come to see—how impoverished human resources are. That insight is what prompted G. K. Chesterton to say, "Christianity isn't difficult—it's impossible."[5] In other words, what Christ calls us to do we cannot do apart from his empowerment. Once Jack comes face to face with his own limitations, he'll be more open to hearing about the One who has the power to transform his heart.

How did the opportunity arise to speak to Jack about Jesus? First, I didn't give him a sermon; I just showed up. Going on *his* turf showed him that my husband and I genuinely care about him. Second, listening to his songs enabled us to understand him better. I could hear his questions and struggles through the lyrics of his songs. I saw where he was hurting. There is great wisdom in the old adage "Scratch where it itches." Once I knew where his itch was, it was easy to help him see that not only did Jesus care about his struggles but Jesus had something relevant to say on the subject! What I hope will eventually draw Jack to consider Christ is that he saw, even if for only a moment, that Jesus understands the practical struggles of his life and cares about his pain. It was only a small beginning but a promising one.

The last thing Jack said to me was "I hate being controlled by my anger."

"Ah, there's the rub, Jack, because whatever controls us really is our god—even if we hate it."

"Well, I sure need to be controlled by a better god than this," Jack replied as he left.

The person who seeks power is controlled by power. The person who seeks acceptance is controlled by the people he or she wants to please. We do not control ourselves. We are controlled by the lord of our life.

If Jesus is our Lord, then he is the one to whom we submit, for he has the ultimate power. There are no bargains. We cannot manipulate him by playing "Let's Make a Deal." If he is Lord, the only option open to us is to do his will, to let him have control. Jesus remains Lord whether we accept him or not. His lordship, his essence, is not affected by what we choose. But our lives are drastically changed by our choice.

Jesus' ownership of our lives is not a control that manipulates us or takes away our dignity. Jesus never presumes things or decides things for people. He does not abuse or bully people. In fact, we find Jesus asking as many questions as people asked him. He does not decide what people need and then give it to them. He asked the blind beggar Bartimaeus, "What do you want me to do for you?" (Mk 10:51). He asked the paralytic, "Do you want to be made well?" (Jn 5:6). He asked Peter, "Who do you say that I am?" (Mt 16:15), "Do you love me?" (Jn 21:15) and "Do you also wish to go away?" (6:67). And he told his disciples, "If you love me, you will keep my commandments" (14:15).

Jesus always preserves our freedom. He allows us to choose him over all others. Jesus will not control us in the wrong way. Nor will he control us in the easy way, by making every decision for us. He governs our lives in the right way: by being who he is without compromise and by insisting we become all that we are meant to be. And he tells us this can occur only through following him, obeying him and maintaining a living, passionate kinship to him.

We are to reflect Christ and obey him not only because of who he is but because of who we have become. The very nature of God dwells in us now. As Oswald Chambers has said, "Jesus is ruthless in His demands and uncompromising because He has put into us the very nature of God."[6]

Summarizing God's purpose for human beings, the Westminster Shorter Catechism tells us that we are created to glorify God and enjoy him forever. God created us for himself. If we are living with any center other than Jesus, we will be living incompletely. So Jesus continually tries to help people see who or what controls them. That is why Jesus is far more interested in people's lives than in their God-talk. Your life, more than your words, will reveal what really controls you.

Jesus aimed for the point of control in his conversations. He knew that faith meant submitting to his authority, not merely getting him to do what we want. Jesus knew people liked him, enjoyed him, thought he was stimulating and really desired for him to be on their team. Jesus also knew that those are not the rules of the game.

There are problems in this issue of control. Either we are controlled by the wrong thing or we try to control Jesus by limiting him to our terms. Jesus will accept our faith, but he will never accept our controls.

Is Jesus' desire to be the Lord of our lives some little fetish of his? Why is it so important to him? Why should we want him to have control of our lives? Besides the fact that he deserves it because of who he is, he knows he is the only one in the universe who can control us without destroying us. No one will ever love you like Jesus. No one will ever know you better, care more for your wholeness and pull more for you. You don't need fifteen years of analysis to discover you are unrepeatable. The last breath Jesus breathed on this planet was for you. Jesus will meet you wherever you are, and he will help you. He is not intimidated by past failures, broken promises or wounds. He will make sense out of your brokenness. But he can only begin to be the Lord of your life today—not next Monday or next month but now.

And the great and joyful paradox is that while he totally transforms us, he makes us more ourselves than ever before.

4

A Question of Love

....

Being Radically Identified with the World

A person who earnestly desired to share Christ's love with his friends told me, "Don't give me any new formulas to witness naturally. I've tried everything. It just doesn't seem right to use surveys or steps on someone you know."

This person is typical of many. Christians say they want to communicate their faith naturally instead of seeming artificial or contrived. So in their pursuit of this they investigate every witnessing technique on the spiritual market.

"I'm not going to suggest a new formula," I said, "because I feel as you do that techniques aren't the most effective, especially for friends. Have you ever thought about looking more deeply at the life of Jesus? If you live by the same values and priorities he had, you will find evangelism happening naturally. It becomes a lifestyle and not a project."

When we develop a way of living that places a special emphasis on people, that demonstrates holiness and a dedicated obedience to God, we can't help but be effective witnesses. Evangelism will flow from our lives instead of

56 / OUT OF THE SALTSHAKER

from memorized techniques.

But this puts the burden on us. What did Jesus value? How important was love and compassion? What was his notion of holiness? What role does obedience play?

We can and will answer these questions in the next three chapters by looking at Jesus. In this chapter we will consider the way Jesus associated openly with notorious sinners and how this love of his can shape our evangelism. In the following chapter we'll examine Jesus' clash with the Jewish leaders of his day due to his very different definition of what it meant to be holy and to stand apart from the world. Then in chapter six we will see what difference it makes according to Jesus to know God not in a merely academic way but in a way that leads us to live out the truth we know.

All three of these areas are vital in evangelism. Let's begin then with the emphasis Jesus placed on love.

What Jesus Regarded as Important

There was a widely accepted notion among the religious people of Jesus' day that religious activity was what was truly pleasing to God. Jesus smashed that notion. Through both his life and his teaching Jesus proclaimed that the primary way to please God was through proper relationships.

Jesus was wholly concerned with God and wholly concerned with people. That is, according to Jesus, the human cause is God's cause. Jesus' lifestyle arose out of the simple truth of loving God, our neighbors and ourselves. His life was a constant celebration of the supreme value, dignity and preciousness of human life.

Malcolm Muggeridge once said in a lecture, "That there is more joy in heaven over one sinner who repents is an antistatistical proposition." Jesus had an antistatistical approach to people. He loved sinners. He demonstrated that everyone is someone to God. There were no little people, no hierarchy. He was not impressed with a pecking order (Mk 10:42-45) but with servant-hood (Jn 13:1-20). He identified with the unimportant, the weak and sinful, the poor and powerless. And because he identified with them, to his critics he became one. At his resurrection the first to witness his appearance were women, the powerless in his culture.

He once met a blind beggar, Bartimaeus (Mk 10:46-52). To everyone but Jesus, Bartimaeus was an insignificant pauper who wanted to interrupt the schedule of the king. But Jesus stopped everything and asked the people who had shouted at the beggar to get lost, to bring the man to him. Jesus not only served this beggar; he asked those who considered him insignificant to serve him too. What a humiliation for them!

Jesus took time to talk to children and to hold them (Mk 10:13-16). Children seemed to have a habit of crashing his meetings with adults. The disciples scolded them and told them to go away. After all, this was Jesus they were trying to see, a very busy and important man. But Jesus scolded the adults and told them their values were wrong. The disciples thought only "important people" should see Jesus. It took them a long time to understand that for Jesus any person was of supreme importance.

The teaching that life is relationships did not begin with Jesus. It is a fundamental biblical principle. To be is to be in relation to someone. The Trinity evidences this. In Genesis we see that God sought relationship with us. Then he gave Adam a mate because "it is not good that the man should be alone" (Gen 2:18). It is interesting to note that modern psychology is turning away from seeing mental health in terms of solitary individuals and instead viewing it in terms of the adequacy of human relationships. Since the advent of atomic physics the assumed idea that physical reality was one of particles floating in an empty void has been challenged and changed. At the heart of science itself "community, not competition, is the metaphor that most deeply informs the work of many biologists. Among physicists, the atom is no longer seen as an independent and isolated entity but as . . . a set of relationships reaching out to other things."[1] In other words, what scientists have discovered is that reality at its very core is communal, involving relationships. This new approach that we see in science and other fields is in some ways a return to the ancient Hebrew-Christian understanding of reality in the first place.

Why did Jesus so stress and demonstrate the necessity of a life that bears the stamp of profound love? Jesus said it reveals his Father's essence. Jesus was not loving and kind to others merely because he happened to be warm and considerate and had good role models at home. He loved people the way he did because he was doing his Father's will and demonstrating his character. He taught friends and foes alike that God has an extravagant, endless kind of love for people.

Royalty in Rags

In one exchange with the Pharisees (who were very troubled by Jesus' contact with sinners) Jesus painted the bleakest possible picture of their understanding of a sinner. He told the story of a Jewish boy who insulted and humiliated his father, left home and squandered his inheritance on immoral living. If that was not bad enough, he got so hungry that he found a job tending pigs. (What was a nice, orthodox Jewish boy doing around swine?) But then Jesus went one step further. This boy, no doubt raised in a kosher kitchen, got so hungry that he wanted to eat the pigs' food! Imagine the orthodox crowd's response to this wretched story. And finally the boy became so hungry that he decided to go back to his father because he was sorry and he knew his father would feed him. Hardly the most abject repentance we have ever read about!

And what was the father's response? Jesus has given us one of the most moving pictures of God in the New Testament. He told the Pharisees that even while the son was a long way off, the father saw him, broke into a run and with outstretched arms embraced him, kissed him and proceeded to dress him like a king. He did not care about getting his robes dirty. The boy had come home; that was all that mattered. It was time to celebrate, and the father threw a party.

Suppose a neighbor was to walk by this scene. Let's imagine this is what happened. He doesn't know that the father has just bestowed clothes and jewelry upon the boy. He sees the father standing with a guest garbed in an ornate robe used only for very special guests, usually royalty. Then as the young man gestures with his hand, the neighbor sees a jeweled ring sparkling in the sunlight. He notices sandals on his feet and a fatted calf being prepared for a feast. Then it hits him. The young man must be a prince! All the details add up: the robe, the ring, the festivity and excitement.

The neighbor wants desperately to go over and say hello, if only he could get up his nerve. But he is only a commoner, a nobody. Yet the father who owns the house seems so kind and generous that the neighbor decides to drop in for a minute and sneak in a hello. Maybe he can even get the guest's autograph. He slowly creeps up behind the two men. The father's arm is still around the shoulders of the younger man as they walk. They talk, but mostly the father listens intently to the young man. His eyes are wise and kind, and occasionally they brim with tears—it seems for joy. The neighbor thinks he has never seen anyone as delighted to see another person.

He decides that if the father is that excited to see this man, then he must be a very important person. So he approaches the two men and speaks hesitantly, asking if he can have the privilege of meeting this most honored guest. The father nearly bursts with pride and delight. The father would love for him to meet his guest. Slowly the beautifully robed young man turns around. But what the neighbor sees frightens him so that he nearly jumps back in disgust. For there in these beautiful robes, exquisite jewelry and sandals is a young man who looks half dead. He is grimy, unshaven and smelly. His face is sunken, and his jaundiced skin seems barely to hang over his bones. He looks diseased. The neighbor begins to feel a bit nauseous and makes a quick excuse to leave. The father is so full of joy that he scarcely notices that his uninvited guest has left abruptly.

Jesus made profound statements in his story. One is that all of us look like that prodigal son when we stand next to the Father. We all look diseased. But when we come to God and become his children, he dresses us in his royal robes of righteousness. The exciting thing Jesus teaches here is that once we come to him, once we belong to him, we are royalty walking on the earth. All of us have specks of his royal gold in us. We are all made in his image. That image has been marred, but never so marred that the specks of gold have been obliterated. And never so marred that God by his grace cannot redeem us and adopt us as his own special heirs. When we go out into the world, we ought never forget that we are interacting with potential royalty. We may be conversing with an heir apparent.

Jesus revealed the nature of God and the tremendous value he places on human life. He also made a powerful statement about the depth and magnitude of God's love for one disease-ridden sinful person. Jesus reached out to others in love and asks us to do likewise because we are called to mirror the nature of God himself. This is not a call to be affectionate and affable and sweet because it is such a nice thing to do. It is a call to love as God loves.

So deeply did Jesus stress the importance of having a love relationship that he said if we are at the altar and realize we are not at peace with a person, we are to quit doing anything religious. We are to leave the altar, and to the degree it is possible we are to become reconciled to that person (Mt 5:23). Jesus went further and said we are to love the unlovely, our enemies (v. 44). We are to love those who do not know the law, not curse them. God's love in us must extend across all boundaries.

A Neighbor's Love

Jesus also taught about the call to relationship in his conversation with a lawyer in Luke 10:25-37. An intellectual lawyer had come to Jesus with a rather ponderous question: "What must I do to inherit eternal life?" This reminds me of the five delightful years I worked with InterVarsity Christian Fellowship at Reed College in Portland, Oregon. Reed students by their own admission have a mentality all their own. They are brilliant, intense, verbose; they love spending hour after hour discussing ideas. They are devoted to study. They love probing the sublime, the esoteric and the metaphysical. The more obscure it is, the better they like it. Practical questions are considered a bit gauche; direct answers, unfortunate and simplistic. They would rather probe for the rare, esoteric pearls. The longer I have studied Pharisaical lawyers, the more I am convinced that the man talking to Jesus had the perfect profile of a Reed graduate.

These lawyers insisted on the primacy of learning. They delighted in any abstract discussion of the law. Ancient Galileans were constantly amazed that the Pharisees could spend hours discussing whether it was mint or rue that ought to be tithed. So along came an intellectual lawyer. He was theologically sophisticated and probably thought he would trap this rather naive carpenter into a great theological debate and dazzle him with his brilliance.

"What must I do to inherit eternal life?" Counsel asked. He probably had anticipated Jesus' every response except the one he actually got. Jesus did the one thing he had not counted on. He did not give him an answer but asked him a question instead (a model in evangelism we could well apply).

"What is written in the law? What do you read there?" Jesus asked.

Counsel answered, "You shall love the Lord your God with all your heart, and with all your soul, and with all your strength, and with all your mind; and your neighbor as yourself."

"You have given the right answer; do this, and you will live," Jesus replied.

Becoming defensive, Counsel asked, "Who is my neighbor?"

And so Jesus told him the now familiar parable of the good Samaritan. The dynamics in the story are fascinating.

Imagine the most brilliant person you know approaching Jesus rather smugly with an enormous theological question. Jesus responds with a question that forces him or her to recite an answer that person learned as a child. It is like saying, "That's a very good question. Now can you remember what you learned in third grade?" He or she answers quickly, feeling somewhat embarrassed and defensive. Now can you think of anything much clearer than the statement "Love your neighbor"? One would like to think a brilliant theologian might grasp its meaning.

What was this lawyer really reacting to? He wanted a nice, abstract religious discussion. He wanted to parade his knowledge before Jesus. But Jesus called him to act on what he knew. This is not an example of Jesus putting down intellectual thought. On the contrary, Jesus was a supreme intellectual here, for he knew that truth must be evidenced in one's life, not put away in cold storage. But for the lawyer it felt awkward and annoying. He wanted something sublime and esoteric—a rare pearl—not to be told to love some bland and insignificant neighbor!

So when Jesus became specific (as he always does), the lawyer tried to find a way to crawl out. "Well, what does it really mean to love my neighbor? The whole thing is so complex," he retorted. "I don't want to rush into anything. What if I went out and loved someone and he turned out not to be my neighbor? I think we need to study this, have a conference on it."

Instead, Jesus told the lawyer a story about neighborliness and asked him to identify the real neighbor. Then he concluded the conversation with these words: "Go and do likewise."

Jesus summed up life here in terms of a love relationship to God, to our neighbor and to ourselves. Before any religious activity, our lives are to bear the stamp of profound love. The priest in the parable of the good Samaritan did not stop to help the victim, perhaps because he was on the way to the temple. In other words, he thought more of religion than he did of that man. His actions reflected his theology.

It is always that way. Our sociology reflects our theology. The way we treat others reveals what we think God is like. Imagine the implications this has for evangelism! The way we treat others is critical. People will understand as much of the love of God as they see in our own lives. The first Bible many people will read will be us and how we live.

We are called, therefore, to mirror the love of God—a love that is so extravagant that we must never keep it to ourselves. We must spread it around. It is not a mushy love, all sentiment and no action. Jesus' love drove him deeply into the lives of people. He cared for their wholeness. When he went out into a day, he did not ask himself, *Is this my social action day, or do I give them the salvation message?* Jesus cared for people as he found them. So must we care for their wholeness—spiritual, social, psychological, you name it.

And how are we to love and be a neighbor to those whom we do not know (which constitutes the bulk of the world's population)? Love must be aggressively translated into simple justice. The call to a love relationship will involve much more than emotional empathy. It requires fighting against injustice. Again, our actions as Christians will reflect how just we believe God actually is.

But are we really supposed to love the unlovely? Are we meant to get involved with those whose lives are lived in opposition to God's standards? Shouldn't we stand apart from sinners and let our lives testify to God's holiness? Jesus and the Pharisees clashed over just this issue: does obeying God's laws require us to have only distant relationships with unbelievers? To understand this better we first need to examine the Pharisees, a religious lay movement in Jesus' day.

The Pharisees cared deeply about God and had more in common with Jesus than any of the other theological schools of thought of his time, yet some of them were his severest critics. Thus they have received a lot of bad press. There is a legitimate and necessary concern in much contemporary scholarship to portray Judaism (and Pharisaism) fairly and in its own terms. There is also a difference of opinion among scholars as to whether the conflict stories recorded between Jesus and the Pharisees were really as vociferous as many have portrayed them.[2] Nevertheless, the deep tensions and alternate visions of the destiny and responsibilities of Israel that Jesus and the Pharisees represent cannot escape our attention. Furthermore, as one scholar said, "The broad picture of the Pharisees in conflict with Jesus seems well rooted in the Gospel tradition. It also seems consistent with, and inevitable in the light of, their different understanding of the divine will."[3]

The irony of the Pharisees, who cared enormously about obeying the ceremonial laws of purity, is that according to Jesus they did not take the law seriously enough. The basic problem of the Pharisees, it appears, was that most of them were less concerned with the prophets (such as Hosea, Amos, Isaiah and so on) than they were with the priestly ceremonial laws (found in Deuteronomy, Leviticus, and so on).

What was the result of their exclusive emphasis on obeying the ceremonial laws of purity and their seeming neglect of the moral law—what Jesus called the "weightier matters of the law, justice and mercy and faith" (Mt 23:23)? It fed and eagerly encouraged the already existing social hierarchy. Their fervor for ceremonial purity led to an apartheid-type response to almost anyone who was not a part of their exclusive sect. There was strict separation from Gentiles and from Samaritans, and there was even an aloofness from fellow Jews who did not have the leisure to study the law as they did. The Pharisees desired solidarity with the educated, powerful and wise, and utter separation from the rest.

So why should we concern ourselves with an inner-Jewish debate that occurred two thousand years ago between Jesus and the Pharisees? Because their conflicts reveal issues that most religious people wrestle with even today. In particular, how involved should believers be with their unchurched friends? Furthermore, the list of warnings of the temptations faced by the spiritually mature are sobering: hypocrisy (Lk 11:38-41), distorted perspectives (v. 42), ostentation (vv. 43-44) and self-righteousness (18·0 14).

Most importantly, just as we must not abandon the law (including all of God's moral law in the Bible as well as the Ten Commandments) thinking it only has meaning for the people of ancient times, so neither does our obedience to God's law excuse us from having relationships with unchurched people. The call to relationship and the call to honor God's laws actually go well together. Our love for God, others and ourselves, and all the actions that this relationship entails, mirrors what the law is all about and what it is preparing us for. We honor God's standards because we have fallen in love with the Lawgiver!

If the Pharisees had properly understood the whole of the law, they would have understood the call to relationship. In fact, one of the most well-known passages of Old Testament law highlights this: "Hear, O Israel: The LORD is our God, the LORD alone. You shall love the LORD your God with all your heart, and with all your soul, and with all your might" (Deut 6:4-5). Instead, some of the Pharisees denied their relationship, as the young prodigal did to his father and subsequently as the elder brother did to his younger brother. And consequently the Pharisees had no message to the lost.

People or Programs?

I remember being with a Christian student on a beach during an evangelism training week. Bob and I met several religious skeptics and began talking about all sorts of things. Eventually the conversation got around to Christianity, and it was a lively and invigorating discussion. We even exchanged addresses before leaving. I was feeling very good about the conversation, but Bob seemed very quiet.

When I asked him what was wrong, he said, "I thought it was an absolute failure. There are four major points to the gospel and you only brought in two of them, and they weren't even in the right order!"

I said, "What were the names of the three people we met this afternoon?"

"Oh, I don't know," he said. "What in the world difference does that make? There were two females and one male. Or was it the other way around?"

I stared at him in disbelief and sadness. Here was a young man who genuinely loved God. He was exceedingly religious and sincere. I doubt that he ever missed his daily devotions. And yet he had missed the entire point.

He was sure his agenda, his four points, were the supreme value. Yet his program was so rigid that real live human beings could not penetrate it. We must beware of this kind of pharisaism, for it is so frequently the disease of the devoted. This student was so busy rehearsing his four points of salvation that he forgot that he was speaking to the very people Christ had come to save.

We must never forget that to be a follower of Jesus is to be dominated by love. We may not be well versed in Scripture or have a seminary background; we may be timid and unsure of ourselves; but we have arms and hearts that were meant to be used. We must ask ourselves, *Do I treat people as royalty walking the earth, including even my parents, my spouse, my roommate, the student on the floor that I can't stand? Do I believe that by merely seeing me God would break into a run and embrace me? Does my life reflect only religious activity, or does it bear the mark of profound love?* When our lives are characterized by the love of Christ, we can begin to interest people in the gospel.

It bears repeating: if we are going to arouse seekers' curiosity in Jesus, then we must demonstrate the love of Jesus. One of the challenges in learning how to love people is seeing beyond their emotional baggage and into their hearts.

A few years ago I was returning home after speaking at a conference. It was late, and I was exhausted and eager to get home. Initially I didn't notice that there was anything wrong with my car, but once I was on the interstate, I saw smoke coming from my engine. As I pulled over, I saw that the car behind me was pulling over too.

A couple got out of the car and asked what they could do to help. The man said that he was starting to pass me when he realized that I was having serious car problems. He said, "I told my girlfriend that if you were my sister I sure wouldn't want her to be stranded on the interstate at eleven at night."

I was overwhelmed by their kindness to me. We locked up my car and they drove me to a restaurant. From there I called a towing service and was informed that it would be at least one hour before a truck could come. (As it turned out, it was two hours.) I thanked the couple for all their trouble and told them to get on with their plans for the evening. But they insisted on staying with me until help arrived. So we sat down at a booth, ordered coffee and began to talk.

His name was Kurt, and he was a truck driver who drove all over the country. Her name was Carla. They had been dating long-distance for a year. She had just flown in to spend the weekend with him. As we began talking, they told me they were both divorced and both had children. Just by observing them I realized that they were in love but frightened about making another mistake.

Initially Carla was reserved, but as I began to ask about her life and especially about her children, the tragedy of her life came pouring out. She was heartsick over her daughter Val whose life experience had been one of unbelievable demonic darkness. Val had been on drugs since she was twelve, married at sixteen, and though she was only twenty-one years old, she had already been married twice and had attempted suicide three times. One of the most bizarre aspects of her daughter's short life was how many deaths she had witnessed. Both of her husbands had been killed, and Val's only child had a deadly disease. I've been told many painful stories in my life, but this truly was one of the worst.

"Carla, how on earth are you coping with so much pain? Where do you get the resources to handle all of this?" I asked.

"I don't think I am handling it well. I can't sleep at night. I smoke five packs a day. I just don't know what to do or how to help her," she answered in despair, inhaling deeply on her cigarette.

"Well, first you begin by caring for yourself. You won't be able to give much to Val unless your own cup is filled," I answered.

About this time Kurt received a telephone call on his cellular phone and excused himself to answer it.

Carla went on, "You know, Becky, I've done everything I can think of to help my daughter. Several years ago, when Val was still living at home, I realized that I had to get my own act together if I was going to be able to help her. I decided to change jobs so I could be there for her."

"What is your job now?" I asked.

"Oh, I'm a bartender. I just knew I had to have something with more stable hours," she answered matter-of-factly.

Of course, the obvious question was, What in the world did she do before she decided to clean up her act and become a bartender? I didn't have to wait for the answer.

"You know, a lot of my friends thought I was crazy to change jobs. You know, since my other job had shorter hours and better pay. I dunno, somehow I just didn't feel being a stripper was a good role model for my daughter," she said in utter seriousness.

It may have been my imagination, but I gulped so hard on my next sip of coffee that I was sure everyone in the restaurant heard it. But by God's utter grace, I don't think my expression changed.

"Well, I can certainly see your point. What you did sure makes sense to me," I answered as if I heard this every day.

"I just don't know where to turn. Val was just released from the hospital last week after trying to take her life again. Oh, Becky, I love her so much and I feel so helpless," Carla said as tears began flowing down her cheeks.

It was amazing to behold. At first glance Carla had an appearance that was hard, almost cold. Just one look at her and it was obvious that her life had been very difficult. Yet as she began to share her life, with all its catastrophic pain, her entire countenance changed. Her appearance became soft and vulnerable. What did I possibly have in common with a stripper-turned-bartender? Carla had a mother's heart. She loved her daughter just as I love mine. That connection alone was a powerful one.

"Listen, Carla, all I can offer you is what has helped me through the most difficult times in my life. Carla, you were never intended to go through this much pain alone. Nobody is expected to handle all of this without help."

"You mean, I should see a shrink or something?" she said as she wiped the tears from her cheeks.

"First, you need to turn to God. He's there, Carla, and he loves you very much. Before you can offer Val comfort, you need to be comforted by the Lord."

"You know, I do believe in God even though I don't know him very well. The other day when I got the call that Val had slit her wrists, I asked myself, *Does God ever get involved in the messes we make in our lives?*"

"Oh, Carla, getting involved with our human mess is God's specialty! In fact God *solved* the human mess by sending his Son, Jesus. Jesus got right down into the trenches of life with us. He died for all of our messes, Carla. And he wants you to turn to him and let him carry this horrible burden for you."

"How would I even start with God? I've made such a complete screw-up of my life."

"You start by telling God exactly that. Tell him you are sorry for all your sins. Ask him to forgive you. Thank Jesus for dying on the cross for your sins. Then ask him to come into your life. From that point on, you will have God's Spirit living and working through you. You won't be trying to help Val alone; God will be reaching out to her through you. But you can't minister to Val unless you allow God to minister to you first," I said.

"I can't imagine what God must think of me," she said sadly.

"Carla, God sees everything about all of us. He sees where you've blown it. But he also sees how much you care and how hard you are trying to help your daughter. He knows that you were willing to change jobs just to help Val. He loves you, Carla. And he wants to come into your life so he can make you the Carla you were intended to be. The Bible says that when we become Christians, he makes us into oaks of righteousness. We become strong and centered and people can come and find rest and comfort in our branches, because we are rooted in the love of Christ."

"Oh, how I would love to be an oak," she said wistfully. "How do I find out more about this? What can I read? And what can I give to Val that will help her?"

"The most important thing you can do for Val is to make your own commitment of faith. But I was thinking about what to send you as a thank-you gift for your enormous kindness to me. May I send you a Bible in a translation that's easy to understand? And I'd like to send you a book of the psalms for Val to read. It's a paraphrased version that I think will speak to Val's heart. Would you like me to send it?" I asked.

"Oh, very much! Let me give you my address. Well, come to think of it, the place where you should send it is to my bar," she answered, looking sheepish.

"Sure, just give me the address," I answered as I got out my pen.

"Uh, well, it's not exactly something I'm proud of. But we named the bar something that would get people's attention," she said. Then she told me the bar's name. Suffice it to say, it verged on the pornographic.

As I was writing it down, Kurt came back to the table to tell us that my help had arrived. As we walked into the cold winter's night, I turned to both of them and thanked them from the bottom of my heart for their generosity and kindness. As I was about to leave, Carla suddenly hugged me with an intensity that almost made me cry. Then she whispered, "Do you think hotel rooms still have those Gideon Bibles? I thought I might start reading it tonight."

My continual amazement, as I engage in the task of evangelism, is how profoundly I am blessed. It is not an experience in which I have something to give but nothing to receive. It's not an experience in which they are changed but I remain unchanged. The truth is, I am as affected by my encounter with them as they sometimes are with me. As I engage in evangelism, I find it's not only *their* needs that are met; *mine* are too. God's intention is to bless us both—the giver of the truth and the receiver. I was incredibly moved by the selfless sacrifice that Kurt and Carla made. They helped me in a real time of need. Imagine, they were on their way to a romantic interlude, and they interrupted it because, as Kurt said, "What if that stranded woman were my sister?" When we allow others to minister to us, it makes our relationship with seekers more authentic.

That isn't to say that the experience of evangelism is always painless. As I enter into the stories of others and listen to their pain, it is very difficult to hear of lives so torn apart by the destructiveness of sin.

Furthermore, as I listen carefully and try to understand their questions about faith, it sometimes feels threatening and uncomfortable. But there is fruit from such an experience. For it forces me to delve deeper into the Bible to try to understand what the Scripture teaches in light of their questions. It makes me more dependent on God as I ask him to show me the way with the particular person I am talking to. The result is that I almost always come away with a deeper understanding of the richness of the gospel. I am changed by our encounter because now I understand biblical truth in a fresher or deeper way than I did before. There are no two ways about it: evangelism is exciting!

Evangelism is also rewarding because it blesses other believers too. The first thing I did the next day was to go to my favorite Christian bookstore and send Carla her gift. There is a marvelous woman working at the store who truly has the appearance of the quintessential "little old lady"—but looks are deceiving! She often sends books for me after I've been on a speaking trip, so when she saw me, her face lit up and she said, "I can't wait to hear the story!"

She loved the story, and as she was about to write up the order, she said, "OK, now where am I mailing this to?" I suddenly remembered the name of the bar and I was horrified at the thought of telling her, especially at her age. "OK, brace yourself," I said as I told her. She immediately burst into the most glorious smile and said, "Can you *imagine* this Bible going to any better place? Praise God!" Then she lifted the Bible in the air, and waving it heavenward, she prayed, "Lord, let your word go forth and bring light, healing and the saving knowledge of Jesus Christ as it goes to . . . to . . . to . . . well, I'm not going to say where, but you know, Lord!" Now that's my kind of Christian!

5

A Question
of Holiness

....

Being Radically Different from the World

I recently saw a remarkable film called *The Apostle* whose central character, Sonny, is a Southern, "Holy Ghost-filled" evangelist and preacher. Sonny is a fiery, vital man whose relationship to Jesus is equally passionate in nature. Sonny loves his church; he loves to preach the gospel, to evangelize and to pray. We see him lead people to Christ, and in one of the most moving scenes in the film, we watch him respond to the greatest crisis of his life by wrestling with God in prayer through the night.

His crisis comes when he discovers that his wife (the church organist) is having an affair with a younger pastor. In an unguarded moment Sonny picks up a baseball bat and hits the young pastor so hard it knocks him unconscious. (Eventually the young pastor dies from the blow.) Knowing he will be arrested and possibly sent to prison, Sonny escapes to a faraway place, leaving his wife and children behind, and becomes a fugitive from the law. There he has a "dark night of the soul" experience, and though it's unclear exactly why, he emerges feeling cleansed and restored in faith.

He starts a new church in a new town, and it soon becomes evident he has not lost his flair or fire. The church worship scenes are so authentic that it feels as if Robert Duvall, the director, writer of the screenplay and actor who portrays Sonny, simply let the camera roll during genuine praise services. It's that real. Duvall is brilliant in his portrayal; he knows his character, Sonny, from the inside out.

If the film's focus had dealt primarily with the common struggle every believer faces of how to be holy and human, it wouldn't leave the Christian viewer, at least, feeling strangely troubled. Or if the film had ultimately painted Sonny as a blatant hypocrite—which would have been very unsatisfying—it would have at least resolved the questions we are left with. But Sonny is portrayed as a genuine believer. So what's the problem?

First, one can't help but love Sonny. His emotional intimacy with the Lord is irresistible. Neither do his sermons stray from the truth, only his life. What is hard to fathom is how a man with a faith that large doesn't have a commensurate sensitivity to sin and commitment to obedience. Sonny's praise life may have been Davidic in nature, but his confessional life fell far short. Even in the pivotal scene after his escape, in which he prays and fasts while temporarily living in a pup tent, we never hear Sonny struggling with much depth or comprehension about the sins of his life.

For example, Sonny never seems to be very disturbed by the fact that he's been a married womanizer—there's just a wink and nod to his self-acknowledged "wicked, wicked ways." There's even a suggestion that he may have been physically abusive to his wife. He starts a romance with a woman in his new community with whom he has a definite spiritual influence. Yet he never tells her that he is actually still married. Nor does he wrestle much with the moral implications of fleeing from the law. He's surely preached sermons on reaping what you sow, yet he's not inclined to pay the consequences. His flight from the law is illegal. Yet Sonny prays from the heart with such warmth and humanity that he makes us want to close our eyes and forget about all the contradictions between his faith and his behavior.

Part of the power of the film is that, whether intentionally or not, it brings us face to face with the impact of modernity. It's all the more devastating because it's seen through the life of a believer. Modern people just don't grasp that there must be a connection between belief and behavior. Why isn't

Sonny's faith evidenced by more godly behavior? Therein lies the contradiction: Sonny is a holiness preacher who isn't holy. The unspoken message regarding his private sins is this: The rules don't apply to me because I am so sincere in my faith. There are no consequences to my actions because in my heart I didn't mean to hurt anyone. My only responsibility is to do the Lord's work and build a church, not bear the consequences for past actions.

It isn't Sonny's faith that is troubling, it's that his beliefs have not been translated into his behavior. *Holiness* isn't a word used much in modern parlance. It sounds too judgmental and narrow to our ears. Yet, as William Bennett writes in his book *The Death of Outrage,* "There is a vital link between reasonable judgment and authentic compassion. Without judgment, there can be no common ethic. . . . No rules to govern behavior. No wise counsel on how best to live. . . . We see every day the human cost of 'tolerance' and 'openness.' Moral judgments need to be made, not for the sake of satisfying a 'Puritan passion' or a 'rigid moralism,' but because we human beings live better, more noble, more complete and satisfying lives when we hold ourselves to some common moral understanding."[1] In Sonny's case his "common moral understanding" was the Scriptures. Sadly, his love of biblical truth was reflected far more in his preaching than his lifestyle.

That film represents one side of the problem. If our lives do not give testimony to the radical difference that knowing Christ makes, our evangelism will ultimately be ineffective and hollow. However, there is the other side of the coin. Sometimes we reduce the call of holiness to trite and legalistic behaviors, such as the man I mentioned earlier who said he could swim on Sundays but not dive.

Holiness External and Internal

Once I was visiting Oregon State University for several days and was trying to get to know the nonbelievers who lived in the dorm where I was staying. One night I learned there was an excellent movie on television and, suspecting there would be a large crowd, I went. The room was packed with students, popcorn and Coke. During commercials we laughed and talked, and I answered why I was visiting their campus. Friendships began to form between myself and several others. A majority of those students came to hear me when I gave a campus talk later that week.

While we were watching television, however, a Christian student walked by and looked at us a bit disapprovingly, then saw me and left bewildered. Later she came to me and wondered why I would do such a frivolous thing as watch TV when it wasn't even a Christian program. Didn't I feel it was wrong? Shouldn't I have been upstairs praying for them and my talk rather than living exactly as they did? Was I giving them a worldly model instead of a spiritual one?

This incident raises some very important questions for us in evangelism. For example, what does it mean to be holy? How much are we to identify with the world? When are we in danger of being indistinguishable from the world? Many times I've seen Christians keep themselves at arm's length from their non-Christian friends because they thought they were thereby being spiritual. But when our understanding of spirituality isolates us from people as well as our culture, then we have misunderstood true holiness. If we grasp Jesus' approach to holiness, we will not be isolated from others, but neither will we be identical. Holiness, in fact, is not merely a concern of Jesus'; it was vitally important in the Hebrew Bible as well.

For example, the Old Testament is a profoundly moral book. Through Moses came the first major expression of the depths of God's concern for morality, for instance, in the Ten Commandments. Nathan boldly rebuked David concerning moral fault with Bathsheba (2 Sam 12:1-9), and Elijah confronted Ahab concerning Naboth's vineyard (1 Kings 21:17-19). But the moral nature of God is chiefly brought home to us through the prophets Amos, Hosea and Isaiah. The Old Testament indeed dealt seriously with the question of inner sin and morality.

Also, it is a common misconception that the law only referred to external conformity and not a conformity of the heart in regard to holiness. The facts are otherwise. As Gustave Oehler says, "The law insists on the disposition of the heart, when it says in Exodus 20:17, 'Thou shalt not covet'; when it binds men to love God with the whole heart and soul, to be placable toward their fellow men, and the like, Deut. 6:5; Lev. 19:17."[2] H. W. Robinson adds a similar note, "Even the Priestly Code, with all its elaborate precautions for ceremonial holiness, is still in large measure, a moral document, the outcome of a passion for perfection that shall be worthy of Yahweh."[3]

Finally, the holiness code in Leviticus begins in chapter 19 with, "You shall be holy, for I the LORD your God am holy" (v. 2). Then toward the end of chapter 20 the LORD says again, "You shall be holy to me; for I the LORD am holy" (v. 26). Just examining what Leviticus 19 and 20 have to say about what constitutes holy behavior is enlightening: Revere your parents. Do not steal or lie. Be a good neighbor. Be reasonable with your neighbor. Pay a decent wage. Do no injustice. Be not partial to the poor or defer to the great. Give honest weights and measures.

Holiness, from God's perspective, is intimately connected to how we treat people. Holiness is rooted in relationship.

As we have commented previously, not all of the Pharisees were critical of Jesus. But those who did criticize Jesus for not being a holy man tended to concern themselves with the external ceremonial manifestations of sin. Even though biblical teaching showed otherwise, they behaved as if evil came only from the outside. When one's concern is only for external evil, then the logical way to avoid being "contaminated" is to avoid the object altogether, or worse, to blame the object for causing the problem.

Take the problem of lust. Both Jesus and the Pharisees agreed it was wrong. But if one sees evil as externally imposed, then the culprit is not one's desire but the person desired. One very orthodox sect called the "Bruised and Bleeding" Pharisees thought lust was evil. So they determined they would avoid the source of the problem, namely, women. And whenever they came into the presence of a woman, not only would they avoid talking to her, but they would close their eyes so they could not see her at all. Of course, this caused them to run into walls, and hence their name. Can you imagine the shock of an exceedingly pious member of the "Bruised and Bleeding" sect walking by and discovering Jesus deeply engaged in conversation with a prostitute? Activity like this made it difficult for them to believe that Jesus was a holy man.

And so the critics of Jesus failed to see the devastating power and effect of such internal sins as pride, jealousy and uncharitableness. We would do well to learn from their lesson.

Jesus' Understanding of Holiness

Both Jesus and his critics agreed that being holy was of fundamental importance. They agreed that God's historical purpose was to call out a people for himself; that this people would be a holy people, set apart from the world to belong to him and to obey him; and that their holiness or difference would be seen in all their behavior and outlook. Jesus demonstrated in his Sermon on the Mount how clearly he believed that we were to be different. In Matthew 6:8 we read, "Do not be like them." Our character is to be completely distinct from what the world celebrates.

Jesus required a righteousness to exceed even that of the scribes and Pharisees, and to be demonstrated in the totality of his followers' lives—both in ethical behavior and in their religious devotion. Jesus took holiness seriously, but he and the Pharisees radically differed over the nature of holiness. Let us look at Jesus' understanding of holiness.

Radical Identification, Radical Difference

The Pharisees understood holiness in terms of ceremonial purification and separation from the masses. But Jesus demonstrated what holiness is through his radical identification with and his radical difference from the world. As A. T. Robertson comments, the Pharisees "were aloof in spirit and built up a hedge around themselves to keep off infection. Jesus plunged into the midst of the disease and sin to root both out."[4] Jesus walked alongside of people. He was approachable. He allowed a prostitute at Simon's banquet to express her love and devotion to him by touching him (Lk 7:36-50). He accepted people as they were.

But we must remember the other side too. Jesus called his disciples to be different as well. He identified, yes, but he was never identical with the world. My fear today is that we may enjoy talking of the Christian's pharisaic problem while we ignore the call to be different. We must never try to escape from the truth that there is a fundamental difference between Christians and non-Christians. If we ignore or minimize this difference, we will be of little use to God or to the world.

Jesus tells us that we are salt and light (Mt 5:13-16). Jesus does not say that we are to become light. Jesus says, "You are light." So we must begin reflecting who we really are and not try to hide it.

Perhaps our mistake is to settle for a far too superficial difference, one that focuses mostly on externals and personal disciplines. If you asked religious skeptics what they felt made a Christian different, their answer probably would be frightfully inadequate. Once in an evangelistic talk I asked some seekers what they thought the big issues were for Christians, what we truly fight for.

In utter seriousness a male student answered, "Judging from what I've seen, you stand against swearing, dirty jokes and rowdy parties. Isn't that right?"

"I think there are larger issues than that for Christians," I said. "For example, Christians are against murder."

Everyone laughed, and he said, "I hardly think anyone wouldn't be, but that issue doesn't come up very often."

"Oh? Do you know how Jesus defines murder? He says it's murder when we destroy people with our words. It's murder when we put people down and treat them as insignificant." I was referring here to Jesus' Sermon on the Mount, especially Matthew 5:21-22.

There was an instant hush in the audience. He said, "I had no idea that Christianity had to do with how you treat people. I thought it was merely do's and don'ts and being sure you don't swear."

What a stunning rebuke when the world believes that the only difference between us lies in *their* ability to better handle hearing barnyard expletives. Imagine how powerful our witness would be if unbelievers saw that the real "language issue" for Christians is that we refuse to gossip and speak judgmentally of others. If only we lived like that! Jim Cymbala, the pastor of Brooklyn Tabernacle Church, said in an interview with *Leadership* magazine (1993) that what most sapped the Christian's witness and spiritual power was grieving and quenching the Spirit's power through gossip and slander.

How, then, are we to be different? John Stott in his treatment of the Sermon on the Mount summarizes this portion of Matthew and consequently defines our "difference" this way: (1) a Christian's character (for example, we thirst for righteousness, we are peacemakers, we are pure in heart); (2) a Christian's influence (we are salt and light in our communities); (3) a Christian's righteousness (we are conformed to God's moral teaching); (4) a Christian's piety (which is marked by our sincerity of devotion); (5) a Christian's ambitions (we seek first the glory of God instead of self-centered material wealth and possession); (6) a Christian's relationships (we do not judge others but we serve them); and (7) a Christian's commitment (we obey Christ as Lord).[5]

I frequently hear that the call to be holy and the call to demonstrate love to sinners are mutually exclusive. (As if love is the antithesis to holiness.) Jesus welcomed and loved sinners; he did not drive them away by too much affectation of righteousness. He showed genuine compassion for people, but he was also direct and uncompromising in denouncing sin. Jesus had compassion, but there was also toughness in his love. He won them without sacrificing the purity of his life.

The paradox of *agape* love is that we accept our neighbor unconditionally and with open arms and at the same time desire God's very best for their lives. If Jesus is our Lord, our compassion will be shaped by his moral absolutes. Christ both was merciful and made judgments. Some things, he said, were immoral and destructive, but he never ceased to love. Indeed, it was his love that prompted his judgment.

But Jesus could keep that delicate balance of expressing love and truth without crushing people, we say. How can we ever achieve such a thing? How can God use us to bring conviction of sin without our coming off as judgmental and unloving?

The truth is, it is the Spirit of God who convicts a person of sin, not us. Nevertheless, God uses us to mediate both his love and his holiness to others. By our being prisms of his presence, a conviction of sin may come. But how?

I know a Christian woman who has cared deeply for a non-Christian woman who has indulged in more sins than I care to count. Her life is a mess. One day this woman said to the Christian, "It's funny, my pagan friends tell me they accept me. They say it doesn't matter what I do. I'm free. Yet it's only with you that I feel loved and safe, and I know I could always come to you. But it's also only with you that I feel remorse for what I'm doing, and I long to clean up my act and get my life together."

That is holiness. Sometimes the very presence of the Holy Spirit within us brings conviction of sin to another, without our ever saying a word. This is especially true when we pray for that person. God's love in us never abandons; it identifies deeply with individual people. But it also brings the reality of God's presence, the purity of his holiness. It is not intimidated by, nor does it flee from, the crisis of sin; neither does it deny the reality of sin's existence.

But sometimes it is the very love of God that demands that we speak painful truth to a friend. For example, a seeker friend of mine was committing adultery. I agonized over what to say to her. I knew how negative her experience with Christians had been. I knew I could easily lose her friendship if she thought I was writing her off because she was sinful. At the same time it was clear to anyone who looked at her that she was miserable. Indeed, she sometimes pondered aloud why she couldn't seem to find happiness. So I prayed and asked the Lord to show me what to say.

The next time she mentioned how depressed she was, I said, "I know you are unhappy. Yet I wonder if you realize that what you are searching for is exactly right. You want to be loved and cherished, and for the ache and emptiness in your heart to go away. The trouble is, you are looking for answers in the very places that are destroying you. Breaking your marriage vows and getting a quick love-fix is not the answer. It's only adding to the problems you already have. You already know I'm going to say this, but I believe the only thing that will fill that void inside of you is God."

That was the first time I had ever mentioned what I thought about her affair. But instead of being defensive or angry, she thanked me for loving her enough to tell the truth. We need to be very prayerful about if and what we say and whether we have gained enough trust to speak frankly. Yet my experience has been that as we ask God to show us what to say, he will help us communicate painful truth in a way that they can hear. They may not receive it, but at least they know that we love them too much to silently stand by and watch them destroy themselves.

There are other ways that God's holy presence in us can be expressed to the world. One of the greatest differences about Christians is that we know we are sinners. Therefore, we have the freedom to admit our sins and weaknesses. We are also free to share how God is helping us overcome our temptations.

Our honesty with seekers about our struggles does several things. First, it punctures the stereotype that Christians think they are perfect. We don't excuse sin by rationalizing it. Indeed, it's because we take sin so seriously that we try to develop a realistic understanding of who we are, warts and all. Our self-honesty, however, leads us to hope, because we see that God is changing us, not overnight and not without setbacks, but slowly and surely.

Our honesty before others also shatters the stereotype that all Christians are judgmental and critical people. By sharing our weaknesses, we acknowledge that we not only understand the human condition but we too must overcome it! We are not "finished products," yet we rejoice that by God's grace we are being strengthened to change. Owning our sins and temptations can actually lead seekers to experience conviction for their sins.

Jake, who is in recovery from substance and alcohol abuse, told me that when he first became a Christian he tried to cover up his past problems. He particularly feared that his admission of being a recovering alcoholic would lessen the power of his testimony to unbelievers. But slowly he realized that, by hiding his past and the fact that he needed to go to recovery meetings weekly to maintain his sobriety, he was actually neutralizing the power of the gospel. What he was inadvertently communicating was that God wasn't great enough and loving enough to forgive him.

Jake recently made a long car trip with Randy, a skeptic friend who is also in recovery. During the trip Jake told Randy about his pilgrimage with Jesus. Along the way they made a stop to Jake's parents' home. "You have no idea what a big step that was for me, Becky. When I was in high school," Jake told me, "I would never let my friends drop me off anywhere near my home. My family is so profoundly dysfunctional. I was mortified to think anyone would discover the truth. But since I've been walking with Christ, I've slowly come to accept my roots and not feel that I must cower in shame."

Amazingly, it was that act that opened his friend's interest in the gospel. Jake's friend also came from a deeply dysfunctional family, but he detested them. Randy was fascinated that Jake's belief in Jesus freed him to own the truth about himself and to love his family.

"Why aren't you ashamed to let me meet your family?" Randy candidly asked.

"Because I've finally learned where my true worth comes from," said Jake. "Yes, my parents are very broken people, and I grieve for them, but no human being can tell me who I am. Only God gives true identity and lasting worth."

The "holy difference" that Randy saw in Jake was not that Jake never struggled with temptation or that his life was free from suffering. What he saw was that, in knowing Jesus, Jake was finding the strength not only to overcome his addiction but also to accept the most painful elements of his life with love, grace and serenity.

But let's remember that God's holiness in our lives can be expressed in joyful ways too. We do much to further the kingdom of God when people see that we know how to celebrate life. A Christian friend of mine, Jody, told me she has a neighbor who is a devotee of the New Age because, she says, "they only emphasize the positive. There is none of the negative stuff you get with Christianity."

One day Jody called me, laughing and reciting the following story: "My neighbor called me and she said, 'Jody, you have really convicted me of something.' Becky, I was alarmed because I knew how defensive she was toward anything she considered negative, especially from Christians! Then she continued, 'You have really convicted me,' she said, 'that I don't know how to have fun.'

" 'What?' " asked Jody, as puzzled as she was stunned.

" 'Jody, you enjoy life. You know when to stop working and relax. You just have more fun living life than I do. All I do is work and worry. You're going to have to teach me how to lighten up! Do you think it has something to do with your faith?' she asked.

"Becky, I had hoped that my life was a witness to her. But if you asked me to guess how I was influencing her view of Christianity, I would have never dreamed it had anything to do with my 'fun quotient,' " Jody confided. So let us remember as we witness to others what Ignatius wrote: "The glory of God is a person fully alive."

So we must ask ourselves, *Do I identify enough? Do I welcome people, or am I a member of the holy huddle, the local God squad? Do I hang around people of various beliefs and mores? Do I love the unlovely? Or, on the other hand, am I different enough? Am I Christlike? Do I bring this aspect of Christ's holiness, of his moral standards, of the fruit of the Spirit to my relationships? Or, out of my sincere desire to identify and to love, have I become culture-accommodating?*

Jesus had the ministry of the towel but he also had the ministry of the whip. Our lives as Christians, if we are to be effective evangelists, should reflect that same dual stance toward the world.

6

A Question
of Obedience

....

Another Way of
Knowing God

When we listen to someone explain how we get to know God, we hear frequent references to believing on Jesus, opening up our hearts to him or asking him to come into our lives. We are to make a decision for Christ or pray a prayer or walk down an aisle. Of course, these things—believing, deciding, accepting—really are essential.

But how often do we hear references to a genuine change in the direction of our lives? How often do we ourselves, as we tell someone about Jesus, point out that obedience to Christ as Lord is also involved? Cathy, the seventeen-year-old runaway I met on a bus, for instance, could have avoided making fundamental mistakes if she had understood the importance of obedience.

The Pharisees' View of Knowing God

The Pharisees studied God. They memorized the Scriptures and knew every word. They even devised games with their scrolls. They would throw a dart into a rolled-up scroll. The word would be read where the dart landed and they would then have to recite the rest of the verse. They felt that through study they could find God and that knowledge was the avenue to transformation. Jesus himself commented to the Pharisees, "You search the scriptures, because you think that in them you have eternal life" (Jn 5:39). To know the Scriptures is to know God, they thought.

There are two points to be made about this. First, knowledge is not enough for salvation. The Pharisees considered themselves supremely righteous because of their vast knowledge. But they misunderstood a vital point. Mere information makes no one righteous; it only makes us responsible for what we know. It is impotent to effect real and lasting change within us. One may be overeducated and untransformed.

The Hebrews' understanding of knowledge, however, is that the degree to which we know something is the degree to which we have integrated it into our everyday life. It is of no use to say we believe in something when our actions betray our beliefs. To know is not only to verbalize or intellectualize, it is to submit in obedience with our lives as well. The Pharisees are a positive model for us in this regard. They knew that if they spoke of faith in God, there must be evidence or fruit in their lives to demonstrate this faith.

So the Pharisees took obedience seriously. They tried to obey the ceremonial laws. In fact, they could hardly obey enough. They constantly kept adding new laws. But they understood one very important thing: we are responsible for what we know. Knowledge must automatically translate into obedience, be it words or action. And so the Pharisees tried to integrate into their lives the part of Scripture they chose to focus upon.

So the key question is, What does it mean to obey? "The word 'obedience' does not mean slavish, uncritical adherence; it comes from the Latin root *audire*, which means 'to listen.' Obedience requires the discerning ear, the ear that listens for the reality of the situation, a listening that allows the hearer to respond to that reality, whatever it may be."[1]

We must learn from the Pharisees' mistakes here. There are three basic issues. The first issue is: what do we obey? Jesus told them they sought life in the wrong place. "I am the way, and the truth and the life," Jesus said. Those who sought truth were invited into a relationship with him. The Scriptures pointed to him, but they were not to be worshiped. That's because to know and obey the truth comes not from a superficial quest for facts but from entering into a relationship of intimate trust and obedience with Jesus. Truth is known in relationship to God through Christ.

Jesus also pointed out the irony that the Pharisees claimed to revere Scripture yet rejected the very person that Scripture proclaimed. If they really believed Scripture, they would have believed in Jesus, and they would have been drawn to worship him. So an attempt merely to obey the laws of the Bible is not enough. We must obey Christ. Indeed, it is our failure to obey God's law that drives us to realize that we need the inner transformation Christ offers.

The second issue is: why must we obey? The motive for our obedience is as important as the act of obedience itself. God requires heart obedience that is motivated by our love and sincerity of devotion to him. Merely to obey rules at a superficial level and not to allow God total access to our person prevents us from having deep contact with God. We do not obey in order to earn our salvation. We must not obey out of pride. Rather, we obey because of who God is and the marvelous work he has done in seeking and saving us. It was something we could never have done on our own.

The third issue is: how broad is the scope of our obedience? The answer is absolute and universal. We are called to obey the whole revelation of God. Jesus tells us to. We must not pick and choose what we will obey. We cannot focus on the aspects of Scripture we find appealing and ignore that which is hard or uncomfortable. That was the heart of Jesus' criticism of the Pharisees.

It is true, of course, that none of us can encompass the depth of all God's desires for us as expressed in Scripture. We are finite. But what we know we must obey. We are called on to meditate on his Word consciously and regularly, to ignore no portion of it by design or planned blindness, to read both Old and New Testaments, both the Law and the Prophets, both the Gospels and Epistles. It is only by such a sweep that we can help prevent the sort of blindness evidenced by some of the Pharisees.

Jesus' View of Knowing God

How do we find God and grow in him? Jesus was adamant at this point. He said we must do what he says. We must put into practical obedience the knowledge we have. He continually asked people to drop their nets, to sell all they had and to follow him.

We might say that Jesus had a theology of obedience. And the object of this obedience was a living person—not a historical norm, not a code of laws, but himself. He called people to be accountable to God whether they were believers or skeptics who were searching. For example, he told his disciples, "What is the point of calling me, 'Lord, Lord,' without doing what I tell you to do?" (Lk 6:46 Phillips).

To the Pharisaic lawyer who came to trap him in debate, Jesus' response was no different (Lk 10:25-37). "What must I do to inherit eternal life?" the lawyer asked. And Jesus told him to recite what he understood, which was to love God totally as well as his neighbors as himself.

This lawyer was not a follower of Jesus, and his motive in the conversation was "to put him to the test" (v. 25). So how did Jesus help him understand the true way? Well, by many standards of evangelizing, Jesus did a rotten job. Jesus did not have the lawyer "pray the prayer." Nor did Jesus ask him to read a tract on the five points that lead to salvation. He simply said, "Go and do it." In other words, "Begin to put into practical obedience what you understand." He called him to be responsible to the light he had already received.

Jesus knew that obedience to his and his Father's words yielded faith, that revelation is based upon obedience. Over and over again Jesus called people to faith and obedience. If I had to sum up one's response to the gospel message, I would say it's "paint or get off the ladder." Jesus approached people exactly like that. He told them to pick up their brush and paint something.

Do you want to discover who Jesus is and deal honestly with your doubts? Jesus' style is not to suggest that you go and ponder the virgin birth for three months but to begin doing what he says. This challenge can mean much to us as we engage in evangelism.

Jesus' emphasis on obedience is greatly needed today. Unfortunately much of Western theology is overintellectualized. Biblical teaching, on the other hand, is intimately connected with action and life; it is associated with the situation we live in. If some of the Pharisees thought that through knowledge and legalistic obedience one could know God, our present generation may be in even worse shape. We tend to think of knowledge only in cerebral terms, as facts to be memorized rather than truth that demands our transformation.

When I worked with InterVarsity Christian Fellowship, I used to ask college students if they had learned much at a weekend conference. They would often answer, "Oh, yeah. You should see how many notebooks I filled."

And my response would be, "You don't have to show me your notebooks. If you learned anything, I'll see it in your life."

Jesus was not the originator of the call to obedience. In the Hebrew Bible as well as in the New Testament there is a consensus. Indeed, Yahweh's purpose is that we should learn to say, "I delight to do your will, O my God" (Ps 40:8). God seeks our fellowship with him through our moral obedience. H. W. Robinson writes, "This is salvation in the deeper and more spiritual sense of the Old Testament. . . . But even in the religion of the Law, . . . obedience to the revealed will of Yahweh is recognized as the supreme end of man and the supreme glory of God. The attitude of Jesus to the will of God and his emphasis on the absolute worth of obedience as the supreme 'value' of human life are the best illustrations of what the Old Testament indicates as the purposes of Yahweh in creation and providence."[2] Obedience is critical because it reveals a harmony of purpose between the human will and the divine. And Jesus is our supreme example of one who was utterly obedient to the Father's will.

Jesus' emphasis on faith and obedience also helps us understand the role of repentance in conversion and discipleship. Too many people believe a Christian is a person who has simply "prayed the prayer" and "decided for Jesus." But many such "Christians" do not live as if they are under new management. They may claim that they once made a decision, but everything else in their life is unchanged. What a superficial understanding of what it means to be a Christian!

Too many people have stopped at the door that leads to conversion. The door (be it a prayer, a decision or whatever) is simply that—a door. It was closed and it has been opened for one express purpose: so we can go through it and get involved in life on the other side. But some see conversion and discipleship as a revolving door that will allow them to stay there without ever actually participating in life on the other side. They have come to glorify their experience of the door when it was meant only as an avenue of passage to a new life. In fact, it is not our "door experience" but our new life that demonstrates whether we have been converted.

A true disciple of Jesus is one who does what Jesus does—obeys the will of God. When Jesus called people to obedience, he was calling them to be accountable to God, to begin living for him as he desires. To know Jesus doesn't mean we keep the religious compartment of our lives separate and then engage in other forms of knowing as if there were no connection. "To convert means far more than to experience the psychological, emotional aspects of change through an inner experience," writes Jim Wallis. "The biblical accent is clearly on a reversal of direction, a transfer of loyalties, a change in commitment leading to the creation of a new community. . . . It is a radical change in the whole of one's life and in all of one's relationships to the world. . . . We have forgotten that a relationship to Christ means a relationship to the purposes of Christ in history."[3]

Why did Jesus call to obedience even those who were not following him? Perhaps so that their experience of conversion (that is, one of obedience) would teach them what it means to be a disciple. The more I read the Gospels, the more I realize how vital it is for skeptics to understand this. Frequently I meet skeptics who are not ready to pray and ask Christ to be the Lord of their lives. What are we to say to those who want to know if Jesus is the way but still need to "check Jesus out" before they are guided by the Spirit into conversion?

Based on my understanding of the gospel, I now say to nonbelievers, "Tell God (or the four walls, if that is the one you think you are speaking to) that you want to find out if Jesus is truly God and that, if you could feel more certain, you would follow him. Then begin to read the Gospels every day. Each day, as you read, something will probably hit you and make sense. Whatever that is, do it as soon as you can." In other words, I call them to act on whatever strikes them as true and to do it if they are sincerely seeking God. Then they learn from the beginning that seeking God is not simply an academic quest for facts that challenges our mind, perhaps, but leaves our inner self detached and uninvolved. They come to see that to know the truth they must practice obedience to the truth. Truth always requires us to submit. Truth transforms us.

The Battle of the Desk

When I was working in collegiate ministry, a very bright student, Sue, came to me. She told me that she was an agnostic but that her best friend, Larry, had become a Christian. He talked to her a lot about his faith and did not neglect her after his conversion. Instead, he brought her to his campus Christian gatherings and introduced her to his new Christian friends. He made her feel comfortable and a part of his very different Christian world. He answered as best he could her many intellectual questions about his faith. And most importantly, he loved her.

"I've seen what faith in Christ has done for Larry," she told me. "I see the love these Christians have for each other and for me. I've seen what Jesus is like in the Gospels and a lot of my questions have been answered. But I still don't believe. I'd like to find God, but I'm plagued with doubts. Please don't ask me to pray to receive Christ; it'd be dishonest. What should I do?"

I suggested what I mentioned above, read the Scriptures and look for an opportunity to put it into practice. She gulped and said, "That's radical. But I'll do it."

So she began having what she called her "pagan devotions." And the Christians around her prayed that God would speak to her in the Scriptures and give her concrete situations in which she could obey. Several months later she said she wanted to talk to me. Here is Sue's story:

"One day I read in the Bible, 'If someone steals your coat, don't let him have only that, but offer your cloak as well.' For whatever reason, that verse hit me between the eyes. So I said to the four walls, 'Listen, walls—or God, if you're there—I'm going to do what this verse says, if the opportunity arises today. I want to remind you that I'm trying to do things your way in order to find out if you exist and if Jesus really is who he says. Amen.'

"The day went by and I forgot the verse. Then I headed to the library to continue working on my senior thesis. Just as I sat down at my designated thesis desk, this guy comes up and starts yelling at me. He told me the school hadn't given him his thesis desk, so he was going to take mine. (Everyone knows how important your thesis desk is for your work. The school only gives you one.) I started yelling back, and pretty soon we caused quite a ruckus. But it was when he glared at me and said, 'Look. I'm stealing it from you whether you like it or not,' that it suddenly hit me.

"I just looked at him and moaned, 'Ohhhhh, no. No. I can't believe it.' And to myself I thought, 'Look, God, if you're there, I do want to know if Jesus is God. But isn't there some other way of finding out besides obeying that verse? I mean, couldn't I tithe or get baptized or give up something else? But don't take my thesis desk! I mean, with my luck, I'll give up the desk and then discover that you don't exist.'

"But I couldn't escape the fact that I had read that verse the very same day someone tried to rob me. Before, I had always been amused to see how Jesus aimed for whatever was controlling the person in his conversations with people in the Bible. But now it didn't feel so funny. I took a deep breath, tried not to swear and said, 'OK, let me think about it.'

"He looked bewildered. But just at that moment the librarian came up. She said she'd heard the conversation and was angered by his behavior. But he immediately began swearing at her and intimidated her so much that she told us we had to see his thesis adviser. So we trotted over to his adviser's office. It was clear to me by now that this guy carried around a lot of rage and was probably a troubled person. The more the guy ranted and raved, the more agitated the adviser became. Finally the adviser said, 'Well, what does Sue think we should do?'

"All this time I kept thinking about what I'd seen in these past several months. I'd seen Larry's life changed. I'd seen something beautiful in this Christian fellowship, something so real I could almost touch it. Even though I was not a Christian, I had been loved by these people. And I'd seen Jesus in the Bible. I felt so drawn to him. I realized that, even without a thesis desk, somehow I still had more than this poor, pathetic guy. I told the adviser that he could have the desk, and the meeting was over.

"When we walked out the door, this guy grabbed my arm and asked me why in the world I let him have it. I told him he would think I had flipped out, but I was trying to discover if Jesus was really who he claimed to be. In order to know if Jesus was really the way to God, I was attempting to obey the things he told us to do. 'So I've been reading the Gospels. And today I read that if somebody tried to rip me off, I was supposed to let them—and even throw in something extra to boot.' All I could see were the whites of his eyes. 'So I'm going to give you the desk, but don't press your luck about something extra.'

"Then he asked, 'Why in the world would Jesus say such a crazy thing?'

"Then I said, 'Hey, if there's one thing I've learned from reading about Jesus and meeting these Christians, it's that Jesus wants to give us a whole lot more than a thesis desk if we'd let him. I think the basic idea is that it's knowing Jesus that makes us rich, not owning possessions. So that thesis desk is yours.'

"Becky, as I said those words, I just simply *knew* it was all true. I knew it from the inside out. I kinda felt like God was saying, 'Well done. That's the way I want my children to behave.' "

There were a lot of things that Sue did not understand about being a Christian when she became one. But there was one thing she did know: to follow Jesus, or to *know* Jesus, we must do what he says. I am not suggesting that we must do this with every skeptic we meet. But this understanding that to know truth will require us to change by submitting to obedience, must permeate more of our evangelism. Obviously we must be sensitive to what the Holy Spirit is doing in a person's life. But we need to call people to as much commitment as they have been prepared for.

Not everyone we meet is ready to accept Christ as Savior, but everyone is on a continuum in their relationship to Christ. Our task is to draw them closer to the point where they choose to become disciples. One way to do this is to call them to accountability for what they know. We do not need to be belligerent. A gentle suggestion can be devastatingly effective.

The Call to Repentance

Jesus calls skeptics to obedience for another reason. The call to obey can also be a call to repentance. Jesus told the lawyer in Luke 10:37 to go be a "neighbor" like the good Samaritan. Superficially that sounds like sheer humanism. Jesus seemingly forgot to tell the lawyer he was the Son of God, that salvation rests in him alone, indeed that it is only through Jesus that we can truly love our neighbor anyway! But maybe Jesus had a different strategy. Jesus called him to obey the light he had been given.

Suppose the lawyer went out and sincerely tried to love his neighbor in ways he had never tried before. And since his consciousness had been raised, he would be more sensitive to failure than ever before. Suppose he realized he could not cut the mustard. The harder he tried to love, the more he was aware of his inadequacies. Perhaps on a return visit to Jesus he would say, "I need help. I can't do it. I tried to do what you said. Where do I go to get help?" I have a hunch Jesus' second conversation would be very different from the first.

To encourage people to reach out to God, to put him to the test, to do what he says (as a means of finding out if God is there) is to communicate that God is alive. We must live by our belief that the kingdom of God is at hand. We believe God is living and at work. Our faith is not in a historical model; it is in a living Lord. This sense of the aliveness and nearness of God must permeate our evangelism. As Chesterton writes, "Plato has told you a truth; but Plato is dead. Shakespeare has startled you with an image; but Shakespeare will not startle you anymore. But imagine what it would be to live with such men still living, to know that Plato might break out with an original lecture tomorrow, or that at any moment Shakespeare might shatter everything with a single song." The person who lives in contact with the living God is a person "always expecting to meet Plato or Shakespeare tomorrow at breakfast."[4]

Our evangelism will be more vital and substantial, and our efforts will be longer lasting, when we help our skeptical friends see that God is alive and present, that they may discover him by putting his commands into practice and that real conviction that Jesus is God is evidenced not by sentimental feelings about God but by obedience to him. Indeed, it is through obedience that we discover who God is as well as deepen our knowledge of him.

A Lifestyle of Evangelism
In this and the previous two chapters we have looked at Jesus' lifestyle and priorities as demonstrated by his values in three areas. We saw, first, that his

life was marked by a deep love for God, his neighbor and himself. Then we noted how his holiness was reflected through his radical identification with the world as well as his radical difference from the world. Finally, we saw how his love and devotion to the Father were evidenced by his obedience to the Father's will.

If we are to be followers of Jesus, his values must permeate our values. We need to be concerned more with how our lives reflect his love, his holiness and his obedience than with the latest witnessing techniques. When we live as Jesus did, in his power and with his presence, seekers will be drawn to us. Evangelism will not be a dreaded task to be ticked off every Wednesday. Rather, sharing Jesus will become a true delight and evangelism will become a lifestyle.

7

Christ
with Us

....

I t is easy enough to say that when we live our lives by Jesus' values,
evangelism will come naturally. But how do we live our lives like Jesus?
It seems too much to ask. Jesus, after all, was God incarnate. I am just a
human being—frail, frightened and essentially unable to live up to this ideal.

Of course, you alone can't live up to the ideal. Neither can I. But God knows
this, and he has not left us to go it alone. Jesus is with us, and by the power of
the Holy Spirit, he calls, equips and motivates us for ministry. This is the first bit
of good news. The second is like it. The presence of Christ brings us his power
and ability to use our limited resources in his limitless ways.

Third, Jesus is with us, not only by being in us through the indwelling of
the Holy Spirit but by being a part of those to whom we are called to minister.
All people have been created in God's image. When we meet them in a real,
personal encounter, we are meeting something of Christ. We are indeed not
alone. And that's what we want to see more clearly now.

Jesus in Us
We may recall that Jesus told the Pharisee lawyer to be "a neighbor." So is

that all there is to being a disciple of Jesus? Is it merely to be kind and loving to the people next door? Is it simply to begin serving others? Luke apparently did not think so, for he followed this story with the familiar Mary and Martha passage (Lk 10:38-42).

Immediately after reading how Jesus told the lawyer to go and serve others, we find Martha doing exactly what Jesus requested. She was serving others by preparing a meal. But, we are told, she was "distracted with much serving." Why was this? Was she not doing all that Jesus required? Why couldn't she serve with peace and joy? Perhaps because she failed to do what Mary did. Mary allowed Jesus to serve her first. And Jesus said Mary had made a better choice.

This passage emphasizes that serving others is not enough. Indeed, our ministry to others is dependent on our being fed by Christ himself. And it is the Holy Spirit who makes Jesus alive to us and nourishes him in us. Therefore, the Spirit of God is an absolute requisite for what we are called to do. We can learn all sorts of counseling skills, acquire techniques and develop razor-sharp programs in evangelism, but we will have no lasting impact unless God's Spirit is central in our ministry. We must ask for God's Spirit to anoint us and equip us for the ministry he calls us to. We can no more make a person become a Christian than we can make ourselves new people.

That is the frustration of the law. It can show us what to do, but it cannot make us want to do it. Only the Holy Spirit (and our obedient will) can bring about transformation. We must pray, first, for a renewal of the Holy Spirit in our lives as we seek to minister, and then for his activity in the lives of the people we are seeking. And in a mysterious way, prayer frees God's Spirit to move.

Indeed, prayer is another absolute requisite for evangelizing, for through prayer God changes us and our friends into the likeness of Christ. Just as we pray daily that God's Spirit will renew us and equip us for the ministry he has called us to, so must we pray daily for the conversion of our friends. And not only for the long-range goal of conversion but also for the step-by-step process of gradual acceptance that will result in conversion.

It is helpful to have a prayer partner, perhaps one other Christian on your dorm floor or in your neighborhood who wants to love that community through you. We need to be diligent and persistent in praying for those God brings to us.

When I was in Spain and knew I would be studying at the University of Illinois in the fall, I asked God to bring the most open seekers and seat them next to me. For three months in Spain I prayed for those whom God would put to my right or my left in class.

When I arrived home, I called Beth Goldhor Domig, a good friend, and asked her if she would pray with me. We dreamed together, prayed together and set goals together. One goal was that after the first month of school we would begin an investigative Bible discussion. One month later we started a study for our skeptic friends. Four of the ones I brought had sat next to me the first day of class. Beth brought those she befriended on her dorm floor the first week.

Ask God to show you just one or two people whom he wants to seek through you. Find someone who will pray and share that dream with you as Beth did with me. And remember in all of this prayer and activity that great mystery of the indwelling of Jesus—"Christ in you, the hope of glory" (Col 1:27).

Jesus with Us

When we begin to realize the reality and power of Jesus' presence in our daily living, our evangelism takes on fresh force. The failure to see how dramatically Jesus' presence affects a situation is, however, a problem his followers have always had.

In Mark 6:30-44 we read how the disciples had just returned from a successful preaching and healing journey. They were tired and Jesus suggested they go away in the boat to find a place to rest. But as they started to dock, they saw five thousand people waiting on shore for Jesus. (I am not so sure the disciples gave the crowd a big smile on first glimpse of them!) Jesus felt compassion for them since they looked like "sheep without a shepherd." So he taught them all day.

When it grew dark and dinner time came, the disciples told Jesus to send the crowd away. When Jesus asked why they could not feed them, they responded cynically, "Oh, sure, with the thousand dollars we just happened to bring along?" But Jesus told them to divide the multitude into groups of hundreds and fifties. He took five loaves and two fish and thanked God for them. (No doubt Jesus was the only one who was grateful for so small an amount!) He touched the food and fed the five thousand.

How did the disciples fail here, and what can we learn from it? First, they failed to offer their limited resources. They looked at the task and their meager supplies and concluded it was impossible. They forgot that Jesus could take natural elements and do supernatural things with them.

Jesus did not look at the five loaves and two fish and say, "This is terrible. Such a tiny amount of food for all these people! I'll just have to do a miracle and whip up some food from nothing." It is significant that he worked with what the disciples had.

When we find ourselves in situations that seem beyond our limits (actually we should look for such situations!), we must not hesitate because we feel inadequate. We must not complain about our limited resources. God tells us he is glorified in our weakness. God's Spirit will take and multiply what we have.

Second, the disciples failed to see the power of Jesus' presence. Jesus prayed and then touched the food, and there was more than enough for everyone. Because of who he is, when Jesus touches anything, there is blessing.

But what about us? When we follow Jesus, his Spirit abides in us. That means he is a part of what we do. Everything we touch Jesus touches. If he touched the fish and multiplied them, then how does he touch our activities? He is with us when we gather for Bible discussion, when we eat and dance and work. And Jesus reaches out and touches others through us.

Maggie, a student at the University of Oregon, was struck by Jesus' feeding of the multitudes. She decided to reach out to her dorm floor by having an ice cream party. She bought the ice cream, borrowed a scooper and said, "God, I have trouble believing that you can work through this ice cream party to tell others of your love. But you dwell in me, so this isn't an ordinary ice cream party. You are here. Love these people tonight."

I went to the party and the room was packed with hungry students. The atmosphere was lively and fun. To my knowledge, no one had a spiritual discussion. Afterward she told me, "Well, it was a failure. I don't think Jesus was working here."

"Why?" I asked.

"Because no one even talked about him. All we did was have fun!"

Maggie demonstrated several misconceptions. First, that having fun was a waste of time. She felt every minute had to be used in serious spiritual pursuit. She did not believe that God would approve of lively spontaneity. Second, she believed that spiritual ministry only occurs when one is speaking about God. If that is true, then God has to work with severe limits. But it is not true. God works as powerfully through the nonverbal as he does through the verbal. We, too, must offer both. We need to let Jesus loose! Remember that Jesus is reaching out to everyone you are. He wants to speak through everything that you do, not just your verbal witness.

The sequel to the ice cream party shows this. Maggie told me the next day that eight students came to her. One girl said, "I couldn't believe you spent your money so we could eat! It was so much fun. You made our floor feel like a family for the first time. Why'd you do it?"

Another said, "My roommate and I had a great time. We decided we're going to have a party next week!"

And another said, "It was so nice of you to do that. You know, I felt love bouncing off those walls. What are you into?"

Then Maggie said to me, "I told you Jesus wasn't at work at that party—that he wasn't showing people who he was. I am the Christian and never noticed him there, but my non-Christian friends did. They don't know who he is yet, but they sensed his presence. I wonder how much I've been limiting Jesus all along?"

When, through the power of the Holy Spirit, we let Jesus reach our dorm floor or neighborhood, he will create a family atmosphere. Jesus will give people a sense of worth. And his love is contagious; people will imitate it. They will be drawn to us at first without knowing why. What we must not forget is that we incarnate Jesus! Whatever our life intersects with, so does Jesus. Whomever we touch Jesus touches. We do not simply give the gospel—we are the gospel.

Jesus in Others

We know we are called to reach out and care for people, but some of us feel so painfully shy that we die a slow death in starting a conversation. Some of us do not feel naturally drawn to people. Reaching out to them seems foreign and makes us uncomfortable.

Learning to care for others requires several things. First, it demands practice. The disciples developed compassion very slowly. For most of them it was a long, hard process that required self-denial and work.

Second, it requires us to look outward. To be consumed with shyness or indifference may have emotional roots or it may mean one is consumed with self. Disciples of Jesus must focus their attention outward in servanthood. We do not listen to others or serve others because we happen to feel like it; we do it out of obedience. I usually find that my compassionate feelings follow obedience (if they were not there at the beginning).

Finally, learning to care for others requires sound theology. Nothing should warm our hearts more than remembering what Jesus is like. We cannot love him long without loving what he loves. We must not forget that Jesus was an agent of creation. His image, however marred now, is stamped in each one of us. That means that whomever we touch bears his image.

The late Mother Teresa, an Albanian nun who set up a home for the dying in Calcutta, India, discussed this point in a talk she gave at the Forty-First International Eucharistic Congress in Philadelphia.[1] She said that after Mass one morning she spoke to a group of sisters. "During the Mass," she said, "you saw that the priest touched the body of Christ with great love and tenderness. When you touch the poor today, you too will be touching the body of Christ. Give them that same love and tenderness."

Several hours later a young nun came to Mother Teresa, her face radiant. "I have been touching the body of Christ for three hours," she said. Mother Teresa asked her what she meant. "Just as we arrived, the sister brought in a man covered with maggots. He had been picked up from a drain. I have been taking care of him. I have been touching Christ. I knew it was him," she said.

"That young sister understood what Jesus meant when he said, 'I was sick and you comforted me,'" Mother Teresa commented. "Jesus comes to us as the sick and the homeless, he comes to us in the distressing disguise of the poor."

We are reminded here of Jesus' own comment to his disciples as he took a child into his arms: "Whoever welcomes this child in my name welcomes me, and whoever welcomes me welcomes the one who sent me" (Lk 9:48). This is a radical statement. It requires that we treat human life as sacred and precious, not to be manipulated on the basis of our whims or desires. It reflects what we noted above, that there is something of God's image in every person. Furthermore, when God became flesh in Jesus Christ, he showed graphically the value and dignity of all human life. No matter how distressing the disguise, Jesus tells us that when we receive one such as this, we have received him.

C. S. Lewis made the same point when he wrote,

> It is a serious thing to live in a society of possible gods and goddesses, to remember that the dullest and most uninteresting person you talk to may one day be a creature which, if you saw it now, you would be strongly tempted to worship or else a horror and a corruption such as you now meet, if at all, only in a nightmare. . . . There are no ordinary people. You have never met a mere mortal. . . . But it is immortals whom we joke with, work with, marry, snub, and exploit—immortal horrors or everlasting splendorous. . . . Next to the Blessed Sacrament itself, your neignbor is the holiest object presented to your senses.[2]

We must see in our neighbors their inherent worth and dignity. In an article in *Campus Life* magazine a young nurse writes of her pilgrimage in learning to see in a patient the image of God beneath a very "distressing disguise."[3]

Eileen was one of her first patients, a person who was totally helpless. "A cerebral aneurysm (broken blood vessels in the brain) had left her with no conscious control over her body," the nurse writes. As near as the doctors could tell, Eileen was totally unconscious, unable to feel pain and unaware of anything going on around her. It was the job of the hospital staff to turn her every hour to prevent bed sores and to feed her twice a day "what looked like a thin mush through a stomach tube."

Caring for her was a thankless task. "When it's this bad," an older student nurse told her, "you have to detach yourself emotionally from the whole situation. Otherwise you'd throw up every time you walked into her room." As a result, more and more she came to be treated as a thing, a vegetable, and the hospital jokes about her room—room 415—were gross and dehumanizing.

But the young student nurse decided that she could not treat this person like the others had treated her. She talked to Eileen, sang to her, encouraged her and even brought her little gifts. One day when things were especially difficult and it would have been easy for the young nurse to take out her frustrations on the patient, she was especially kind. It was Thanksgiving Day and the nurse said to the patient, "I was in a cruddy mood this morning, Eileen, because it was supposed to be my day off. But now that I'm here, I'm glad. I wouldn't have wanted to miss seeing you on Thanksgiving. Do you know this is Thanksgiving?"

Just then the telephone rang, and as the nurse turned to answer it, she looked quickly back at the patient. Suddenly, she writes, Eileen was "looking at me . . . crying. Big damp circles stained her pillow, and she was shaking all over."

That was the only human emotion that Eileen ever showed any of them, but it was enough to change the attitude of the hospital staff toward her. Not long afterward Eileen died. The young nurse closes her story, saying, "I keep thinking about her. . . . It occurred to me that I owe her an awful lot. Except for Eileen, I might never have known what it's like to give myself to someone who can't give back."

What struck me about this nurse and about the young nun is that they knew the poor in their midst. I wonder how many of us really know the poor? Mother Teresa asks the hard questions:

> Do we know the poor in our own family? Maybe the members of our family [or church or college fellowship] are not hungry for a piece of bread, maybe they're not naked or homeless, but do any of them feel unwanted or unloved? . . . The Missionaries of Charity care for the crippled and the unwanted, the dying and the hungry, the lepers and the alcoholics. But the poor come to all of us in many forms. Let us be sure that we never turn our backs on them, wherever we may find them. For when we turn our backs on the poor, we turn them on Jesus Christ.[4]

8

Practicing
the Presence
of Christ

....

I was walking through O'Hare Airport in Chicago one day when my purse slipped and everything tumbled out. As I was stuffing things back inside, a young woman with a baby stopped to ask the time. Then she nervously bit her lip and asked, "You don't know where I could get a drink, do you?"

I didn't. But as I searched her face, I saw that she was distraught. So I stood up and initiated a conversation.

She quickly interrupted with, "Do you know how much a drink would cost here?"

I could see that we were getting nowhere, and suddenly I heard myself saying, "Gee, I don't know, but would you like me to go with you to find the bar?"

"Oh, would you? I would really love the company," she responded.

Off we went. And all the way I was kicking myself for it—going to a bar at noon with a perfect stranger. How unorthodox! Then I thought, years before it became a popular slogan, *I wonder what Jesus would do in a situation like this?*

That is just the point. What would Jesus do? In the previous chapter we saw the power and the perspective that Christ's presence brings into our lives. But what is our responsibility in being good stewards of the gift of Christ's presence? In this chapter we will look at four ways we can practice the presence of Christ: seeing people as Jesus does, loving them as they are, loving them as we are, and being salt and light in the world.

Seeing People As Jesus Sees Them

Often we are blind. We act as if those around us were not really people like us. If we see them bleed, we pretend they aren't really hurting. If we see them alone, we tell ourselves that they like it that way.

But Jesus wants to heal our sight. He wants us to see that the neighbor next door or the people sitting next to us on a plane or in a classroom are not interruptions to our schedule; they are there by divine appointment. Jesus wants us to see their needs, their loneliness, their longings, and he wants to give us the courage to reach out to them. If we are to do that, we need to do two things: we will have to take risks as well as get beneath the surface of people's lives.

To take initiative opens us up to the risk of rejection. To let people inside our lives is a frightening but essential ingredient in evangelism. It is risky to abandon our security blankets in order to penetrate the lives of others. At O'Hare I wondered what I should do now that I was in the bar with the nervous woman I had just met. I realized that Jesus would probably be more concerned about why she needed a drink than about going into a tavern. I knew that if I couldn't be at ease around her when she had a drink in her hand and allow God to lead me into what he perceived as a mission field, then I wouldn't be very effective in communicating God's unconditional love.

After we found the bar, it took only minutes before she began sharing that she had decided to leave her husband. Her husband, unaware of her decision, would be meeting her at the airport in Michigan. She was petrified at facing his response and felt totally alone. "Oh, but it's ridiculous telling this to a complete stranger. How boring this must be for you!" she would comment and then talk on.

The saddest part was her obvious inability to believe anyone could care for her. She trusted almost no one. When she mentioned a problem with which I told her I could identify, she said, "Oh, so that's why you act as if you care. Listen, aren't you afraid of picking up strangers like me? You really should be more careful."

As I began to tell her who God was and that he was the one who brought me into situations like this, she seemed to hang on every word. Soon we were walking to her plane, but I felt torn. I wanted to reach out to her and tell her how moved I was by her problems and that God cared deeply for her, but she was so cold and defensive that I feared her rejection. Finally at the gate I took her hand and said, "Listen, I want you to know that I really care about you, and I'll be praying for you the minute you get off the plane."

She just stared blankly. Then, turning away, she said, "Um . . . I'm sorry—I just don't know how to handle love," and walked away.

The encounter wasn't a smashing success, but I felt I had been obedient. Being a Christian means taking risks—risking that our love will be rejected, misunderstood or even ignored. Now I'm not suggesting that you race to your local bar for Jesus. But if you find yourself in a situation in which you believe God has put you, then accept the risk for his sake.

Seeing Beneath the Crust

A second way to practice the presence of Christ is to see beneath the crust. We must never assume that a person will not be open to Christianity. Again and again I have had to learn that the least likely looking people have been the most open to God.

Once when I worked with InterVarsity I was on a bus sitting next to a woman in her late sixties. Her face was hard, she was chain-smoking, she wore thick make-up and her eyes were vacant. I initiated a conversation, but her responses were blunt and cold, so I quickly stopped and began working on a talk I was preparing. I thought I would have plenty of time to do paperwork because she was so spiritually closed.

A few minutes later, to my surprise, she said, "What in the world are you doing? You look very busy. What are you writing?"

I tried to avoid answering her question directly because I was certain she would not understand. But she said, "Sure, it's a nice day. But what are you doing?"

I gulped, then told her what I did for a living and that I was preparing a talk for a Christian university students.

"You work for God, huh?" she answered cynically.

I knew that was a dead end, so I said, "Tell me your name. And what do you do?"

She said, "I'm Betty. Listen, I'm really busy too, just like you. I've got lots of friends. I just never have a moment to myself. Of course, I . . . uh . . . well, I live alone. But I have so many hobbies that I never seem to notice." Her answer was sadly revealing.

"You know, I've never yet lived alone. I guess I'm kind of afraid I'd get lonely," I said.

Suddenly she spun around in her seat and looked at me with great intensity. "Look, girl. You talk about lonely? I'm so lonely I want to die. Half the time I feel I already have. What I said about having lots of friends? Yeah, well, I don't. Nobody cares. My heart is bad, and when I feel funny, I run outside, 'cause if I die, at least somebody would know.

"You talk about God. I'm gonna tell you something. I came here to see a guy. I think he kinda liked me. He was lonely like me, and we just got on. I called his apartment and he didn't answer. So I called the landlord and asked him if Jack was there. He told me to hold on. When he came back on the line, he said, 'Oh, Jack is here. But he's dead. Looks like he died a few days ago. That's a shame. I'll take care of it. Goodbye.' Is that what'll happen to me? I just lie dead on a floor for two days and nobody knows? What's your God say about that?"

As pitiful as Betty's face was, it was the most alive I had seen her during the whole conversation. Pain had forced her out of her deadness and defenses. She hurt too much to be complacent; she had to be real. It seemed as if she were coming up one more time for air.

Trying to identify with her feelings, I said, "Makes you wonder if there really is a God, doesn't it? Makes you wonder where in the world Jack is now."

She answered, "I keep asking those questions. But I got no answer. Been asking those questions over and over since it happened."

"When did you learn that Jack had died, Betty?" I asked.

"Last night," she said. "And I been up all night . . . just askin' the silence for an answer."

I wanted to weep. Not only for her tragedy but also for my blindness and for the goodness of God toward her anyway. I had sat next to a woman whom I dismissed on sight as being unopen spiritually, but she had been up all night asking ultimate questions. I had wanted to ignore her so I could write my talk on evangelism, but she was asking questions from her depths, and God was reaching out to her.

I told her that I grieved for her pain. I shared that someone very close to me was also going through a time of excruciating loneliness. I told her how this person felt God was meeting her in her brokenness. Betty looked hopeful for a few seconds, then wistfully said, "You are so young, so young."

The conversation moved on to other things. I tried to think of some way to reveal God's love. It was clear that for Betty words were cheap. Later in the conversation I said, "Listen, I get to Salem fairly regularly. What if I visit you when I come?"

It was the second time she brightened. Her eyes lit up and she said, "You don't mean it? Sure, you could come! Listen, I'm a great cook too! And you could meet my dog. We'd have a great time!"

But when we arrived in Salem, Oregon, she had become tough again. As we got off the bus and she opened the door to the bus station, she said, "Well, kid, it's been OK meetin' you. See ya around." And she walked off. Then as she approached the other side of the station, she stopped, turned around, and looking at me in desperation, said, "Oh, God, Becky. Don't forget to call. Oh, please, don't forget me." And she left.

I sat down in the terminal and wept.

I wish there was a happy ending to Betty's story, but there isn't. I visited her. I spent nights with Betty and her dog. I brought students over to meet her, and they loved her far more consistently and faithfully than I. To my knowledge Betty only took; she never gave. Perhaps she was unable to. In fact, she used us. She was so starved for love that she could only gulp it down and grab for more. She came to know about the source of our love. She knew about Jesus. But she never chose to follow him, at least while we knew her.

I met her and I left her a woman alone.

Betty was not a waste of our time. She was important to God and important to us. We did not fail God with Betty. But we cannot make anyone become a Christian. We are not judged by our success but by our faithfulness and obedience, though it was a costly and painful obedience for us.

We must never assume that people are as they appear. All of us have needs. Like Betty, most of us have experienced some form of rejection. We long for things we are scared to death to ask for. We long to be touched, to be appreciated, to be told we are special, but we do not know how to ask. When we have been hurt, we have tender areas like open sores that make us deeply fear being touched and exposed. Still, that is what we long for most of all. What we need is for someone to act like Jesus, to put arms around us, to reach out to us and say, "Come home with me. I care about you. I want to be with you."

And that is also what we are called to do. We must not wait until we are healed first, loved first, and then reach out. We must serve no matter how little we have our act together. It may well be that one of the first steps toward our own healing will come when we reach out to someone else. When we get beneath the surface of a person, we will usually discover a sea of needs. We must learn how to interpret those needs correctly, as Jesus did. Jesus wasn't turned off by needs, even needs wrongly met, because they revealed something about the person.

The Samaritan woman had had five husbands and was currently living with a sixth man. The disciples took one look at her and thought, *That woman become a follower of Jesus? No way! Why, just look at her lifestyle.* But Jesus looked at her and came to the opposite conclusion. What Jesus saw in her frantic male-hopping wasn't just looseness. It wasn't her human need for tenderness that alarmed him but rather how she sought to meet that need. Even more, Jesus saw that her need indicated hunger for God. He seemed to be saying to the disciples, "Look at what potential she has for God. See how hard she's trying to find the right thing in all the wrong places."

That blows the lid right off evangelism for me. How many Samaritan women and men do you know? Everywhere I am, I see people frantically looking for the right things in all the wrong places. The tragedy is that so often my initial response is to withdraw and assume they will never become Christians. We must ask ourselves, *How do I interpret the needs and lifestyles of my friends? Do I look at their messy lives and say 'That's wrong' and walk away? Or do I penetrate their mask and discover why they are in such trouble in the first place? And then do I try to love them where they are?*

We can show people that they are right to want to fill the void, and then they may be surprised by joy to discover that the emptiness inside is a God-shaped vacuum.

Loving People Where They Are

In order to establish trust with people, we must love them with the baggage they bring with them. We need to accept them where they are without compromising our Christian standards. Jesus accepted the "gift" from the prostitute at Simon's banquet (Lk 7:36-50). He shattered his "testimony" by allowing a loose woman to touch him. But he did not ask her to demonstrate her love for him and sense of forgiveness by exegeting Ezekiel. He allowed her to offer a gift that she was comfortable with.

We too must live with the tension of being called to identify with others without being identical to them. That may mean that we demonstrate our support by affirming a friend's motive even if we cannot participate in the deed.

When I lived in Portland, Oregon, a woman moved in below me in my apartment building. Every time I saw her, she was on her way to another party. We always exchanged friendly words, and one day she said, "Becky, I like you. You're all right. Let's get together next week and smoke a joint, OK?"

I replied, "Gee, thanks! I really like you too, and I'd love to spend time with you. Actually I can't stand the stuff, but I'd sure love to do something else."

Of course, she looked a bit surprised, not so much because I didn't smoke marijuana but because I had expressed delight at the thought of spending time with her. I could have told her, "I'm a Christian and I never touch the stuff," but I wanted to affirm whatever I possibly could without selling short Christian standards. Too often we broadcast what we "don't do" when we should be trying to discover genuine points of contact. Most of us tend either to overidentify and blend in so well that no one can tell we are Christians or we separate ourselves and play it safe by having little contact with the world. We should recognize what our tendency is and work against it.

There are, of course, some things we should not do. One test is whether the activity violates a scriptural principle. Another is whether we are violating our own sense of purity. Here it is important to know ourselves.

We must be aware of where we are vulnerable. Under most circumstances it is dangerous to talk ourselves into what we know is a real temptation but say we prayed God would give us strength to overcome. Often people tell me they entered perilous situations because they felt they were the only person who could witness. I believe we must take risks as Christians, but God will not call us into situations he knows we cannot handle. He can find someone else to go who does not struggle in that area.

Loving Others as We Are

Our message is not that we have it all together. Our message is that we know the One who does! That means we have the freedom to fail. It also means we have the freedom to be ourselves—plus.

Let God make you fully you. Rejoice in your God-given temperament and use it for God's purposes. This point cannot be emphasized enough. We must be authentic. If we try to be someone we are not, people will see it instantly. A man I know with a larger-than-life personality talks about God with anyone he meets almost upon immediate contact. He doesn't have to warm up the subject; he simply talks about the Lord's goodness to him and about how grateful he is to be a Christian. It's so effortless that it is a joy to watch. His smile lights up his face, and his manner is so infectious that I've never seen anyone offended. People can sense his authenticity and they enjoy his style because it's so utterly him. Yet if someone else, with a different kind of personality, tried to do the same thing in the same manner, it would fall flat.

Much has been written about various temperaments.[1] Most of it is helpful, even though I personally resist oversimplified categories that put people into slick personality boxes. Of the many personality distinctives that have been drawn by researchers, one of the most obvious is the extrovert-introvert distinction.

God made some of us extroverts. These are the types who get energized by talking and interacting with people. They are usually comfortable relating to the outer world. They can talk about personal issues with relative ease. I am by nature an extrovert, though over the years I have found I need much more alone time to process and make sense out of my inner world. Nonetheless, my tendency is to figure things out by talking them through. And I love meeting people and discovering their stories.

God made others introverts. These are the ones who get their energy replenished by being alone. They tend to be more comfortable with the inner world than the outer world. They need to meditate and think things through first before they are comfortable speaking. They are often more private and prefer to share personal information with a select few.

We should praise God for these differences and take them seriously. In regard to evangelism it means we need to express our faith in ways that are consistent with who we are, as well as be sensitive to the person to whom we are speaking. At the same time we must remember that no spiritual growth occurs without our being stretched. Being an introvert isn't an excuse to never share the gospel. Rather, it means finding ways to share the love of Christ in a way that fits who we are. The key is that we don't become so stretched that we violate how God has made us.

For example, I have a friend, Amy, who is an introvert by nature. Being a mature Christian, she takes seriously Jesus' call to share her faith. At the same time she has had to learn how to express her faith in a way she is comfortable with.

Amy told me, "I'm not a person who can verbalize my deepest thoughts easily. Nor am I very quick on my feet verbally. So I ask the Lord daily to allow the Jesus who lives in me to love those people I come into contact with. I've been amazed by how often a person will say, 'I can't believe how much you care about me.' Yet I don't feel I've done anything that extraordinary. But as I share who the source of my love is, and as I pray, things happen."

In that example alone there is much to learn. First, this is an illustration of the power of listening. Knowing my friend, I'm not surprised people feel loved in her presence. She has an unusual capacity to listen with depth and compassion—more than she is even aware of. Listening well is a powerful way to share the love of Christ. Second, this illustrates the power of prayer. When we ask God to let people experience the love of Jesus though us, something happens that can't be quantified or easily explained. That's because prayer involves mysteries that happen to the soul. As you listen and pray for your seeking friends, it will open doors for God to penetrate.

Amy loves to paint and takes art classes whenever possible. Her art classes have provided her with a great opportunity to bring, as she says, "the aroma of Christ" to others. "How do you do that?" I asked her. "Art classes provide a safe environment for people. As we paint, people talk easily. Part of my influence in the class was that I shared things of a more personal nature. For example, if I was worried about one of my children, I'd say so. But I'd also add 'I pray for them every single day and, boy, does it help!' Or when I discovered I needed surgery, I was honest about my anxieties. But I also felt free to tell them how grateful I was that my church was praying for me."

"Pretty soon they began to share more of themselves as well. If someone said she was upset over a problem, I would write a note and tell her I was praying for her. Over time they began to see how my relationship to God impacted how I handled the daily concerns all of us share," Amy said.

"By the end of the class," Amy continued, "several felt free to come to me privately with their spiritual questions or personal problems. One woman started going to church, another went out and bought a Bible, another asked me to pray for her. But I don't feel evangelism is my gift by a long shot. I'm not very good at wrapping things up and closing the deal," she said.

While we can improve on the skills Amy felt weren't her strength, the truth is that some people genuinely are more gifted than others at "closing the deal." These are people with the gift of evangelism. That doesn't mean those who don't have the gift of evangelism are free to remain silent or will never lead a person to Christ. Just look at the fruit of Amy's witness! She shared authentically how Christ made a difference in her life and people were drawn to Christ. Amy did what the apostle Paul wrote to the Thessalonians: "So deeply do we care for you that we are determined to share with you not only the gospel of God but also our own selves" (1 Thess 1:8).

But what if you fear the "stretching process" will be too much for you as you learn to share your faith? A remarkable collegiate woman told me once that, though she was an extreme introvert, she knew she had to find ways to share her love for God. She was perceptive and realized she shouldn't ask God to suddenly make her a boisterous extrovert. Rather, she asked him for the freedom to look outward, not to look at herself and be paralyzed by fear. She told me she got a summer job as a waitress because it would force her to talk with people.

When she returned to the university, she applied some newly learned lessons. When she was eating in the cafeteria, she would ask her table, "I'm going back for milk. Can I get anyone anything?" Usually a few would reply yes. When she returned with what they requested, it almost immediately opened up a conversation and they asked her questions. She said the fact that they were both focusing on the extra milk she had in her hand reduced her fear of eye contact. Her being able to focus on something else (even if it was a glass of milk!) kept her from focusing on herself. That led her on to discovering other ways to serve.

She had a plant that everyone admired. So when someone said she had a beautiful plant, she would say, "Thanks! Let me give you a cutting." That offer opened conversation but kept her focusing initially on the plant, which helped her fears. She also offered to help students preparing for tests if they were in her field or needed a paper typed. Eventually, after much practice and continually raising the stakes, she became more and more at ease around people. It was a learned skill. But what freed her and helped her to love and accept herself and others was learning that she could take initiative in ways that were reasonably comfortable for her and that people responded to her. She was still reserved but not so desperately afraid. She loved people powerfully but quietly.

What struck me about her was the effectiveness of her nonverbal witness. She told her friends about Jesus, but she demonstrated him in beautiful ways too. She worked on overcoming her timidity but discovered eventually that she had the gift of serenity. People were drawn to her because her presence brought a sense of peace. She would have never realized this gift if she had not gone through the excruciating process of taking initiative. She worked on some of the "limits" in her temperament (just as an extrovert would need to learn when to use restraint), but in the process God blossomed in her the gifts of her temperament.

What these last two examples illustrate is that being an extrovert isn't essential to evangelism—obedience and love are. Since I am an extrovert, my personal illustrations already reflect my own style of witnessing. The joy of these various examples, however, is that God needs all of us to reach all of his children. The lesson is that God isn't glorified in our lives if we try to wear our best friend's personality. We must be who we were created to be. And we must reach out to others in a way that is both sensitive to the person with whom we are talking and consistent with our own personalities.

But regardless of our temperaments, we all must become initiators. The mark of a mature Christian is whether she or he chooses to be the "host" (the initiator) or the "guest" (the receiver) in relationships where being a host is most appropriate. There are, of course, times when those who are ordinarily hosts should be guests. The point is that the call to love those around us is in part a call to identify their needs. Once we have some understanding of their needs, we must find ways to meet them that are natural for us.

"But," you may say, "the fact is that to take initiative in itself is not natural for me. I'm just a shy person." Actually, the ability to get outside of one's own skin and serve another is not natural for anyone. But sitting back and doing nothing is not an option. We are called to love, to serve, to identify need and to respond. That is not easy for anyone, but it is what the Holy Spirit helps us to do so that we can become more like Jesus. Nonetheless, in the way we exercise our love, the way we choose to demonstrate it, the way we share Christ with others we can choose a style comfortable for us.

The Christian must be the one who loves, cares and listens first. We all can take initiative, whether quietly or openly.

Being Salt and Light

We must not become, as John Stott puts it, "a rabbit-hole Christian." When I worked with collegiates, the form it would take was this: A Christian student leaves his Christian roommate in the morning and scurries through the day to class, only to frantically search for a Christian to sit by (an odd way to approach a mission field). Thus he proceeds from class to class. When dinner comes, he sits with the Christians in his dorm at one huge table and thinks, *What a witness!* From there he goes to his all-Christian Bible study, and he

might even catch a prayer meeting where the Christians pray for the nonbelievers on his floor. (But what luck that he was able to live on the only floor
with seventeen Christians!) Then at night he scurries back to his Christian
roommate. Safe! He made it through the day, and his only contacts with the
world were those mad dashes to and from Christian activities.

If you're not in college, that description may sound ridiculous or irrele-
vant. But how often do we in the church imitate the same behavior? The most
common objection I hear when I am training churches in evangelism is this:
"All my friends are Christians! With work, parental responsibilities, church
activities, there's no time left to form a friendship with a seeker."

Life does get more complicated with greater responsibilities as we get
older. Yet to have no time to be "the aroma of Christ" to an unbelieving
neighbor, friend or colleague means we aren't taking seriously God's command to "go and makes disciples."

What an insidious reversal of the biblical command to be salt and light to
the world! The rabbit-hole Christian remains insulated and isolated from the
world when she is commanded to penetrate it. How can we be the salt of the
earth if we never get out of the saltshaker?

Christians, however, aren't the only ones to blame. Even the world
encourages our isolationism. Have you ever wondered why, on a typical
television program, everyone always "behaves" when the minister comes to
visit? Suddenly their language changes and their behavior improves. Why?
They want to do their part to keep the Reverend feeling holy. They will play
the religious game while he is around because he needs to be protected from
that cold, real world out there.

Sometimes non-Christians will act oddly around us because they are
genuinely convicted by the Holy Spirit in us, and that's good. But all too often
they are behaving differently because they feel that is the way they are
supposed to act around religious types.

I am often put in a religious box when people discover what my profession
is. During the days when I ministered to collegiates, I had a clergy card that
sometimes enabled me to travel at reduced rates. The only problem was that
occasionally ticket agents didn't believe I was authorized to use it! A young
female just wasn't what they had in mind when they saw a clergy card. More

than once I was asked, "OK, honey, now where did you rip this off?"

Once when I was flying from San Francisco to Portland, I arrived at the counter and was greeted by an exceedingly friendly male ticket agent. "Well, hello-o-o there!" he said.

"Uh . . . I'd like to pick up my ticket to Portland, please."

"Gee, I'm sorry. You won't be able to fly there tonight."

"Why? Is the flight canceled?"

"No, it's because you're going out with me tonight."

"What?"

"Listen, I know this great restaurant with a hot band. You'll never regret it."

"Oh, I'm sorry, I really must get to Portland. Do you have my ticket?"

"Aw, what's the rush? I'll pick you up at eight."

"Look, I really must go to Portland," I said.

"Well, OK. Too bad though. Hey, I can't find your ticket." He paused, then said, "Looks like it's a date then!"

"Oh, I forgot to tell you, it's a . . . special ticket," I said.

"Oh, is it youth fare?"

"No, um, well, it's . . . uh, clergy," I whispered, leaning over the counter. He froze. "What did you say?"

"It's clergy."

"Clergy!" he shouted as the entire airport looked our way. His face went absolutely pale as he was horrified by only one thought: *Oh, no. I flirted with a nun!*

When he disappeared behind the counter, I could hear him whisper to the other ticket agent a few feet away, "Hey, George, get a load of that woman up there. She's clergy." Suddenly another man rose from behind the counter, smiled and nodded and disappeared again. I never have felt so religious in my entire life.

As I stood there trying to look as secular as possible, my ticket agent reappeared and stood back several feet behind the desk. Looking shaken and sounding like a tape recording, he said, "Good afternoon. We certainly hope there have been no inconveniences. And on behalf of our airline, we'd like to wish you a very safe and pleasant flight . . . Sister Manley."

As humorous as this incident was, I think it shows how difficult it is to maintain our authenticity before the world. The challenge is not to allow ourselves to become more or less than human.

We know, in short, that Christ desires to have a radicalizing impact upon us and our relationships. But that impact is greatly aided when we live as we are called to live: no longer regarding anyone from a human point of view but desiring to see beneath the crust, to love people as they are with the gifts they have to bring, and to care in ways that correspond to who we are as well. We are not insulated and isolated from the world, but neither are we complacent and blind to its agonies and sorrows and the darkness of its heart. We are salt and light. We make a difference because we are different. And when we live before God as we truly are, he will change the world in which we live.

9

Developing
Conversational Skills

·······················

Once a college professor and I were having a stimulating conversation on a plane. The talk was lively and comfortable—until he asked me what I did for a living. When I told him I was in Christian ministry, he looked at me quizzically as if he were thinking, *Funny, and she seemed so intelligent.*

Clearly taken aback, since he assumed he had been talking to someone normal, he began trying to find the right words to say to a religious type. In a stilted manner he finally said, "I'm sure it must be very . . . uh . . . rewarding."

"Well," I said, "I'm not sure it's as rewarding as it is intriguing."

Almost in spite of himself he said, "How do you mean, 'intriguing'?"

"I think one of the hardest issues a Christian must face is how in the world we know that what we believe is true. How do we know we are not deluding ourselves and worshiping merely on the basis of need rather than truth? Or that some psychologists are not correct in saying we worship a glorified version of our father figure. To have to deal honestly with those questions is exciting and intriguing."

He looked at me in surprise and said, "Well, I have to confess, though I haven't thought much about faith in a long time, those are the very questions I have. OK, how do you know it's true?" For the rest of our flight we discussed the evidences for and the message of the Christian faith.

Frequently, when I'm traveling to speak, I am asked what I do for a living. You might think I'd try to hide the fact that one of the books I've written is on the topic of evangelism. It is quite the opposite. Often I respond by asking, "Have you ever been offended or buttonholed by Christians trying to share their faith with you?" That's all I have to say. Everyone seems eager to share a war story.

Once they discover I've written a book that examines how to more effectively communicate the Christian faith, I usually ask them, "How do *you* share your deepest convictions with others, without betraying your beliefs yet without seeming intolerant or arrogant?" That nearly always opens the door to a provocative discussion of faith. People are especially interested to know how Jesus spoke about faith to those who didn't believe. So even the topic of evangelism, if handled sensitively, can be a door that opens a discussion about faith. But what opened that door was my mentioning one of their "hot buttons" regarding faith before they did.

These examples reveal one kind of conversational skill. It involves being the first to suggest the defenses that our unchurched friends may have. Walls are torn down and bridges are built when we suggest their own objections before they do. It's also important to acknowledge that their objection is often quite legitimate.

In this chapter we will look at ways of moving conversations from discussions of ordinary topics to spiritual ones. We will examine a variety of ways of communicating our faith. However, one thing needs to be made clear. Good communication skills cannot convert anyone. It is the power of God and his divine initiative that penetrates and converts the seeker's heart. Jesus said, "No one can come to me unless drawn by the Father who sent me" (Jn 6:44).

So why do we bother building our communication skills? Because we want to be sure that our style of communicating the gospel isn't blocking the seeker's ability to hear it! It is one thing when skeptics take offense at the gospel; it is quite another when their offense is over a blundering, aggressive, insensitive or even an apologetic style. The way we communicate must reflect what we communicate. In fact, the two cannot really be separated.

Once I had lunch with a woman named Mary who told me her office mate was close to accepting Christ. Mary was especially concerned because she was being relocated by her company, and she felt her office mate needed Christian friends. When Mary introduced me to her, she looked at her office mate and said, "Now I'm having Becky meet you because you really need friends. You'll never make it with God unless someone sticks close to you. So I asked Becky to keep an eye on you when I'm gone."

I wanted to crawl under her desk. But as I tried to think of some cover, the office mate looked at me, smiled and said, "You know, she really, really loves me. And it always shows."

Although love covers a multitude of conversational sins, there are some principles that will help us be better communicators of our faith.

The Importance of Attitude

We cannot overestimate the importance of our attitude. Our attitude and style communicate content just as do our words. If we notice that skeptics seem embarrassed, apologetic and defensive, it is probably because they are picking up our attitude. If we assume they will be intrigued to discover the true nature of Christianity, they probably will. If we project enthusiasm and not defensiveness, and if we carefully listen instead of sounding like a recording of "Answers to Questions You Didn't Happen to Ask," seekers probably will become fascinated.

Why are we sometimes embarrassed or apologetic when we share the gospel? Maybe it's because pockets of unbelief still reside in our souls. Sure we believe, we say, but not so much that we are willing to stick our necks out and take a risk. Ironically, the one sure way to build faith in God is to acknowledge our fears and doubts and then be willing to take a risk in spite of them.

Or we assume our friends won't be interested in spiritual matters, so we don't expect a positive response. Granted, there is often a high level of mistrust among skeptics toward the institutional aspects of Christianity. Recently a poll was given asking Americans to rank their level of distrust for various professions. Television evangelists came in next to prostitutes and organized crime! But my experience is that there is a great deal of openness toward any expression of faith they consider to be real.

Last, our discomfort is due to our own stereotypes of the unchurched. In the evangelism training conferences I have given around the world I never cease to be amazed by how consistent some responses are, regardless of which country I am in. For example, once I was giving evangelism training in India and a beautiful woman in a sari raised her hand during the question-and-answer session and said, "One problem, which I believe may be unique to us Indians, is that we fear offending people when we do evangelism." I assured her that I hear that comment more than any other no matter what country I am in.

There is a role-play exercise I do in evangelism training in which I say, "Turn to the person on your right and assume that person is a Christian who has just asked you, 'How was your weekend? What did you do?' Tell that person about this event and one thing you have learned from being here so far." There is always an immediate buzz of conversation as people excitedly share what they have learned.

After a few minutes I say, "Now reverse the roles so the other person has a chance to answer. Remember to tell what this event was this weekend and one thing you've learned from being here. Only this time pretend that the person asking the question is a non-Christian acquaintance."

The silence following my second set of instructions is only equaled in drama by the "you've got to be kidding" look on their faces. The feedback after the exercise is always telling. "How did you feel going from the first exercise to the second?" I ask. The answer is always the same: "Terribly uncomfortable!" Their reasons generally are the following: "Because I knew he wouldn't understand a thing I said"; "she'd think I was crazy"; "he'd think I was pushy"; "she'd take offense"; "my church friends would understand me, but I knew he wouldn't"; "they'd think I was a religious fanatic to use my weekends to go to a Christian conference"; and so on.

To varying degrees and with only one or two exceptions, I have received those responses from all over North America, Latin America, Asia, India, Europe and the Middle East! I have heard these responses from Catholics,

Orthodox, Protestants, mainline and evangelical denominations. What's the problem here? First of all, it's small wonder that we feel uncomfortable with evangelism with paranoid preconceptions like that floating around in our heads! Our fear seems to be that if we dare say a word about God, most people would gladly eat us for breakfast! In other words, what cripple our effectiveness are our *own* stereotypes of others.

But Jesus tells us not to judge others. That means we must refuse to assume a person is closed to God. In fact, why not assume the opposite? Sure, this person may have been turned off by a false and distorted picture of the Christian faith—but that's good news, not bad. Has he ever been exposed to true faith? Does he know what Jesus is really like? Why not assume the best and believe this person might be very open to God? And if we can't pull that off, then at least we must remain agnostic. That is, we must remind ourselves that we really have no basis for assuming the negative.

Here is one thing I've found helpful, especially in avoiding an us-versus-them defensive mentality. When you are speaking to a person about the gospel and you begin to feel your fear level start to rise, pretend that you are talking to a Christian. If you thought you were talking to a believer, you would be much more relaxed and you'd act like yourself.

Unfortunately, our insecurities and fears are often misinterpreted by seekers. When we act stilted and awkward, they mistake our sense of inadequacy for arrogance. What they *think* they are hearing is "Well, I'll *try* to explain this to you, very slowly—but I'm sure you're too unspiritual to really grasp it." It would be far better to acknowledge our fears instead of pretending we don't have any.

No Question Is Unacceptable

Learn to delight in all questions seekers may pose, especially the ones you can't answer. No questions should be regarded as too hostile. I often tell people I'm very grateful that God is using them to sharpen me intellectually when I am stumped by a question. I tell them I don't know the answer but can't wait to investigate it. And usually I do investigate and learn in the process. What we model by this approach is that we love Christ with all of our minds. A question we can't answer is not grounds for abandoning our faith but for further exploration. Our message is that the truth of faith may be above reason but it is not contrary to reason.

We get into trouble when we feel it's up to us to defend God and prove by our own wits and wisdom that we are right and they are wrong. Of course, there is a legitimate place for debate. But if our style with seekers is to always "argue them down," we may be winning the argument and forgetting the purpose of evangelism: to introduce the gospel to our hearers in the confidence of *God's* power to convert.

Or perhaps our fear is that we must have all the answers. I often meet sincere Christians who honestly believe they can't share their faith because, as they say, "What if someone asks me a question I can't answer?" Of course people will ask us questions that we can't answer! What has that got to do with evangelism? The gospel does not need our aid in its defense; it is quite capable of defending itself. As Luther said, "Let us not be anxious, the gospel does not need our help; it is sufficiently strong of itself."[1]

It is the Spirit's role to convict of sin and convince the seeker of God's truth. Our task is to share the story of Christ and to ask the Spirit of God to make the message of faith credible and knowable. Yes, we take their questions seriously and answer them as best we can. We work hard to relate the gospel to the cultural context of our hearers. We want to make the Christian position intellectually viable to searching persons. But to refrain from sharing the most glorious news ever announced to humanity because we might be asked a question that stumps us is a tragedy.

Exposing and Imposing

Next, we can learn to expose our faith, not impose it. As we have seen, we cannot make someone a Christian. Only the Spirit of God can truly change a heart. Consequently, though we are called to let our faith be known, we are not called to force it on others. In fact, if our evangelism reflects an aggressive style, it could indicate our misunderstanding of the role of the Holy Spirit. We could not convert anyone if our life depended upon it.

Evangelism, then, is not employing a super sales strategy with shrewd salespeople. Why? Because the gospel is not for sale! It is a free gift of grace for those who will accept it. God's Word, as theologian Karl Barth said, "does not compete with other commodities which are being offered to men on the bargain counter of life."[2]

We don't force our faith on others; neither do we manipulate others into listening. Instead, we tell the good news of what God has done for us and the whole world in the life, death and resurrection of Jesus Christ. We simply share our faith in love, hoping that God will act upon their hearts so that they may receive the truth we profess.

I used to worry constantly after witnessing to someone whether I did it right, if I should have said this or that, and so on. The Scripture calls us to excellence, but it also says the Spirit will give us what we need for tough situations (Mk 13:11). To be anxious about whether we have witnessed in exactly the "right way" implies there is some outside perfect standard that we are being judged by. There *are* things that are very helpful to understand as we engage in the task of evangelism, and we will examine them in the next several chapters. But there is no magic formula; there is no absolute and correct way to witness every time. We are called to do the very best we can and then trust the Holy Spirit to speak to a person through what we say and do. We witness in the confident expectation that God will move and act upon our hearers in his way and in his time. Donald Bloesch sums it up best when he writes, "Evangelism is not the imposition of a point of view but the overflow of a thankful heart."[3]

Taking It Easy

There is an inevitable tension in evangelism. On the one hand, we should feel an urgency about sharing the gospel. The more we care about our friends, the more we long for them to know God. We want to share the good news because we care about their total well-being. I agree with Bonhoeffer, who wrote, "To tell men that the cause is urgent, and that the kingdom of God is at hand is the most charitable and merciful act we can perform, the most joyous news we can bring."[4]

At the same time we need to learn to relax. Since it is the Holy Spirit's job to convert, that should ease some of our anxiety. We are called to be a witness to the truth of God's good news and to share what we have experienced in simple, personal terms. Jesus did not say, "Go and be theologians";

he said, "You will be my witnesses." Being a witness for Jesus Christ involves our words, and it also involves the way we live our lives, but it does not mean that we are called to be flawless philosophers or apologists. We simply trust the power of God to work through our obedient efforts. I am not saying we should not seek to arouse curiosity in the gospel nor to relate the gospel to the situation in which seekers finds themselves, but we will probably be more effective with an initial, casual reference to God than nervously wondering about whether we are doing it exactly right.

We need to remember that evangelism is a process. Conversion may take place in a moment, but God will use many people, events and experiences to lead a person to himself. People need time to think, watch, listen and talk through their questions. Our witness is invaluable, but it is still just one aspect that God will use to draw a person to Christ.

When I train churches in evangelism, one point of anxiety that is frequently mentioned is the question of timing. When is it appropriate to proclaim the good news? It is a valid concern, for I have met seekers who were turned off by an approach that was too abrupt or too impersonal or in which they felt cornered and manipulated. Our burden for a person's salvation does not excuse insensitivity.

I remember one young man saying, "I have a friend who works in my office. We play golf together and are becoming friends. I really want to witness to him, but I keep wondering when the right time is. I mean, at what moment should I tell him? How will I know when the exact time is to finally witness?" By the time he had finished his question, he had me feeling as uptight and intense as he was. And I could not help but sympathize with whomever the recipient of this talk would be. That kind of anxiety and intensity would scare a person to death!

How do we know if we are speaking at the right time and at the right place? In order to know if there is an "opening" to proclaim the message of Christ, we need to listen carefully both to God and to our friend. We need to ask God, even as we are conversing with our friend, to give us wisdom and a word of knowledge (1 Cor 12:8). Then we need to test the waters with the person. Have we sensed on his part any interest in the spiritual comments we have made? Did she seem genuinely interested and ready to pay attention? Jesus warns us against not giving what is holy to those who are uninterested in it (Mt 10:14).

It is far more effective to first toss out a few casual comments about your relationship to God or about how Jesus views a particular subject. There is something very appealing about openness. Say, "Hey, I'd like you to meet a friend who's in this fantastic Bible discussion I'm in" or even, "We had an interesting study this week on how Jesus related to women. He sure was ahead of the culture of his day in his attitude toward women." And then see what happens. Their responses will guide you in how to proceed.

Getting Rid of God-Talk

We should talk the same way to non-Christians as we do to Christians. In the past I used to ask my host before I spoke to a crowd, "Are there many skeptics in the room?" Then one day it dawned on me that, regardless of the answer, it wouldn't change the nature of my talk. Truth is truth, and its appeal is universal. Of course, we need to speak truth in ways that are relevant and arouse the curiosity of our audience, but in most instances we should be able to tell both groups the same stories or experiences or thoughts. We should not assume that our unchurched friends will not be interested in our spiritual side. We need to invite them into our lives, to share what we share, enjoy what we enjoy. We must not act superior because we know God or have more information.

But when we explain the Christian message, we should do so in plain language, preferably in fresh and creative ways. Few things turn off people faster or alienate them more easily than God-talk. Without realizing it, we use words or clichés that have a correct understanding only among Christians.

When I worked with college students, I gave many evangelistic dorm talks. I remember one in which a skeptical but seeking student asked me, "What does it mean to be a Christian?"

A Christian student who really desired the other student to understand replied, "It means you have to be washed in the blood of the Lamb." The first student paled and looked confused. The Christian continued, "That way you will be sanctified and redeemed."

Another student, seeking to help his Christian brother, said, "And the fellowship is so neat. Praise the Lord! You really get into the Word and get such a blessing."

By the end of the evening, it was clear from the skeptic student's face that he felt Christians came from another planet!

To the world, religious clichés are often either red flags or else the meaning is imprecise. Of course, we must not dispense with biblical words and concepts. Instead, we need to develop fresh and relevant ways to express what they mean. Frequently I will describe what a word means, then say, "That's what the Bible means when it talks about sin." If we do it in that sequence, we can arouse curiosity and dismantle defenses.

For example, I attended a film with a woman who is a psychologist. She is a genuine seeker, and I had chosen the film because it raised central issues about what it means to be human. Later, as we sipped coffee, I said, "The film suggests that the human situation is tragic. From all your experience as a therapist, do you agree?"

She responded, "I think people get into awful messes with their lives, but I'm not sure I'd call it tragic. Would you?"

"Well, the Bible says the human situation is tragic . . ."

"Oh, I know," she interrupted with a tone of cynicism. "You Christians say we are all sinners."

"But Joan," I responded, "do you know why? The Bible says it's because something very, very precious has been broken. If we weren't so significant, if we didn't have so much meaning, then it wouldn't be so sad. It's only when something precious has been broken that we can say, 'How tragic!' That brokenness is what the Bible calls sin. That's why God hates it so much. Sin caused something extremely precious to become dehumanized."

"What do you think are concrete evidences of sin in a person's life?" she asked.

"Pride, envy, narcissism, self-deception, perfectionism—anything that makes us less than we were created to be," I answered.

"What, then, is the source of sin, according to the Bible?" she asked.

"We are control freaks. We seek to live our lives calling all the shots instead of answering to God's rule. We have a 'God complex,' and judging by all the people that flood your office, I'd say it isn't serving us well. We've been created to be God-centered, and we are hopelessly self-centered. Sin has left us addicted to ourselves," I answered.

Our conversation lasted for hours as we discussed what the Bible says is the true source and the solution to the human problem. As we stood up to leave, she said, "Becky, I've got a lot to think about. I've just understood for the first time what Christians mean by sin. I know I don't have any psychological explanations for the source of human ailments that comes even close to the depth of the biblical analysis. Let's get together soon after I've had time to think. But I want to thank you, not only for speaking to me about spiritual things, but for saying it in English!"

We need to first understand for ourselves the meaning of biblical words, then we need to translate them in ways that people can understand. I read somewhere that Albert Einstein once said, "You don't really understand something unless you can say it in a really simple way." Here are some other common Christian terms we should learn to express in fresh ways: *grace, salvation, justification, sanctification, regeneration, redemption, born again.* Your Christian group may well have other phrases meaningful only to the initiated. Learn to translate them.

Asking Leading Questions

We can learn to ask good questions. Too often we allow ourselves to be put on the defensive. The dynamics are greatly changed when we turn the tables and begin to direct the conversation by asking questions. My friend Dale Hanson Bourke and I once led an investigative Bible discussion for women who wanted to know more about the Christian faith. When I asked one of my most skeptical friends to come, she at first answered, "It might be interesting to look at the life of Jesus, but I know I could never be a Christian. My commitment to scholarship makes any consideration of Christianity impossible. It's irrational, and the evidence supporting it is totally insufficient."

I answered, "I'm so glad you care so much about truth and that you really want evidence to support your beliefs. You say the evidence for Christianity is terribly insufficient. What was your conclusion after carefully investigating the primary biblical documents?"

"Uh, well, you mean the Bible?" she asked.

"Of course," I said. "The New Testament accounts of Jesus, for example. Where did you find them lacking?"

"Oh, well, look, I remember Mother reading me those stories when I was ten," she replied.

"Hmm, but what was your conclusion?" I continued and as a result discovered she had never investigated the Scriptures critically as an adult. This is all too often the case. But we can arouse curiosity in others to investigate the claims of the gospel when we help them see that their information and understanding about Christianity is lacking. Just her realization that she had based her beliefs on impressions formed as a child made her eager to come to the study.

Another person I invited to the investigative Bible discussion, a woman who was quite hostile to what she perceived was Christianity, told me, "Why should I come when I can't stand those hypocrites who go to church every Sunday. They make me sick."

"Yes," I responded, "isn't it amazing how far they are from true Christianity? When you think of how vast the difference is between the real thing and what they do, it's like worlds apart. The more you discover what Christianity is really about, the more mystifying it is that anyone could settle for less. That's exactly why I'm inviting you to come, so you can examine for yourself the real thing."

"Uh, the real thing? Well, what do you mean by that?" she asked. We then talked about what basis we must use to evaluate what genuine faith looks like. She, too, came to the study when she saw that to fairly evaluate Christianity she had to be willing to examine the life of Jesus. But her hostility was changed into curiosity because she was asked questions, not preached sermons.

God has made us curious, so let's learn to ask questions.

These principles of conversation are applicable to most of our dialogue with seekers. They can be applied anytime and any place. Now we need to explore the larger picture of the task of evangelism.

10

Three Ways
to Witness

....

The heart of evangelism is sharing the story of Christ, the good news of how God took upon himself the sin and shame of the human race so that all who believe in him might be saved.

This message is the most liberating news to ever grace this planet. The question is, then, why aren't we more eager to share it? Why don't we race out to share such joyful news? The psalmist tells us, "O taste and see that the LORD is good" (Ps 34:8). Once we know that truth from the inside out, we will always have something to tell others.

Motivation shouldn't be a problem. But perhaps one reason we feel gun-shy about proclaiming the gospel is because we have never led a person to Christ before. Leading someone to Christ is an awe-inspiring experience that changes us forever. It confirms the truthfulness of the gospel and the reality of God's presence as few other things do. In case you feel inadequate, let me tell you about my first experience.

Born Again in Barcelona

After my failure with Mary in Barcelona, which I mentioned in chapter one,

I asked God to help me be more brave the next time around. Ruth Siemens kept telling me that, when the time was right, I should ask my friends if there was any reason they could not become Christians right now. The Bible discussion I had started for seekers was nearing an end for that year, and all of us were studying for finals. After one exam Todd and I went for a cup of coffee in a student restaurant.

Of all of the students in the discussion, he was the most cynical to the gospel. He made Mary, in her agnostic days, look like Mother Teresa. Initially he came only to disrupt the discussion, but we befriended him, and eventually he came every week. There was only one more discussion left, and I felt I had to ask somebody in that group to become a Christian. I was sure Todd would never become a Christian (I really did not think I would be instrumental in anyone's conversion till I was at least eighty!), so Todd seemed safe.

I said, "Todd, you've been part of this discussion all semester. You've heard a lot about God, but you've never decided what to do with God. One of these days, Todd, you're going to have to decide. Sooner or later God is going to speak to you and say, 'Decide now.' And what are you going to say?" I was feeling so proud for sounding firm (even though I knew my confidence stemmed only from the fact that he would never respond) that I failed to notice how serious his face became. "Yes, sooner or later, Todd, God is really going to speak to you. And when he does, in that year, I hope you will say yes."

I think I was still speaking when Todd said, "You're right. God is speaking, and I am saying yes."

But I went right along without inhaling, "That's right, Todd. One of these days God will reach out . . . uh, w-what did you just say?"

"I said, 'God has been speaking to me right now. And I said yes,'" he answered.

I paled. "Oh, Todd," I answered weakly, "you have such a sense of humor. But really, you shouldn't scare me like that."

"Becky, I'm not kidding. I've been thinking about this for a long time. And I'm ready now," he replied.

"Todd, listen to me. You can't rush into this. I mean it's a huge decision. And it'll change your life so much. You better think it over and then go see Ruth."

"Look, Becky. This isn't an emotional decision. I know I put up a good front, but I've been thinking about God for a long time. Now, look, I want to become a Christian!" he nearly shouted.

"Right here? In the restaurant? In front of everybody? Todd, I just, well, I can't."

"Why not?"

"Well, because I've never done anything like this before."

"Don't worry, I haven't either," he answered. "I tell you what. Let's close our eyes, then I'll say something to God and then you do. It'll be over in just a few minutes."

So we did, right there in a restaurant in Barcelona, Spain. When I opened my eyes, I still thought it was only temporary. But even if his conversion only lasted a few hours, it would have been enough for me. I said, "Now, Todd, something Ruth always says is that conversion is a matter of your will. It doesn't matter if you don't feel any different," since I was sure he didn't (talk about the sin of unbelief on my part!). "It's your will that you've given to God. The emotions will come later. But there is just one thing I wanted to ask you," I said.

"Sure, what is it?"

"Uh, do you feel any different?" I asked.

"You bet I do!" he roared.

I looked at him in utter shock. "Todd!" I cried. "Oh, my goodness—*it works!*" So off we went to my apartment to tell Ruth and Kathy.

While we were there, Stephanie, another agnostic friend in the Bible discussion, called and asked us to do something that night. During the evening I kept thinking how flabbergasted she would be when Todd told her, especially since he was one of her best friends. We were in a restaurant when she looked at Todd and said, "You know, you've really changed. You just look happier, more peaceful. Spain must really agree with you."

And Todd responded, "It isn't Spain, Steph; it's God. I've become a Christian."

Thinking he was joking, she said, "Yeah, right. I'm Santa Claus. You shouldn't joke like that in front of Becky."

"Stephanie, I'm serious. I've given my life to Christ. I intend to follow him."

She looked incredulous and then terribly anxious. He was the least likely of all of them to turn to God. If Todd could, then what did that mean about the others? She grew quiet and serious as Todd told us of his spiritual pilgrimage, that he always had hid behind his sarcasm and seeming indifference. We took a cab home. Stephanie decided to stay over with me. We walked into my room and she said, "I want to know how he did it. What do you do when you become a Christian?"

Now I could have lived off Todd's experience for a good twenty years. But when I saw how seriously she asked me that question, I thought, *Oh, it couldn't be! It couldn't happen again. I just can't handle this.*

So I said, "Steph, would you excuse me for a few minutes?" I casually walked out and shut the door. Then I panicked. It was 1:30 in the morning, and I needed help. Kathy and Ruth were asleep, but I went into Kathy's room anyway. I burst open the door and couldn't think of anything to say. So I cried out, "Pray!" and wheeled back out. Kathy told me she awoke with such a start that she prayed for ten minutes before realizing she did not know what she was praying for!

Back in my room Stephanie and I talked quietly for several minutes. Then she said, "Becky, I've been running away from God for a long time. It's time I start running to him," and she became a Christian that night.

As reluctant and inept as I was, that night changed my life. Before my eyes I saw the very two who seemed the least likely turn their lives over to Christ. Perhaps even as significant as that experience is the fact that today, all these years later, Stephanie is a mature Christian married to a Christian man. I am the godmother of their now twenty-one-year-old daughter. God is faithful. And little did I realize that a feeble attempt to witness to one woman would produce a family who loves God.

There are people around us whom God longs to touch through us—people whom only we can reach with our particular style and personality, people whom we have been called to. We must begin to ask God, "Is this the one? Is she the one you are seeking?" It is a fantastic drama, and God wants to use us to accomplish it.

Since my first experience back in Barcelona, I've seen many people give their lives to Christ. Watching peoples' lives be transformed by God has convinced me of one thing: there simply is no greater service that one human being can render to another. To see people find wholeness, meaning and joy, to be restored to freedom as they walk in the grace and mercy of God, is a privilege beyond the power of language to describe.

In light of such mercy and grace, the only question we can ask is this: how do we communicate the gospel to an unbelieving world?

Once I was in my car waiting at a stoplight with my window rolled down. A car pulled up next to mine, and just as I put my foot on the gas pedal, a piece of paper came rocketing into my window and hit me on the cheek. It didn't hurt, but I was so startled that I pulled my car over immediately. As I unrolled the paper, I discovered it was a gospel tract. I'm sure the person who threw it into my window was well intentioned, but "torpedo evangelism" is not what I see practiced in the Bible!

I shared this story with a friend of mine who said, "It's clear that person didn't have the gift of evangelism or she would have done it better. She'd be better off practicing her own gifts and leave the evangelizing to you!" My friend spoke somewhat in jest, but she uncovered what many believe: if we don't have the gift of evangelism, then it's all right to remain silent. Nevertheless, God commands each and every one of us to "go and tell." That is what makes evangelism unique. Not everyone is called to be a prophet or a teacher, for example, yet even prophets and teachers are commanded to go and make disciples (Mt 28:18-20). In other words, regardless of whether we have the gift of evangelism, we are still called to share the gospel with others.

However, when evangelism is done as poorly as what I've just described above, it forces us to ask, what exactly *is* evangelism? Evangelism in its simplest form is introducing our friends to Jesus. Peter brought his brother Andrew to meet Jesus; Philip brought his friend Nathaniel. Michael Green, the English author who has written extensively on the subject of evangelism, believes the best description of evangelism is this: "a presentation of Jesus Christ in the power of the Holy Spirit so that people will put their trust in God through him, accept him as their Savior, and serve him as their King in the fellowship of his church."[1]

Another question we must ask is this: is there a "right" way to do evangelism? Is one approach better than another? Answer: as long as Christ is proclaimed, the integrity of the seeker is honored and the motive that drives us is the love of God, there is no form of evangelism that can be faulted. However, I believe there are a few things that, if properly understood, will help us become more effective communicators of the gospel: understanding both the ways and the means of how to evangelize, and understanding the natural stages involved in the communication process. In this chapter we will examine the ways. In the following chapters we will examine the wonderful means that God has given that enable us to share the gospel in power.

There are three primary ways that God has given us to accomplish the task of evangelism. Our evangelism is the most effective when we proclaim the gospel, when we demonstrate Christ's compassion through our words and compassionate service, and when we depend on the Spirit and point to the demonstration of the Spirit's power. These ways are not mutually exclusive, and hopefully our lives model all three.

Certainly the primary form of evangelism is the proclamation of God's truth through the sharing of the gospel. However, opportunities to explain the gospel often come only when seekers experience Christ's love through us. Loving acts pique their curiosity, for they verify the authenticity of our message. And some seekers are drawn to consider Christ when they observe the Spirit's presence and power in our lives. One seeker, whose brother's conversion was accompanied by being supernaturally released from a ten-year drug addiction, told me, "I had intellectual answers to refute every argument he proposed for why Christianity was true—except the major one. Who can argue against a completely transformed life?"

Declaring God's Truth

The Bible tells us that true faith comes by the preaching and hearing of the Word of God. "So faith comes from what is heard, and what is heard comes by the preaching of Christ" (Rom 10:17). How are we to tell others? By drumming up a little message of our own? Fortunately not, for God's message of grace has been given to us through the gospel—his revealed message through his revealed Word.

It is not a story of human invention but a God-authored gospel that has the power to save! We are called to give the unchanging message that God sent his Son, Jesus, who took our sinful, broken humanity into himself and made it his own by dying on the cross. He sacrificed his life for us and overcame our sin. Then he rose from the dead so that by surrendering our lives to him our sins may be forgiven, our lives made whole and our eternal destiny made secure!

We proclaim the good news of what God has done primarily through the telling of the gospel. But the gospel is also proclaimed when we tell our story of salvation, for our conversion story illustrates the power of the gospel. Therefore, our task is to tell "his" story and "our" story in the hope that it may one day be "their" story.

Displaying God's Love

Second, Jesus tells us that the world may accurately judge whether Jesus is who he said he is by looking at how we demonstrate Christ's love (Jn 17:20-23). In other words, the communication of the gospel includes sharing the love of Christ to an ailing and lost world through self-giving service. How has God equipped us to do this? God has imparted his divine characteristics to dwell within us through the fruit of the Spirit: love, joy, peace, patience, kindness, goodness, faithfulness, gentleness and self-control. These characteristics of Christ are revealed as salt and light in a lost and needy world, whether by caring about the moral decay of our society, demonstrating integrity in the workplace, fighting for the dignity of the downtrodden or for those who suffer from discrimination, or simply loving our unchurched friends in our college dorms or neighborhoods. Whether we are identifying with the pain of our neighbor or serving strangers in a soup kitchen, we are engaged in the form of evangelism that demonstrates Christ's love for a lost and needy world.

Acts of kindness are a powerful means of grace. They are even more powerful when we reveal, at the appropriate time, the source of our love. To hide the good news of God's salvation and simply witness through loving presence is not enough, for then we would be depriving seekers of the knowledge of where they can find hope. "I have not hidden your saving help within my heart, I have spoken of your faithfulness and your salvation; I have not concealed your steadfast love and your faithfulness from the great congregation" (Ps 40:10).

Demonstrate God's Power

Third, we bear witness to Christ by walking in and pointing to the power of God's Spirit. We know that effectual evangelism can be done only by the regenerating and liberating work of the Holy Spirit. We don't simply impart information when we share the gospel; we need the Spirit's power to give our words meaning and effectiveness. The truth must be spoken in the power of the Spirit. How does that happen? God's means of grace is the gift of the Holy Spirit, who indwells every believer. As we learn to walk in sync with the Spirit, he will give us just what we need in the moment we need it. Besides learning how to avail ourselves of all the Spirit offers, we should also point seekers to the manifestations of the Spirit's power.

In Jesus' ministry the proclamation of the good news was accompanied by the demonstration of God's power. Jesus not only preached to the sick—he healed them. He not only proclaimed salvation to those oppressed by evil—he delivered them. The proclamation of the gospel went hand in hand with a demonstration of the Spirit's power (1 Cor 2:1-5).

"But that was Jesus," we may say. "How on earth are *we* supposed to do that?" Of the three approaches, we may feel the most inadequate in this one. But God has equipped us here too. Through the work of the Holy Spirit we are filled with the fruits of the resurrection victory of Christ. For example, what Christian has not seen God intervene at a point in his life when all seemed hopeless? Or been wonderfully surprised by something God has done when her feeble prayer received a resounding answer? Most of all, we have witnessed lives transformed by trusting in Christ—not the least of which is our own! We have far more in this arsenal than we realize. We must freely point seekers to the demonstration of the power of God wherever we see evidence of it.

Putting It All Together

So now we know that people who say, "I just fix people's cars for the sake of the gospel," or "I show Jesus' love by listening to their problems" are demonstrating the way and means of evangelism that *displays Christ's love.* This is worthy, for it reveals the character of Christ's compassion. Fantastic! Yet there is more. At the right time and the right place, seekers need to be able to connect our kindness with the source of our love by hearing the message of salvation. To witness by loving presence but never reveal the source of our love is not evangelism. Or when a person says, "I preach the gospel, but I leave others to love them into the kingdom," we know this is the aspect of evangelism that *declares God's truth*. Wonderful! But done alone it is insufficient. All Christians are summoned to the practice of love, for it reflects the character of God and authenticates the gospel we preach. Or for the person who says "I just pray and trust God to bring people to salvation" is evangelism that rightfully depends upon and *demonstrates God's power*. But evangelism that never proclaims the gospel or mediates the love of Christ through acts that the seeker can observe is insufficient as well.

Think of all that God provides so that we may share the good news! He gives us his message of truth, he indwells us with his presence so we may mediate his divine love to our neighbor, and he fills and renews us with his Holy Spirit. Evangelism is something that *God* does in people's lives; we are only the instruments he uses. It is the Spirit of God who convicts others of sin and who changes people's lives. It is so liberating to remember that God's initiative *precedes* our response. He is always there before us. Once we understand what evangelism entails and we see that God has provided all we need to accomplish the task, it frees us to share the good news with joy.

Evangelism, then, is most effective when it declares God's truth, when it displays Christ's love and when it depends on God's Spirit and points to God's power. But how do we start? Is there a process? Or do we dive in and start preaching to people, simply throwing out words without regard to people or the situations they are in? No, for to do that would be to subvert our best efforts.

In the next three chapters we will explore each stage of the communication process as we learn how to cultivate, plant and reap. We will also explore how to effectively declare God's truth, display God's love and depend on God's power so that our evangelism may be as fruitful as possible.

11

Cultivating the Soil

....

I believe there is a process in the communication of the gospel that involves three phases. A Christian organization called Sonlife Ministries[1] has phrased this communication process quite aptly as (1) cultivating the soil, (2) planting the seed and (3) reaping the harvest. Or to put it another way, we need to learn "CPR" in order to share the good news effectively. A lifesaving device to save lives eternally!

The first stage of "cultivating the soil" is learning how to "prepare the way" as John the Baptist did for Christ. We do this by arousing the curiosity of seekers so they will want to hear the good news. That doesn't mean we blindly engage in stage one with every seeker we meet. We need to pay attention, for perhaps the curiosity of the seeker has already been aroused. If this is the case, then we may have the opportunity of sharing the gospel, which is the second stage, called "planting the seed." Yet even announcing the gospel is not enough. At the right time we need to sensitively point out that God desires a response or decision to be made. In other words, the third stage is "reaping the harvest," which involves an appeal to the will to make a commitment to Christ. Only God can make the human response positive. But evangelism isn't fully understood unless there is the hope to produce a harvest.

In this chapter we will examine the first stage in the process of evangelism: learning how to cultivate the soil of the seeker. In the next two chapters we will consider the other two stages.

A Disclaimer

All along we have been talking about evangelism as a lifestyle. We have looked at Jesus' life and examined a few practical conversational skills so that we may become more natural and at ease in sharing our faith. I do not now intend to change my basic approach. Techniques can be helpful to some people in limited ways, but they will not make us natural. So what follows is not a new, never-before-revealed technique of lifestyle evangelism.

In fact, learning how to speak and live God's truth, living in the presence of Christ's love and mediating it to others, and walking in the power of God's Spirit not only help us in our evangelism but these graces enable us to live a life of faith. In one sense, evangelism training is simply calling believers to live as true Christians. When we live as we are called to be, evangelism can't help but happen.

But the danger of carefully analyzing something—evangelism for example—is that we can turn it into a rigid formula. We can lose our spontaneity and start worrying, *Oh, dear. Am I supposed to be cultivating or planting right now? I can never keep it straight.* That would be the very antithesis of what I am intending.

My hope is that by exploring the natural stages of evangelism—cultivating, planting and reaping—and by looking at the means we've been given to accomplish the task, namely, living in God's truth, love and power, it will free us simply to be who we truly are in Christ. When we live by grace, we learn how to walk in the joyfulness of God. So what we have to offer others is not a life of rigid self-consciousness but a life of joyful abandonment to God. Life lived this way is the most powerful magnet for evangelism there is.

So, if what I am about to say in this chapter and the next two sounds like technique or makes you feel stilted, then ignore it. I merely want to look at the process of evangelism in the hope that it will clarify your thinking and make sharing the gospel seem less intimidating.

What It Means to Cultivate the Soil

We cannot make people open to the gospel. We cannot coerce them into considering Christianity. So do we just hang around and wait until seekers come to us and say, "By the way, I've always wanted to be saved, but no one ever told me how"? Is there anything we can do to open blind eyes?

There is one sense in which our blind eyes are never fully opened until after we receive faith (Is 35:4-5). But before there is a faith commitment, is there anything we may do as a possible preparation? Eugene Peterson said in a lecture, "As we become practiced in sin, we develop complex defenses against grace. Do we penetrate these defenses by frontal assault? Sometimes, but more often indirection is called for, slipping past the defenses 'on the slant.'" Jesus, for example, used this method of "indirection" when he spoke in parables in order to get through to people.

In Acts 26:18 Paul says Jesus first called him to *open the eyes* of unbelievers, then to turn them from darkness to light and to receive Christ in faith. In other words, Jesus is calling us to arouse the curiosity of seekers before we preach the gospel. If their curiosity is piqued, they will want to hear the gospel message. Remember, we are called to be "fishers" of men and women who throw out bait, not "hunters" who gun people down.

This first stage of "cultivating" is called pre-evangelism. It's what comes before we proclaim the message of salvation. Using our agricultural metaphor, the soil must be cultivated before seed can be planted in order for a harvest to be reaped. How is the soil of seekers broken up or tilled? How is the seeker's curiosity aroused?

Let's examine the three resources that we looked at in chapter ten and see how they can be applied to this first stage of evangelism.

Cultivating the Soil by Declaring the Truth

All truth comes from God. But what aspect of truth is the most helpful to communicate in this "cultivating" stage? Our goal, of course, is to proclaim the message of Christ. But if we speak too quickly or prematurely, we may lose our opportunity altogether. What do we do? We first arouse the curiosity of seekers so they will *want* to hear the gospel. How do we do that?

We need to be careful listeners. We need to discover the questions our seeker friends are wrestling with. We also need to discover how much they already believe. We make a mistake when we assume there will be no points where we may connect in mutual belief. I usually try to find as many points of mutual agreement as possible before we explore where we disagree. This is particularly helpful when in dialogue with those of different religions. When we first establish the points of truth upon which we agree, it not only builds bridges of understanding but also sheds light on the areas where we disagree.

Also, discern what the larger issue of truth is that lies behind whatever issue is being discussed. We need to encourage our friends to ask themselves what truth they base *their* opinion on, and then to consider whether that truth is big enough to build their lives upon.

It is also helpful to know the questions that our culture is wrestling with. A wonderful way to do this is by seeing and discussing thoughtful films with seekers, like I did with my therapist friend mentioned in chapter nine. One the most common threads of conversation between people is "Did you see such-and-such a film? What did you think of it?" But one word of caution: Just because we are striving to relate our message to the problems and issues of the day, that doesn't mean we allow the questions of our culture to reign supreme—because our culture may not be asking the right questions! Yes, we take their questions seriously. We seek to understand what the Bible says in light of their questions. Yet we take far more seriously the questions that God asks of us.

But how do we help seekers move from the questions of culture to the divine questions? One way is to develop skills that enable us to move a conversation from ordinary topics to spiritual ones. Once we do that, we are closer to sharing the good news.

As I have said before, we all have different temperaments. Some of us are cognitive; others of us, intuitive. Some respond naturally to ideas illustrated through graphs or charts; others are repelled by them. That is what makes communication with any person exciting and at the same time complex. So when examining any technique or model, we need to ask ourselves, *Does this correspond to the way I relate to people, or does it seem artificial and feel awkward? And even if it feels comfortable for me, would it be appropriate for the person to whom I am speaking?*

It is important to realize we are at least halfway responsible for how a conversation goes. We have choices in how we communicate. We should want to make our conversation count in representing Jesus Christ. But that brings us back to Jesus' own example. Jesus directed his conversations—for instance, with the woman at the well. He did not manipulate her, yet neither did he allow red herrings to get him off the track. He was not molded by her presuppositions; her alternatives did not keep Jesus from his purpose.

So, to have purpose and ultimate desires for a conversation is not wrong. And it is not wrong to learn a few principles of communication to help us get a conversation going as well as to direct it toward spiritual matters. Here are three models that are not to be understood as rigid techniques but which some have found helpful in moving conversations from ordinary topics to spiritual ones.

Conversational Model A: Investigate, Stimulate, Relate

Investigate. First we must discover who the person is. This requires a genuine interest and curiosity in that person. Jesus was known as the friend of sinners. He loved all types of people and didn't distance himself from those whose lives weren't tidy. It is the love of Jesus that motivates our interest in others. One way we discover what a person is really like is by asking questions. Our culture does not encourage us to ask each other questions. We can fly from Los Angeles to New York and never speak to the passenger next to us. But Christians are not to be molded by their culture. We must learn to ask questions, draw people out, so that it becomes part of our lifestyle and not a technique.

To do that we need to learn how to be listeners first and proclaimers second. It is like rowing around an island, carefully viewing the shoreline for a spot to go ashore—a shared interest or a shared problem. Look for ways that God has made you alike. The more interests you have, the easier and quicker those mooring points are discovered. For the sake of Jesus Christ we need to be interesting! The more we enjoy God's world and develop our gifts, as well as explore new interests, the easier it will be to establish rapport with others.

If we listen for the nuances, we can draw others out without prying. Many people hesitate about giving direct messages because they are not sure anyone really wants to listen or are afraid that they cannot be trusted. Frequently people give clues about what things are bothering them or where they feel need. For instance, in response to "How are you?" someone says, "After last week things could only go up." Or as in the case of Betty when she said, "I live alone; but I have so many hobbies that I never seem to notice," which was an even more hidden message.

Sometimes people give us direct data but do not elaborate. For example, one person, after I invited her to a Bible discussion, said, "Thanks for the invitation, but I can't. I went to a funeral last week, and now I'm bogged down with homework." In both cases the ball has fallen into our court. We must find a way to express concern and give them an opportunity to talk if they want to. We must approach with care any message that we think we hear. If we sense need, it is probably because they intended for us to hear it. Sometimes you may hear a need and feel you are not the person to meet it. Then find a person who can.

Even if you are suddenly tongue-tied and walk away feeling you blew it, it is not too late. Go back later and say, "Listen, I'm so sorry about your grandfather's death. I just couldn't think of what to say to you the other day. But I care and I'm praying for you" (be sure you do actually pray). That may open just as many doors as an initial statement of condolence.

Stimulate. After we have an idea of who we are talking to, we must seek to arouse their curiosity about the gospel. This is one of the most neglected aspects of evangelism. We try to saturate people with information before we have caught their attention. A look at Jesus and Paul to study their fishing techniques will be helpful.

Jesus was often deliberately vague and intriguing with people at first, not giving the whole answer until he had their complete interest. When Jesus met the Samaritan woman (Jn 4:7-42), he told her that if she only knew who she was talking with, she would ask Jesus to give her some of his "living water." He knew that the Samaritan woman wouldn't understand what "living water" meant, which was evidenced by her very practical retort that Jesus could hardly offer her living water since he had no bucket to draw water from! But

Jesus told her that once anyone drank his brand of water they'd never be thirsty again.

Now we see that Jesus' deliberate obscurity was a stimulus and test of her spiritual interest. When she asked to receive this "living water," he did not automatically give it to her because he knew she didn't yet understand. Instead, he sensitively approached the subject of her personal life, which as it turns out was somewhat sordid—as Jesus certainly knew. All of a sudden Jesus' discussion about having a thirst that has never been satisfied begins to make a lot of sense. He did not manipulate her; he sought to arouse her curiosity. There's a world of difference between persuasion and manipulation.

Paul aroused the curiosity of the Thessalonian Jews in the synagogue with his fierce logic and rational arguments (Acts 17:1-8). In Athens he captured the interest of the Greeks by citing their poets to affirm his points: "As some of your own poets have said, 'We are his offspring.'" (v. 28 NIV). Also Paul, after walking through the city of Athens and seeing countless altars to various deities, turned to the people and both cleverly and tactfully said, "Men of Athens! I see that in every way you are very religious. For as I walked around and looked carefully at your objects of worship, I even found an altar with this inscription: TO AN UNKNOWN GOD. Now what you worship as something unknown I am going to proclaim to you" (vv. 22-23 NIV). We too need to develop a style of intriguing evangelism that piques interest in the gospel.

Relate. When we have discovered where people are and have aroused their interest in what we have to say, then we are ready to relate the gospel message. Investigating and stimulating are the necessary pre-evangelistic steps that will enable us to communicate Christ more effectively. But it is not enough to take the first two steps without the third. Paul, for example, knew his audience, found where they needed to grapple with commitment and then proclaimed the gospel (Acts 17:16-34).

The story of the professor I spoke to on the plane (chapter nine) is a good example of this model. As our conversation began, I "investigated" by asking him many questions—about his field, his interests, his life. I took a genuine interest in who he was as a person. We don't take an interest in people in order to trick them into a conversation about Christ. We want to know and understand people because God loves them. Period. It is because of God's love that we also desire to share the good news of Christ. If we take the time to get to know people, it makes it much easier to know how to arouse their curiosity.

Once I understood the professor was an intellectual, it wasn't hard to guess his resistance to faith: that there is no rational basis for believing. When I said, "I don't think my work is rewarding, but it is terribly intriguing," I was using the second element of this model. I was arousing curiosity just as Jesus did when he used the phrase "living water" with the woman at the well. When the professor asked me why my work was intriguing, I had learned enough about him to guess pretty accurately what his objections to faith would be. I answered in a way that was truthful but also relevant to him.

After we had discussed the historical evidence for faith, he said, "I wasn't going to tell you this, but I was raised in faith. Yet the more we talk, the more I realize that as a child I blindly accepted Christianity, but as an adult I have blindly rejected faith. For the sake of intellectual integrity I need to know what I've rejected. I'm not saying I believe the historical evidence, but I can't refute it either. So I'm going to get a Bible and start reading. But I want to tell you something. I think what strikes me most about you is that you seem to be a woman of hope and not despair. Why?"

I answered, "Well, you see, the reason I am a woman of hope and not despair is because I have fallen hopelessly in love with Jesus Christ. I am not the same; I have been made new." At that moment I no longer needed to investigate or stimulate. I was now free to relate the reason for the hope that is within me.

Conversational Model B: Concentric Circles

Another important skill in moving conversations from common interest to spiritual matters is discerning what the underlying issue is that lies beneath the beliefs being expressed. For example, these days we often hear, "I don't care what a politician does behind closed doors—I just care about his or her policies." The unspoken greater issue here is the relationship between public and private morality. Is there a connection? Does compromise in one area affect compromise in another? From there we ask, "Where does our sense of morality come from anyway?" In other words, what began as a belief being expressed moved to the larger issue of the nature of morality and ultimately landed at the theological question of morality's origin.

The model we will examine next has been adapted from Donald C. Smith, who developed this while he was a staff member for InterVarsity Christian Fellowship in Michigan. Conversations, he says, can be like an onion. As we peel off the layers in a conversation, we go even deeper into the mindset of a person. Often conversations begin with general interest questions (What do you do for a living? How many children do you have? What is your major?). Then as the conversation develops and greater trust is established, we ask more specific questions (What do you enjoy about your job? What era of history are you specializing in? What do you think about the present political scandal?). The next layer is the one that we frequently miss, but it is crucial. This is detecting and speaking to what the greater issue or the greater need is that hasn't been expressed (Do you think the old adage is true that we reap what we sow? How does your art reflect the nature of humanity? Are you satisfied with what psychology is teaching you about people?). And then comes the theological layer (What is the source of goodness? What do you think God demands of us?).

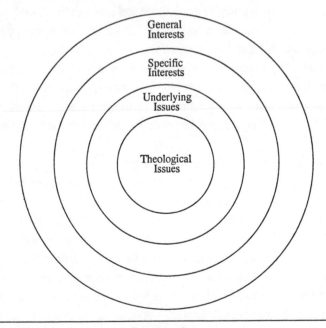

Figure 1. Concentric circles model of conversation

Here's how the model works out in practice. Once I spoke with a college student and asked, "What is your major?" (general interest question).

"Art," Peggy answered.

"I really think that's a great field of study. Why do you major in it?" (specific interest question).

"Well, I guess because I appreciate beauty," she said.

"I do too. You know, I had a biology professor once who said we are nothing more than meaningless pieces of protoplasm. Do you think a piece of protoplasm can appreciate beauty?" (underlying issue behind the interest).

"Mmmm, I've never thought of it before. But we must be more than that. The appreciation of beauty runs so deep in us," she said.

"One thing has always intrigued me. Where do you suppose beauty comes from? I mean, what's its source? And where do we get our ability to appreciate beauty?" (theological issues).

"You mean like God or something? I don't know, but it's interesting to think about."

"Well, is there any evidence to support the idea that God is the source of beauty?"

From here on, one can continue this kind of conversation in many ways. The topic is already spiritual, and it can be natural to raise, for example, the question of beautiful people—like Jesus. When we hear people responding to their God-image (such as saying they appreciate beauty), we can help them see it could be because they were created by a God who enshrines that very quality.

The transitional key in the model is addressing the larger underlying truth issue. It is not stopping at a flat statement of belief but probing deeper. It does not have to be an intellectual, abstract transition. For example, in my earlier conversation with Betty the turning point was the underlying issue. I had picked up that she was lonely. But instead of asking her directly about it (which probably would have frightened her), I talked about my feelings about loneliness. "You know," I said, "I've never yet lived alone. I guess I'm kind of afraid I'd get lonely." In other words, I addressed the unspoken emotional issue hidden beneath her words. She responded by opening up her whole lonely life to me.

It could be that this model is not one you will find helpful. Fine. Perhaps you will find the following model more consistent with your style.

Conversational Model C: Relationships, Beliefs, Source of Authority

This last model deals with the issue of how to keep conversations from degenerating into arguments. What do we say when a person voices an opinion that is in dire contrast to our own, especially an opinion we believe violates God's truth?

I have adapted the following conversational model from Mark Petterson.[2] He says, "In any conversation the content is controlled to a large extent by the questions. If you want to control what is discussed, then you must take the initiative in asking questions." He then defines three areas that conversations (and consequently questions) deal with: relationships, beliefs, source of authority.

Relationships. The first area of conversation is how a person stands with respect to a common denominator (work, school, major, number of children, so on). This is like the "investigate" part in Model A and the "general interest question" in Model B. Conversation in this area is relatively easy and relaxed. We can usually find something of mutual interest.

Beliefs. Everyone has beliefs about politics, love, the meaning of life, God and so on. You might ask, "What do you think about [a recent news story, an upcoming election, an ongoing social issue or Christianity]?" It is in this area of beliefs that conversation can break down. Meaningful interaction is difficult at this level if the beliefs are not shared. Conversations can soon degenerate into argument, each person solidly maintaining his or her previously conceived dogma and not listening or interacting with the other. For example, someone may say, "I think church is full of hypocrites!"

You say, "There may be some who aren't sincere, but I know many whose faith is genuine."

He returns with, "Well, I'm convinced that it's just a vast brainwashing conspiracy!" The other person is convinced to the contrary, the battle lines are drawn and fruitful interaction is ended.

How can we avoid the impasse and move into dialogue? The key is to move the conversation to the third area.

Source of authority. What if the Christian had responded by saying, "Wow, you have some pretty deep feelings about this subject. What was it that led you to have such strong convictions?" In other words, you are asking the person *why* he believes as he does. Asking why makes people disclose their authority. This allows the conversation to continue and very often forces people to admit that what they believe about many important things is mere personal opinion. It may be possible, then, for the Christian to move the discussion on and show how Jesus provides authoritative information. If Christ's claim to be the living God is true, "then his answers to the meaningful questions of life are of the utmost importance," Petterson writes.[3] By asking the question, "Why?" the Christian can often make any meaningful conversation eventually focus on Jesus Christ, who is the central issue.

It is also in this area that Christians must know not only who their authority is but also why he is reliable. That probably means being able to cite some evidence for the historicity of the gospel. We will take up the use of evidence in our conversations in chapter fifteen.

Again, these approaches are simply a means to get conversations onto gospel turf. If this isn't your strength, then forget about it. There are other ways to pique the curiosity of seekers. To arouse curiosity by appealing to issues of truth is an appeal to the mind. But how do we appeal to the heart?

Cultivating the Soil by Displaying God's Love

In this chapter we have been considering how to gain a person's initial interest in Jesus. First we considered cultivating the soil by declaring the truth. Now let's look at how we might do this through the second way mentioned in chapter ten—displaying God's love.

Nothing touches the heart of people more than experiencing God's deep care and concern for them. This is especially true in today's world where there is such profound brokenness. It shouldn't surprise us, then, that people are drawn to consider Christ when they can see the love of Christ demonstrated through us. We are called to live a radically different lifestyle so that the loving presence of Christ within us may be seen in all that we do. As Donald Bloesch writes, "We cannot make people open to the gospel but we can help them to be open to us as persons. In healing and feeding the hungry,

Jesus was engaged in pre-evangelism."[4]

In every stage of evangelism—be it cultivating, planting or reaping—seekers need to see Christ's loving presence in us. But it is especially critical in this first stage. For if seekers do not see the love of Christ in us, then they most likely won't be interested in investigating any further. The famous quote from Emerson feels painfully apt: "Who you are shouts so loudly that I cannot hear what you say."

It bears repeating that most seekers won't pay attention to our gospel before they have seen our love and care for them as persons. If our hearers do not sense that the motive for our proclaiming the gospel message is love, then all of our efforts will be perceived as "a noisy gong or a clanging cymbal" (1 Cor 13:1). Even if we share Christ with virtual strangers, they can tell whether we care about them as persons.

People have amazing radar in this area. They know from our communication whether we regard them as persons to be cared for and enjoyed rather than objects to be manipulated and controlled. They can tell by our style whether they are projects we are working *on* or persons we are working *for.* If we are going to arouse their curiosity about Jesus, then we have to start behaving like Jesus!

I'm frequently asked how to be a witness in the workplace or with our family members or roommates. First, our colleagues must see that we are honest, truthful, reliable, that we don't engage in gossip and that we encourage and praise our colleagues' achievements—even in a very competitive workplace. Then it will be much easier to interest them in the gospel.

Likewise, our family members and roommates will initially look far more at our behavior than they will listen to our words. If they see in our behavior unselfish service, kindness and patience, it will have an impact in drawing them to consider Christ. When I first became a Christian, I made many mistakes in witnessing to my family. But I recall overhearing one family member say, "I knew Becky was converted when she offered to do the dishes—and it wasn't her turn!"

There are many creative ways to cultivate interest in the gospel by displaying Christ's love. Often the most natural expression flows from doing the things we love.

A friend of mine named Pat is an avid gardener. For the past three years she has organized something she calls a Garden Faire. For two days in early summer she opens her magnificent garden to the public. As friends, neighbors and strangers wander through her riotous poppies, hollyhocks and larkspurs, they can't help but read the thoughtful plaques she has placed throughout her garden. One says: "All I have seen teaches me to trust the Creator for all I have not seen." Other plaques have Scripture verses like, "See! The winter is past; the rains are over and gone, flowers appear on the earth; the singing has come" or "The whole earth is full of His glory" or "The Lord will guide you always; he will satisfy your needs in a sun-scorched land and will strengthen your frame. You will be like a well-watered garden." Just the sight of the glorious flowers next to such glorious verses would have made a convert out of me!

As you leave the garden there is a verse that reads, "The grass withers, and the flowers fall, but the word of our God stands forever." No one walking through that garden could have left without knowing that Pat gardens to the glory of God! This is a beautiful example of cultivating evangelism, for it is low-key, sensitive and also a natural reflection of who Pat is.

Pat also volunteered to be the one who welcomes people to her community. When newcomers arrive, she brings them a basket of flowers, freshly baked bread and a list of the neighborhood activities. One of those activities just happens to be the Bible discussion she leads!

Another way to cultivate friendships and practice the presence of Christ's love is by getting to know our children's friends and the parents of our children's friends. I have followed the example of my dear friend Pamella Bock. Pam hosted a yearly mother-daughter Valentine tea for her daughter, Angela, since she was in elementary school all the way through high school. I have done the same for my daughter, Elizabeth. It's not only a lot of fun, but it enables the moms to get to know their daughters' friends, as well as each other, and it cultivates the soil for future spiritual conversations.

My husband, Dick, says that our workplace and our personal interests should be our target zone for the gospel. As a businessman he says that he was always aware that his employees were watching him. They were observing whether he treated them fairly, seeing if he cared about their safety and well-being, watching how he conducted staff meetings and whether he disciplined employees fairly. Over time they realized that they could absolutely trust him to be fair because they knew he had integrity. They also knew he was a man of deep faith. It didn't take long before his employees began coming in to talk to him about personal problems. Some of his employees' wives even came in to discuss problems at home. It wasn't uncommon to walk by Dick's office and see him praying with his employees and their wives together.

Dick also says that he developed the practice of claiming territory for God. Dick is a great sports lover. So, for example, when he used to play tennis regularly, he would claim the tennis club for Christ every Tuesday and Thursday. And because he walked in expectantly, he often had remarkable conversations about the Lord. He is an avid skier, and he has deliberately taken some ski trips with friends who were not believers. He says that there is something about being in the majesty of God's creation that creates an openness in men to talk about God more easily than they normally would. He's also a sailboat racer. He says many times he'd find himself crewing side by side with a complete pagan. Yet some of his most powerful conversations about Christ were in the wee hours of the night as they watched an awesome thunderstorm.

Look around you, see where your lives naturally intersect with unchurched people. Claim your territory for God! Whether you are a kindergarten teacher, a banker, a laborer, a housewife, a student, an executive or an office worker, you have been given your own plot of soil to cultivate for the glory of God.

We've looked at how we can personally arouse curiosity in the gospel through demonstrating Christ's love. How can churches reveal the love of Christ in this stage of "cultivating"?

Recently I was invited to train a church in evangelism. The pastor told me that his congregation had wanted to demonstrate Christ's love in practical service to their city. They had read Steve Sjogren's book *Conspiracy of Kindness,* and taking the author's advice they had looked at the needs of their city and responded appropriately. In the past two years they had offered free car washes, free Christmas gift wrapping and free auto mechanic help once a month for single moms. They also gave family and teen seminars and did poverty work in the inner city. He said most people were amazed to encounter such generosity and many wanted to know why they were doing such kind things.

Some of his parishioners had made signs that read, "Just the outpouring from a thankful heart." If they were questioned as to its meaning or asked why they were doing these activities, they explained they had encountered the liberating love of Jesus and merely wanted to give something back. The next step, the pastor said, was to be trained in how to be better proclaimers of their faith.

Cultivating the Soil by Demonstrating God's Power

How do we utilize God's power as we seek to "cultivate"? There are times when we point seekers to the evidence of God's power. But we ourselves must be in constant dependence upon the Spirit of God because our most powerful weapons are those that employ not the wisdom of this world but the power of God: "The weapons with which we do battle are not those of human nature but they have the power, in God's cause, to demolish fortresses" (2 Cor 10:4 NJB).

One example of an indispensable spiritual tool that fortifies us to tell others about the good news is prayer. We pray for blind eyes to be opened! Many people are blinded to the gospel. We need to pray that the Spirit of God will open the eyes of the blind so they can understand the truth about Jesus.

I remember bumping into an old friend I hadn't seen since high school. As we sat looking at a dinner menu, Bob asked me if there had been any significant changes in my life since high school. I took a deep breath and began to tell him about my faith in Christ. I remembered him as being intelligent and cynical, and it soon became apparent that in those respects he hadn't changed.

I tried every apologetic approach I could think of, only to be rebuffed with polite but patronizing remarks. Knowing I was getting nowhere fast, I excused myself to go to the restroom. There I prayed a fervent prayer: "Lord, all Bob is hearing is *blah-blah-blah*. Let my words be spoken in the power of Your Spirit. Transmit through me your meaning and speak to his heart. Open his eyes, Lord."

I returned to the table. A few minutes later, in response to a question he asked me, I began telling Bob my conversion story. Initially he listened with the same skepticism. But suddenly it was as if someone had reached inside his head and turned on a light. Bob's whole countenance changed. In fact, he had a look of astonishment. "Wait a minute—that makes sense," he said. He began peppering me with questions about the Bible, about Jesus, about the meaning of the cross. We left the meal several hours later with my challenging him to start reading the Gospels.

The next morning the phone rang. It was Bob saying he'd been up all night and only had the Gospel of John left to read. Soon I introduced him to Christian men who befriended Bob and invited him to a Bible discussion. Six months later Bob gave his life to Christ.

How did it happen? It became clear that God had been pursuing Bob for a long time. Yet I know of no other explanation for what happened in that restaurant other than that the Spirit of God responded to my prayer. Why Bob responded to prayer so quickly, while others I have prayed for have not, is a mystery. But that experience powerfully reinforced for me how vital prayer is to evangelism. We need God's power to do God's work. In this pre-evangelism stage we need to ask God to give us wisdom and effectiveness, but above all we need to ask him to open the eyes and soften the hearts of those we are seeking.

We have looked at the first stage of evangelism and the resources that help us in "cultivating the soil." Now we are ready to examine the next stage of evangelism: "planting the seed."

12

Planting
the Seed

....

The proclamation of the unchanging message of Christ, the second stage, is the very heart of evangelism. "Faith comes by what is heard and what is heard comes by the preaching of Christ" (Rom 10:17). What brings people to faith is hearing the story of salvation, seeing the story confirmed in lives that bear the stamp of Christ's presence and love, and experiencing the story for themselves through the power of the Spirit. Our aim in this stage of the process is to communicate the gospel and to share its truth with clarity and confidence and power.

Once we have cultivated the curiosity of our hearers, the first stage, our next task is simply to introduce the gospel in the confidence that the gospel has its own power to persuade. Let's examine how to "plant" the gospel message, and how, by using the same three ways we discussed earlier (God's truth, God's love and God's power), the seed of the gospel can take root and flourish in the heart of the seeker.

Planting the Seed by Declaring the Truth
There are several ways we proclaim the truth of God's redeeming gospel.

Certainly how we live our lives and the evidence of the Holy Spirit's power in us and around us gives testimony to the truth of God's claims. But the principal channel for conveying God's truth is proclaiming the gospel. It is important to remember once again that we did not invent the gospel. The gospel has been handed down to us. It is a message of revelation, not human invention (Gal 1:16). That is precisely why it is life-transforming! It is *God's* message from start to finish. It is God's personal address, given through his messengers, calling people to repentance and faith.

But the very fact that the gospel has been divinely revealed, not humanly invented, also reminds us of our responsibility. The Bible makes it clear that we are not to tamper with its message (Gal 1:8). We don't have the freedom to water down the gospel to make it more acceptable to modern trends. Certainly we have a responsibility to make the gospel relevant to the contemporary situation of our hearers. We need to use language that people understand. Our presentation needs to be coherent and understandable. But the essence of the message is unchangeable and timeless. Paul told the Corinthian church, "We refuse to practice cunning or to falsify God's word; but by the open statement of the truth we commend ourselves to the conscience of everyone in the sight of God" (2 Cor 4:2).

In other words, we want to make the gospel viable to the world but not palatable. As John Stott once said in a lecture, "For the gospel to be effective it must remain prickly." We aren't called to convince the seeker of our own truth and experience. We are simply called to introduce the gospel in the power of the Spirit with confidence and faith in God's power to convert.

Therefore, we need to have a basic understanding of the Christian message so that when we do feel led to give it we can. It doesn't mean that we will always start at the beginning and work systematically through each point. Nor does it mean that we must get all the facts across in a single conversation. Much depends on where seekers are and how much interest they have. But if we have a working knowledge of the essence of the gospel, it will help us enormously. For that reason I have listed in the appendix some gospel outlines that you may find helpful.

"His Story"

What is the gospel message? Donald Bloesch states it succinctly: "The gospel is the surprising movement of God into human history recorded in the Bible culminating in the life, death and resurrection of Jesus Christ and the corresponding movement of God in the personal history of those who believe."[1] To proclaim the gospel involves telling "his story" primarily, for it illustrates the truth of what the gospel accomplishes.

Why is the gospel called good news? Because the story of Christ addresses how God entered human history through Christ, who took upon himself the sin of the human race so that all who believe might be saved from the judgment we rightly deserve. Our message is that Jesus lived, died and rose again for our sin! We are to repent, believe and receive Christ as King. We are to follow Jesus as the Lord of our lives and to live under his rule. Everything about us, every aspect of our being—physical, social, psychological, intellectual, material—is to be lived for God's glory. Our new purpose is to live in partnership with God, whose desire, as Jesus taught in his prayer, is for his kingdom to reign "on earth as it is in heaven" (Mt 6:10).

Frequently I am asked, "How much information should we share in order to communicate the essence of the faith?" It's a fair question. After all, there are entire books written on the subject. It can easily seem overwhelming. In fact, I've never been a person who can easily reduce profound truth to four or five points.

One thing that must be considered is the context. A person giving an evangelistic message to a crowd, for example, will have perhaps only thirty minutes to share the gospel. If you lead an investigative Bible discussion for seekers, you could have as many as seven or eight weeks to explore the life, the claims, the death and resurrection of Jesus. So to a certain extent, the format determines the amount of time available to proclaim the gospel.

But let's say that a friend or acquaintance asks you in private conversation, "What does it mean to be a Christian? What is it that you believe?" What do you say? Let me share an experience I had recently.

One Sunday evening I came across an article in a magazine that told of a woman who, without having a medical degree, was able to diagnose illness even before it has fully developed. She could sense a tumor for example, even before it appeared in any test. Some doctors were using her "expertise" when they couldn't discern what was wrong with their patients. The source of her insight, she said, came from spiritual power—not necessarily God alone, but a whole team of "spiritual guides." She described hearing voices that guided her to her diagnoses. "I love the invisible power. I can totally change people's lives," she said.

As I read the article, it became clear that what had started as a naive participation in New Age practices had led this woman into genuine occult practices. I couldn't help but reflect on what amazing times we are living in. Today it is commonplace to find reasonable, intelligent people who go to past-life therapists, visit psychics and read their horoscopes while wearing angel pins!

I finished the article feeling terribly sad. I turned to the Lord in prayer and asked, "What do we say to people who are truly searching for you, then read articles like this and get sidetracked into dangerous, even demonic activities? What do we say to those who want an answer for how people like this woman have this kind of prescient knowledge?"

As I prayed, I sensed God was saying, "Don't get involved in futile conversation about how these people know what they know. Simply ask a true seeker, 'What is it that *you* want to know?'"

The very next day, as I walked into an elevator on my way to a doctor's appointment, an attractive woman in her midforties walked in next to me. As we exchanged pleasantries, I noticed she was carrying a book that had the word "Spirit" in the title. I'm always curious to see what people are reading, so it wasn't unusual for me to ask her what the book was about. She responded by asking me if I had seen the article about a woman who was a "medical intuitive." I told her I had read the article carefully. She said that after reading the article she had decided to purchase a copy of this woman's book, and she had done so that very morning.

We had appointments in the same office, and as we walked into the empty waiting room, she introduced herself as Kay. She told me of her astonishment at this woman's apparent ability to discern the physical and emotional ailments of people. How could these "spirit guides" lead this woman into such knowledge? she mused. Where did such power come from?

After listening to her for a few minutes, I said, "Is there any particular reason you are drawn to this book?"

"Well, I guess you could describe me as a seeker," she answered.

I said, "That's interesting. I would have once described myself in exactly those terms. Kay, we could spend hours pondering how this woman knows what she knows. But I think what interests me more is this: what is it that *you* really want to know?"

Kay sighed and looked out the window. Then she answered, "I want to believe there is some force or being out there who has created all of this. I desperately want to believe that this 'God' is good. But what I can't get around is this: if God is good, then how can life be this awful? The front page of the newspaper today had a story dealing with moral scandal at the highest political level, another story was about parents who have forced their little daughter to live in a dog cage, and another article was on why children are murdering children. How can it be this bad? How can God be good with this much suffering? Why is life such a mess?" As she asked the questions the pain on her face was wrenching.

"There probably is no greater question than this one, Kay. I too have searched for God, and that question haunted me above all others. I think the issue is this: is the problem metaphysical or is it moral?"

"What do you mean?" Kay asked.

"Is the source of the problem to be found in God's nature or in human nature?"

"That's interesting. What do you think?" Kay asked

"From the different explanations I've seen, I think the Bible gives the most satisfying answer. It says there is a God and he is good. He created us in his image so we could have intimacy with him because he loves us. He also gave us free will because he loves us. Part of our dignity is that he gave us the capacity to choose. But at some point in history human beings chose the human experiment—we chose to be centered in self instead of centered in God. We chose self-rule instead of God's rule. It's what the Bible refers to as the Fall, and the results have been catastrophic. Evil became a reality on our planet. So life as we see it now is not the way it was meant to be. It was not God's intention that there be this suffering. All of us now remain in the vicious cycle of self-rule, both by birth and by choice."

"You know, I wouldn't find it hard to believe that *we* are the source of the problem," Kay said. "But the difficulty with that explanation is this: how could God have possibly thought it was worth the risk? How could he, knowing that there would be parents who'd lock up their kids in dog cages, still create us anyway?"

"Well, let's just suppose for a minute that the Christian story is true, that God created us in love. But we rebelled and chose to do it our way. And the effect of our rebellion is that it produced a state of deep separateness—from God, from each other, even within ourselves. In our brokenness we couldn't come to God, so God came to us. God didn't stand apart. He didn't abandon us. He sent his Son, Jesus, who became a man and entered fully into the human crisis and died on the cross for our sins in order to solve it, and to seek and save us. Maybe that doesn't directly answer why God created us, but such dramatic attempts on God's part to rescue us certainly reveals his overwhelming love for his creation."

"So you're saying Jesus' coming was like God offering people a second chance? But why would he bother? Becky, how could God possibly love people who are so screwed up?"

"Kay, you've hit the nail on the head. The most amazing part of all is watching what divine love really looks like in Jesus. Nothing could turn Jesus' compassion and love into hatred. He was tested to the utmost, but nothing could overwhelm his love. Just *imagine* the implications if the Christian faith is true! Because of love, God created the world. Because of love, Jesus offered himself as a sacrifice on our behalf. Because of love, Jesus defeated and triumphed over everything that assails us—sin, death and evil!"

Kay looked at me for a few seconds and then said, "What you are saying is profoundly moving. It even makes sense. I don't have any difficulty believing that we are responsible for the human mess. I even understand that we can't resolve the human crisis, even though it's of our own making. God would have to do that too. Perhaps he did by sending Jesus. But then what? Does the Christian just sit back and experience a cozy relationship with God? What about the unbelievable mess of the world around us?"

"You know, Kay, I read a passage in the Bible this morning that may answer your question. It's the very first speech that Jesus gave as he inaugurated his ministry. Obviously a first speech is terribly important because it outlines the mission: it's the person's manifesto statement. In his speech Jesus quoted from a text in Isaiah and said, 'The Spirit of the Lord is upon me, because he has anointed me to bring good news to the poor. He has sent me to proclaim release to the captives and recovery of sight to the blind, to let the oppressed go free, to proclaim the year of the Lord's favor.' Then he sat down and said, 'Today this scripture has been fulfilled in your hearing.'"

"Kay, to be in relationship with Jesus isn't finding a convenient way *around* suffering. It's joining Jesus as he works *through* the sufferings of those who are still in bondage to sinful self-rule. As forgiven people, we may then work in partnership with Jesus as he helps the blind to see, the lame to walk, the oppressed to be free."

Then she asked, "Where has your search led you, Becky?"

"I am utterly, totally, one hundred percent convinced that Jesus is who he said he is. I have committed my entire life to him. Surrendering my life to Jesus hasn't insulated me from life's pain and difficulties, but knowing him has brought a joy that none of life's suffering could ever overwhelm."

"But what do I do? I can't surrender my life to something I'm not convinced yet is true," Kay said.

"I'd suggest two things. First, pray. Tell God that you aren't sure if he is there, but if he is, tell him you are trying to find him. Ask him to show you if Jesus is the way to God. Second, get a modern translation of the Bible and start reading the Gospels. Determine that you won't stop until you discover who Jesus is. Read and pray every day, and ask God to reveal his truth to you."

"What if I come to believe that it's true?" Kay asked.

"Then you confess your sins to Jesus and thank him for dying on the cross, accept in faith his forgiveness and ask him to come into your life as King. Then find a church you feel comfortable with and join the family of faith!"

"I can't say I believe yet, but I *will* do what you've suggested. I just wish it were easier, and I didn't feel so vulnerable."

"Kay, I will pray for you. And I've got wonderful news. As much as it feels like it's all up to you, it's really God who is seeking you! It's God who pursues us, and he promises that he always finds any seeker who is genuinely searching for him. He won't lose you, Kay. You're not going to slip through his fingers. Just look at what happened in this office!"

At that exact moment the nurse opened the door and said, "I'm so sorry the doctor has been running late. Becky, he's ready to see you now."

I have prayed for Kay ever since that encounter. I am not sharing this story as an example of how to perfectly explain the gospel. In fact, afterward I thought of things I should have said and worried about what I hadn't made clear. But I had to remind myself of what I've already said to you: God is the one who converts, not us. We simply do the best we can in the moment God has given us and trust him for the results.

However, what were some of the elements of the gospel message I communicated to Kay? We touched on four areas that comprise main points of the gospel message: God's nature; the human crisis of sin; Jesus' life, death and resurrection; and the appropriate human responses to such good news, namely, repentance, faith and obedience. Furthermore, because of the nature of Kay's questions, I had the freedom to lay the framework of a biblical worldview. The gospel made greater sense to her because she heard it in the broader context of the stories of the Creation and the Fall.

What aspects of the gospel we initially emphasize will be determined in part by the seeker we are speaking to. What struck me about Kay was her sensitivity to the sufferings of the world. That is a perspective more typical, perhaps, of someone in her forties than of someone in her twenties. I believe she came to understand that human suffering is rooted in our sin, not God's neglect. She also wanted to know how faith is lived out—how it really works—which is very typical of a modern person. Judging by her responses, it was hearing about the love of God and Jesus' triumph through the resurrection over every evil that attacks mankind that moved her most.

While she intellectually grasped that the source of human suffering is our sinful insistence on self-rule, I didn't sense in Kay a deep realization of her own sin. But such knowledge will come—indeed, it *must* come—if she is to be truly converted. Nobody understands it all in one shot. We can trust and ask God to enlighten seekers in their journey, just as he does for us.

Our Story

To proclaim the gospel not only involves sharing God's message of salvation, it involves sharing our conversion story as well. However, we need to remember Paul's warning when he said, "We do not preach ourselves, but Jesus Christ as Lord" (2 Cor 4:5 NIV). So what purpose does our conversion story have? Helmut Thielicke helps us to understand: "The witness not only confesses and declares *his message,* he also confesses and declares *his encounter* with the message."[2] When we share our conversion story, it reveals our encounter with God's power and the beauty of his touch upon our lives.

But our story also reveals a terribly important lesson. The only way we ever discover the true nature of Christianity is when we step out and commit ourselves to Jesus. Then we begin to see for ourselves that God is real. There simply is no substitute for direct, personal experience. So long as we remain outside, debating or even believing the truths only in our heads, we can never really embrace the Christian way.

It has often been said that God only has children, no grandchildren. Tradition, in other words, cannot possibly make you a Christian. Only a personal encounter with Jesus as Lord accomplishes that. All of us are required to verify for ourselves what we have been taught on this all-important journey of faith. "The Creed," said Metropolitan Philaret of Moscow, "does not belong to you unless you have lived it."[3]

Therefore, if you have trusted Christ but feel your story is unexciting or inadequate because you were raised in a five-generation Christian home, take heart. Every one of us is absolutely unique. No one could ever duplicate your journey because it is uniquely your own. You need to take your story seriously. There are truths you were raised with, traditions you may take for granted (or even be embarrassed by) that your secular neighbor is starving for. There is such brokenness in our society today that many people can't fathom what it would be like to have had parents who prayed every night at their children's bedside.

Besides taking our own story seriously, we need to learn how to communicate it. And as we do so, we need to be honest and real. We don't have to pretend that we are now perfect or that we never struggle in any areas of our lives. To be able to honestly share what some of our difficulties were, or what inner questions and angst led us to seek Christ, can be helpful to others. But that doesn't mean we need to make inappropriate public confessions. Paul's testimony in Acts provides a helpful model (Acts 26:9-23). He first spoke of what he was like before, then what it meant to meet Jesus and what it meant for him since. Follow Paul's example and write down the story of your journey with God. Practice sharing it, first with friends and then with seekers.

Never underestimate the power of *your* story. It is uniquely your own, ordained by God, and it couldn't possibly be duplicated.

Planting the Seed by Displaying God's Love

One of the biggest challenges in communicating the gospel is how to talk about sin. Everyone wants to hear good news, but how do we communicate the "bad news" without alienating seekers? This is a particular challenge in our happiness-oriented, self-absorbed modern culture. And what exacerbates this problem even more is that we live in a therapeutic age that believes our problems are rooted either in addiction or in emotional wounding. The point is not that this analysis is entirely wrong. Indeed, many *do* suffer from addictive behavior, most people *are* emotionally wounded. But neither analysis uncovers our deepest problem—the problem of sin.

I believe one of the critical issues that the church faces is how to not shrink from naming sin and still be the bearers of grace. Christians have tended to deal with the subject of sin in one of two ways: either by being silent or by being judgmental. Either we skip over the uncomfortable bits and wind up conveying a gospel of warm feelings and cheap, sentimental grace or we behave and speak in ways that appear condescending, judgmental and critical.

How can the whole truth of the gospel be spoken in ways that people can hear? I agree wholeheartedly with Donald Bloesch, who says, "We can only know our sin when we have first been confronted with the depth of God's love for us revealed in Christ."[4] But that's impossible, we say. How do we tell seekers about sin and communicate God's love at the same time? We do it in two ways: by our style of communicating and by the substance of our message.

One way our style reflects the love of Christ is when we properly identify with the problems, stresses and hopes of others. That should not be hard to do since we know that we, too, are sinners who have received forgiveness and who constantly depend upon God's strength to conquer sin. Unbelievers need to see God's effectiveness in our lives, but they also need to sense our understanding and sensitivity to the complexities of their problems. Jesus himself modeled this compassionate understanding toward human frailty. "We do not have a high priest who is unable to sympathize with our weaknesses, but we have one who in every respect has been tested as we are, yet without sin" (Heb 4:15).

Second, we communicate God's love by our message. Our compassion and sensitivity toward others comes directly from our personal encounter with God's grace through the gospel. We share the cross because it was the means whereby we have been set free, and we know it has the power to set others free too. It is a message that acknowledges the problem of sin while at the same time assures us of the possibility of forgiveness.

We communicate grace and truth, then, by our loving and compassionate style and by the substance of our message of salvation. Let me share an encounter I had that illustrates this.

A year ago I boarded a plane and took my seat next to a man who appeared to be in his late twenties or early thirties. I had just finished speaking to a conference, and all I wanted was to sit quietly and read my book. But my seatmate soon introduced himself as Rick and seemed eager to talk. As I put my book away I asked him what he did for a living.

He told me he had been a rather famous race-car driver. In his racing days he thought he had everything: fame, money, all the trappings of success. He felt invulnerable. That all ended when he was in a near-fatal car accident while driving in a race. He was hospitalized for months, his worst injury being his legs, which were severely broken. After a long period of therapy and an extended stay at the hospital, he was finally released. Remarkably, he was able to walk without a limp, but his doctors told him he could never do race-car driving again.

Without his career or a big income to give him identity, he became terribly depressed. He had been a heavy drinker before, but now he became a full-fledged alcoholic. Looking back, he said there were four or five years that he couldn't even account for. Then one night, in a drunken stupor, he crashed his car into a wall. For weeks the doctors didn't think he would live, but amazingly he pulled through. When he was fully conscious, he was informed that both legs had been broken again. He was told he would probably never walk. He knew he'd come to the end of his rope.

Rick said, "I've never been a religious person, but for the first time in my life I cried out to God and asked him to help me. I told him I was sorry I'd made such a mess of my life. I asked God to please let me walk again. I promised that as soon as I was released I would join Alcoholics Anonymous. I also told God that I'd try to find out more about him so we could get to know each other."

Sure enough, after extensive therapy and to the astonishment of his doctors, his severely broken bones mended, the connective tissues healed and once again he was able to walk. He kept his word, and upon being released from the hospital he joined Alcoholic Anonymous. He hadn't had a drop to drink for sixteen months. Not only that, but at the AA meetings he had met a wonderful woman, whom he planned to marry soon.

We talked for a long time about the changes in his life, his goals and dreams for the future and his profound regrets about the people he had hurt during his alcoholic days. What haunted him most was that he had never visited his beloved grandfather while the old man lay dying of cancer in the hospital. His grandfather died while Rick was still in an alcoholic haze; he never got to say goodbye.

Then I said, "You know, Rick, the pain of facing your regrets, now that you are sober, is tough. It's very tough. But I must tell you how much I admire your courage in facing yourself, for owning your problem and sticking with your recovery. I think owning our problems is the hardest work any of us has to do. It's hard on our pride, but ultimately it is liberating, don't you agree?"

"No question about it. The hardest part was to stop blaming everybody else and accept responsibility for what was my problem alone. But you're right; it was freeing to finally own it. Becky, you really seem to understand, and you don't feel judgmental. Hey, are you in recovery too?" he asked with sudden intensity.

I paused for several seconds before answering. "Yes, I am in recovery. But not for alcohol. I'm in recovery for a problem far deeper than alcoholism."

"What do you mean?" Rick asked as his eyes widened.

"I'm in recovery, Rick, from what the Bible calls sin. You know why I don't seem judgmental to you? Because I've learned that the only thing that separates people is their symptoms—but *all* of us suffer from the same underlying disease of sin. It's the one disease everyone needs recovery from."

"I'm not sure I get it. What's the difference between being a drunk and being a sinner? Isn't it the same thing?" Rick asked.

"Alcoholism is the addictive behavior. Sin is what lurks behind the behavior. The *core* of sin isn't so much a set of behaviors as it is having a God-complex. You could never drink a drop of alcohol again, Rick, and still be determined to run your own life rather than let God be in charge. Sin is choosing to be self-ruled instead of God-ruled. And destructive behavior, in whatever form it takes, is always the inevitable result of refusing to let God be God."

"Oh, man, I can really identify with what you're saying. I took such pride in being in charge of my life. No one—not God, not my parents—*no one* could tell me what to do. And look at where it got me! But if AA is the treatment for alcoholism, then what's the treatment for sin?" Rick asked.

"Let me ask you something, Rick. You said that you cried out to God in the hospital. Now you follow the twelve-step program, which means you daily acknowledge your powerlessness over your addiction, which you can't conquer without the help of a 'Higher Power,' right?"

"Absolutely!"

"Have you found the name for this 'Higher Power'?"

"No, not yet," Rick answered. "But ever since I prayed that night in the hospital, my life has been different. I can just tell God has been looking out for me. I'm still searching, though. I want to know more about who God is."

"Rick, I know the name of the Higher Power—his name is Jesus. And the treatment for sin is the cross. All of us have tried to live our lives as if we deserved to be God, and look at the mess we've created! But God sent his Son, Jesus, who took our broken humanity into himself and made it his own. We deserved God's judgment, but Jesus stepped in and took it for us. He sacrificed his life for us and overcame our sin in his own heart so that *our* hearts could be changed. He rose from the dead and he offers to heal our brokenness, to forgive our sins and to make us whole. We just need to surrender our lives to him, to repent and believe."

"Yeah, but I've blown it so bad. I mean, I know God is there; otherwise, I'd probably be dead by now. But how could I ever believe that God would forgive me for everything? Especially after all that I've done—it just wouldn't seem fair."

"That's what the cross is all about, Rick! All of us nailed Jesus to the cross. Alcoholics and teetotalers, church folk and pagans, preachers and prostitutes—all of us are responsible for the death of Jesus. Luther says we carry his very nails in our pockets. But Jesus loved us so much that he voluntarily chose to die for us. Don't you see, Rick, if the cross shows us how serious our sin is, it also shows us that there is nothing we could ever do that cannot be forgiven.

"You think your sins are bad," I continued, "but have you ever considered that you've done something worse than being an alcoholic? You are responsible for the death of God's Son. And so am I. Our insistence on playing God is what drove Jesus to the cross. What could be worse than that? And if the cross shows us that God is willing to forgive us for the death of his Son, then why wouldn't he be willing to forgive us for every other sin? That's the amazing love of the cross!"

Rick was a strong, rough-hewed kind of guy. But for the first time in our two-hour plane ride, he wept. Unbeknownst to me, Rick had boarded our plane with the soil of his soul fully cultivated. All he needed was to hear the proclamation of the gospel. He was wide open and ready to receive Jesus as Lord. As our plane touched down, he asked me how to make a confession of faith. Then he bowed his head in silence for several minutes.

Afterward he said, "Listen, my fiancée will be waiting for me outside. I'd really like for her to meet you. I want to share everything we've talked about with her. And I'd like to start our marriage together in faith. Do you have any suggestions?"

"Well, start by sharing with her what has just happened to you. And may I be the first to send you a wedding present? I'd love to give you a family Bible and a devotional book that you can read together. And I'll send a book on the basics of the Christian faith. OK?"

It was a small airport, and as we quickly reached the waiting area, his fiancée was there. Rick introduced me and began to excitedly tell her everything we had talked about. She looked slightly dazed by his overwhelming enthusiasm, but I couldn't stay to help explain. Since I knew someone was waiting to pick me up, I excused myself and started walking across the airport.

Then something happened that has never occurred to me before or since. As I was walking, my heart overflowing with joy by what had just happened to Rick, I suddenly heard the sound of a chorus of praise and another sound that was like the tinkling of chimes. It was unlike anything else I have ever heard in my life. It was so beautiful, so exquisite, so majestic that I stopped dead in my tracks. I turned around to see where it was coming from, and nothing was there. It probably lasted for several seconds, but I stood transfixed in awe.

The sound ebbed away when I realized someone was calling my name. It was Rick's fiancée, calling me from the other side of the waiting area. By the look on her face it was clear that Rick had told her about his newfound faith. With tears streaming down her cheeks, she shouted across a crowded airport, "Becky, thank you! Thank you! Thank you!"

I cannot imagine a more theologically appropriate benediction to that experience. What else can we say in response to a God of such generosity, such love, such grace, who pardons our sins when we deserve death, who transforms us, fills us with his Spirit and delights to call us His own? The longer I live, the more I have come to see that the only language appropriate for such an awesome God is the response of praise overflowing from a grateful heart—praise that says in awe and humility, "Oh, God, thank you! Thank you! Thank you!"

How was the love of Christ mediated to Rick? How do we communicate God's grace and the tough truth about human sin without alienating people? First, by developing a style of communicating that identifies with the human problem. Seekers don't need to stand alone in their feelings of guilt and remorse. We can stand right there with them. We can identify with their problem of sin because, even though the sins for which we have been forgiven may be quite different from their sin, we still share the same underlying problem. We, too, sent Jesus to the cross.

Second, we convey grace and truth when we share the message of salvation. Rick felt a great deal of guilt for his alcoholism. Ironically what set him free was looking at the cross and realizing that the core of his problem was much deeper than simply taking another drink. The cross always brings us out of hiding because it makes us see that if Jesus had to die, then we have a problem that is far more serious than we ever imagined. Yet the cross also gives us hope. As I wrote in *Hope Has Its Reasons,* "The cross breaks our denial, but only *in the very instant* that it shows us the possibility of forgiveness. It shows us our corruption, but in the same breath it tells us the price has been paid.... The Christian view of sin is radical but not pessimistic because to see sin in Christian terms is to see that sin can be forgiven. That really is freedom. That really is amazing grace."[5]

In reflecting upon my experiences with Kay and Rick, I believe they teach us several truths. First, people are drawn to the gospel for many different reasons. Some are drawn to consider Christ because of crisis or pain, others because of guilt over sin, still others because they long for meaning and purpose for their lives. Second, because people vary and their needs are so different, it's not surprising that they respond to different aspects of gospel truth. Everyone nearly always responds to the fact that God loves them. But beyond that central truth, what people respond to initially varies enormously. Third, because people's needs are so varied, it may actually affect the way in which we explain the gospel. I know that was true in my experience as I shared Christ's victory over evil with Kay and shared the depth of sin with Rick.

Even theologians, in seeking to define the gospel's essence and in examining the meaning of the cross, have emphasized different aspects of its glorious truth.[6] To come to true faith in Christ involves confessing our sins, believing in Christ and receiving God's Spirit as we live our lives in full surrender to Christ as King. But what initially draws a person to consider Christianity will undoubtedly relate to his or her needs and particular situation.

So if you are a person who worries that you never seem to communicate the gospel in exactly the same way, take heart. You are in good company. The New Testament writers were unable to reduce the gospel to a single metaphor. Even Jesus never seemed to repeat himself either. He rarely explained the gospel in the same manner. Sometimes he communicated the gospel using the metaphor of bread, other times he used the word "water," because what he said was in the context of the person he was speaking to.

If, however, you are someone who finds great freedom in expressing the gospel in exactly the same way each time, that is fine too. Just be certain you are truly listening to the other person and try to connect the aspects of gospel truth that will be the most relevant to that person. God wants his truth proclaimed. So long as what we say is motivated by God's love and faithful to the truth of the gospel, that is all that matters.

Planting the Seed by Depending on God's Power

We've already said that our communication of the gospel depends not on human strategies or well-polished techniques or even brilliantly reasoned arguments but on divine initiative. It is the hidden work of the Holy Spirit that gives our words meaning and power and that produces changed hearts. God has also given us powerful spiritual resources that serve us in the task of evangelism. For example, the Word of God is filled with the power of the Spirit and brings life and renewal to those who seek him. The great Reformer John Calvin had a similar position: "God alone is a sufficient witness of himself in his own word."[7]

Over the years I have been amazed by how powerfully God speaks to seekers through the Scripture. God's Word truly does not return to him empty. J. I. Packer said in an interview, "You have liberty and authority when you allow the Bible to talk through you, a liberty and authority you don't have if you're offering your own ideas or cherished notions."[8] I couldn't agree more wholeheartedly.

I have frequently led Bible discussions for seekers in which we examine the life of Jesus. One that stands out in my mind in particular consisted of a group of women who were accomplished and competent professionals. One was a powerful executive who exuded a rather intimidating, no-nonsense air. One week she said, "I haven't been able to get Jesus out of my mind all week.

I keep asking myself, *What would Jesus do with the power I have in my job?* You know, I can spot a person who has complete authority a mile away. And Jesus possesses an authority like no one I've ever seen. Yet he uses his power so beautifully to serve others. I found myself wanting to talk to him about important decisions I need to make this week. But then I said to myself, *Wait a minute, you don't even know if you believe in Jesus!"*

This is exactly what I mean about the way God uses his Word. The Spirit of God speaks through his Word in ways that can't be measured, explained or controlled. God's Spirit's speaks through Scripture and gets into our bones and marrow and sinks into our consciousness in extraordinary ways.

How do we use the Bible in our evangelistic efforts? Christians often feel inadequate in evangelism because they haven't memorized enough Bible verses. Scripture memory is an invaluable tool in developing our Christian character, but frankly I have not found that sharing isolated verses with seekers is as effective as when we share the stories of Jesus or passages of Scripture that have moved us. In my experience that is when the Spirit operates with greater power.

Part of our preparation for doing evangelism is studying and meditating upon Scripture, allowing the Word of God to dwell in us richly. The more we gain insight from a passage and are moved by its meaning, the greater it enables us to communicate God's truth with power and clarity. It's amazing how often God uses our personal daily Bible reading to provide the truths we need to share with the person God leads into our lives that very day.

Another invaluable spiritual resource in evangelism is prayer. As we pray, God guides us into truth and sometimes shows us how to share that truth.

My experience with Kay illustrates how God uses both prayer and his Word. After reading the article about the "medical intuitive," I had asked God what to say to seekers who might be led astray by reading such an article. I felt heartened by the Lord's answer and went to sleep. The next morning the Bible passage I read for my devotions was Luke 4. As I meditated in silence and in prayer on that passage, I was moved to tears by Jesus' profound commitment to restoring and setting people free from the ravages of sin. His purpose is for the blind to see, the lame to walk, the oppressed to be free and the captives to be released! But *never* did I imagine that only four hours later

I would be quoting that very passage to a woman searching for God, a woman who had read the very same article as I had the night before.

I shouldn't be surprised. He is the living God who is always seeking and searching for his lost sheep. But what's important to note is this. Kay's manner while speaking to me was intense and sincere but very self-contained. It was only in the moment that I quoted the passage from the Bible that tears welled up in her eyes. Never underestimate how spiritually alive the Word of God is. I could almost hear its crackling power as I spoke it.

The Spirit chooses to work and speak through our human acts and words. God also speaks through his divinely appointed means of grace, such as preaching, prayer, the Bible, worship or the demonstration of our Christian life. As seekers come into contact with clear preaching, hear the Word of God, watch us at work and worship, and are the recipient of our prayers—watch out! Their lives may be changed.

13

Reaping
the Harvest in
God's Truth & Love

....

All stories of conversion are different. Some conversions are dramatic, others quiet. Some people respond out of crisis, others in calm. But the common element in every story is that, one way or another, God reaches us. He comes through. He does not abandon us. But neither does he barge in uninvited.

In the more than thirty years that I have been a Christian, I have seen many people turn their lives over to God and be changed. And yet the awesome mystery of conversion never fails to move me. Any Christian who walks with God over a period of time witnesses the marvelous acts of God's mercy and power. We see him heal people of illness; we watch him restore the emotionally wounded to wholeness; we see him forgive and release from guilt those who have been in bondage to sin for years. Our lives bear witness to the countless prayers we have seen God answer, meeting the needs of the financially distressed, giving wisdom to those who seek it, giving grace and peace to those who suffer.

Yet for all the abundant evidence of God's power and grace, what could be more miraculous than seeing a person who was once dead in sin become alive to God? I believe the miracle of conversion is greater than the creation of the world. When God created the world, he had no sinful opposition to deal with. But when a person responds positively to God's call—even after the world, the flesh and the devil have all mounted their opposition—what we are witnessing is simply one of the greatest miracles there is. No wonder there is such joy in heaven over one sinner who repents!

Even more remarkable is that God invites us to be part of that process. We are his ambassadors. We not only have the honor of sharing God's message but we even have the awesome privilege of inviting a response.

Let's examine this glorious truth of God's work of transforming us. Then we will look at the marvelous resources God has given us as we learn how to declare God's truth, display God's love and depend on God's Spirit as we enter this final stage of evangelism.

Conversion: Not Information but Transformation

The whole notion of our need for transformation rests on the premise that we have a problem so serious that only God could solve it. But to benefit from the cure we need to understand the nature of the disease. As we saw in the last chapter, the nature of the disease, the ultimate source of human woundedness, comes from the dislocations of not making God the center of our lives. Having put ourselves out of joint with God, we have wounded ourselves as well. In defiance and arrogance we have tried to be equal with God by putting ourselves in the center instead of God. As the great prophet Ezekiel said in the eighth century before Christ, "Though you are a man and no god, you try to think the thoughts of a god" (Ezek 28:2 NEB).

What then can be done about our narcissistic, self-focused nature? We can't reach in and straighten a twisted nature. Though we are responsible for our condition of sin, we are powerless to change it. Can we overcome our addiction to ourselves by sheer willpower? What self-improvement course will give us the power to stop ourselves from being self-centered and self-absorbed?

It's at this stage of the journey that Jesus takes us by surprise. Just when we realize our poverty and our powerlessness, Jesus tells us to rejoice! Why?

Because help is on the way! Only a power that is stronger than ourselves can help us overcome ourselves. That is why Jesus calls it the good news. He knew that the fatal human disease within our nature could only be cured by the Divine Surgeon.

Both the remedy and the proof of God's love and solution to our crisis are seen in the cross and the resurrection. The cross enables us to see our problem and how God solved it. The resurrection is where we see that human nature can be changed. Why does the resurrection give us confidence that we can be transformed? Because the very Spirit of God who raised Jesus from the dead and gave him physical life also enters our being when we are converted and gives us spiritual life. No other cure could solve our spiritual crisis but conversion.

Moral reformation, for example, looks at rules and how to conform. It focuses on our behavior when what is needed is the reformation of our hearts. Spiritual transformation looks at Jesus and how to be transformed into his likeness! That's why moralism and legalism as solutions to sin are woefully inadequate. They may make us nice, but they don't make us new. Christ's cure is not, as C. S. Lewis wrote, teaching a horse exercises so he can jump higher and higher. "Christianity," says Lewis, "is doing an operation on the horse so the horse can *fly!*"[1]

What makes humans fly? Or to put it less dramatically, what enables us to transcend our flawed human nature and live transformed lives? "God's great secret, and the Christians' hope of glory, . . . that secret kept from the generations and the centuries past, is this: 'Christ in you'."[2] When we receive Jesus as Lord and Savior, God's Spirit takes up residence in our souls. That's what makes us a new creation. We now have within us not only our old human nature but also we have God's new nature through his Spirit. This transformation does not happen overnight. But it could not happen *at all* unless God's Spirit indwelled us.

So we cannot be transformed without being indwelt by Christ's Spirit. We cannot be indwelt with Christ's Spirit without being converted. We cannot be converted without surrendering our lives in faith to Christ. That is why our goal in evangelism is not merely to *tell* people about Christ; it is to *lead* people to Christ as well—so that their lives may be indwelt and transformed by God's

Spirit, just as ours have been.

Seeing how vitally important conversion is, should we simply nail seekers to the wall and force them to repent and convert? The truth is, only God converts the human soul. As Jeremiah, the crusty prophet of old, said, "O LORD, You induced me, and I was persuaded" (Jer 20:7 NKJV). Pascal, the great French philosopher, mathematician and Christian, said, "We shall never believe, with an effective belief and faith, unless God inclines our hearts, and we shall believe as soon as he does so."[3]

So, in a strict sense, it is only the Spirit of God who can bring conviction of sin and liberate our will that has been deadened by sin. Does that mean, then, that we are off the hook? Have our responsibilities ceased once we have proclaimed the good news?

The truth is, the announcement of the gospel is not enough. As witnesses and servants of Christ, we are called to seek a commitment to Christ. We don't do this by force or manipulation. But at the right time and the right place we encourage seekers to respond to the truth. As ambassadors for Christ we hope for conversions and even seek them, not by our power but in the power of God. We can be instruments of the Spirit in his work of persuasion and conviction. This doesn't mean, however, that we are responsible for the results. As Methodist authors Eddie Fox and George Moore point out, "The only failure we ought to fear is that of failing to spread the gospel of the kingdom. The results are in God's hands."[4]

Let's look at what we can do then to encourage seekers to commit their lives to Christ.

Reaping the Harvest by Declaring God's Truth

What truths do we need to make clear to a person seriously considering Christianity? How do we help someone cross over the line into making a commitment for Christ? First, we need to make it clear that there is a decision to be made and that only they can make it. God will not force his love on us. He will not require us to have a reconciled relationship with him if that is not our choice.

Let's also help the person considering Christ to understand that making a decision is not only how we enter the kingdom of God but it is also how we continue to grow in the kingdom. We must choose each day to love and serve God, to listen to Jesus and obey him. No one drifts into discipleship, just as no one drifts into God's kingdom. The seeker's need to make a decision simply mirrors what the life of discipleship is all about.

What, then, are the steps involved in making a genuine commitment to Christ? In the New Testament the primary elements of conversion seem to be a response of repenting, believing and receiving the Holy Spirit. To complete reconciliation with him, we must each admit that we have rebelled (Mt 4:17), confess that we cannot be reconciled to God apart from what Christ did on the cross (Jn 1:12), and accept Christ's purpose, rule and power in our lives. Through prayer we can invite him to live in us (Rev 3:20). Let's look at each aspect.

Repent. First, we repent of our sins. This involves asking God for forgiveness for our self-centeredness as well as for our unbelief in not trusting who he is, for refusing his love and having chosen to go our way instead of his way. It also involves turning away from every behavior that we know to be wrong.

Here again, let's help the seeker understand that to put our trust in Jesus does not mean that we will never struggle again with sin. The way we grow as followers of Jesus is by regularly confessing and turning from our sins. We need to be honest that it's not easy to turn from sin. But they can trust that God will help them not only to own and confess their sin but also to overcome it as well, for that is what he has done and is doing for us.

Believe. Second, we confess our faith in Jesus as our Savior and our Lord. To be followers of Jesus means we acknowledge his absolute claim over our entire lives, and we accept that our faith must issue in obedience. We must be willing to give God first place in our lives and live under his rule. Jim Wallis in *Agenda for Biblical People* writes that "the great tragedy of modern evangelism is in calling many to belief but few to obedience."[5] That is why Jesus frequently asked people to count the cost before they made a commitment. He wanted them to be sure they understood what they were committing themselves to.

Again, let us freely share that what is required of the convert is demanded of the disciple. We don't acknowledge Jesus as our Savior and Lord in one second and then live as we please the next.

Two questions about evangelism that are frequently asked at this stage of the process are these: How much does a seeker need to understand in order to make a legitimate commitment of faith? When do we let him or her know about the implications of following Christ as Lord?

These are big issues and not all Christians are in agreement as to the answers.[6] However, one thing seems clear. People who get into the Christian life without understanding the essentials of faith, or who have never been challenged to repent of their sins, are likely to remain stunted Christians at best.

This became painfully clear when I recently spoke to a Christian collegiate national convention. One young Christian student told me, "Look, I cheat on my exams, and I feel kinda guilty about it. But I figure it's all right because I really want to be a lawyer for Christ." This kind of thinking reveals how little he understood of what it means to follow Christ when he became a Christian.

We must be certain that our evangelism is not divorced from an understanding of the content of the Christian faith. We must also help seekers to understand that we can't separate faith from how we live our lives. To follow Christ is to live under God's rule. Following Jesus means every aspect of our beings, every dimension of our lives, will be directed, shaped and transformed by the holy presence of Jesus in our lives.

"But won't such honesty deter people from accepting Christ?" we may ask. My experience has been exactly what Mark Mittleberg, the coauthor of the book *Becoming a Contagious Christian,* describes in an interview with *Leadership Journal:* "There's a rumor that if you want to attract unchurched people, you've got to tell them what they want to hear. We've found just the opposite. People are looking for leaders who have the guts to tell them the truth."[7]

Receive. Third, we receive the Holy Spirit by asking him to come into our lives. With the filling of the Spirit we are strengthened to live as new people who are called into a new way of life. We ask the Holy Spirit to come into our lives, to fill us with his power (Acts 1:8) and to fill us with his presence. The Spirit's presence seals what we have done in receiving Christ as Lord.

However, our need for the Holy Spirit does not end at conversion. As followers of Jesus we will continue to need the fresh renewing of the Spirit to accomplish the various tasks and capitalize on the various opportunities that God gives us.

Potential converts also need to know before they decide for Christ how not to quench the Spirit's presence within them but rather what they will have to do to stay spiritually alive. Daily Bible reading and prayer are essential, as is belonging to a Christian community. Young Christians need to find a church that is faithful and alive, and they should meet with a small group of Christians regularly for Bible study, prayer and fellowship. They are to be baptized if they have never done so. We can help them for the first few weeks until they are more secure. It takes a long time to learn to live in God's world in God's way, so we need to be there to help them begin. And we must bring others along to help them too.

At some point we need to share not only the delightful privilege they have of helping others to find Christ but also the truth that they are called, as Robert Webber writes in his book *Common Roots,* "to participate in Christ's victory over evil, to *extend* Christ's victory in every area of life in which they live and serve, to bring all of life under the reign of Christ."[8]

Taking the Final Step

There is probably no experience more terrifying than the first time we lead a person to Christ. But there are few things more thrilling or that make us more aware of how true Christianity is. To see God's Spirit take control and beautifully change a person's life is one of the greatest miracles we will ever witness. So we must be willing to help people enter into a relationship with God if they are ready.

What do we do when a seekers says, "OK. I would like to be a Christian. How do I do it?" Or if *you* sense that the moment is right, you may say, "Is there anything that would keep you from becoming a Christian right now?"

Listen carefully to what they say. If they say they aren't sure or feel a bit reluctant, ask them if they'd mind telling you why. Once we hear their concerns, it's usually fairly easy to assess their readiness. For example, if they say, "I just feel so unworthy," all we need to say is "None of us are worthy. That's exactly the point. The Bible says 'while we were yet sinners Christ died for us.'" Just be sure they understand that there is nothing any of us can do to make ourselves worthy. It's accepting what Christ has done for us on the cross (not what they can do) that opens the pathway to God.

Or they might say, "I'm not sure I understand everything." This is a good time to review the basic gospel truths. Do they believe they are sinners? Do they believe that Jesus died on the cross for their sins? Do they understand that asking Jesus to come into their lives is making a commitment to live in intimate relationship with Jesus as the Lord of their lives? If they understand and trust those things, they are probably ready.

Sometimes a person considering Christianity says, "I believe the essentials of Christianity, but I still have unanswered questions." We can reassure them that having faith in Christ doesn't mean we have all of our questions answered or that we never entertain doubts. If they seem to understand the essential truths, then we might say, "Faith means you surrender everything that you understand about yourself to everything that you understand about God. Your knowledge of God and yourself are not static. They will always continue to grow!"

After answering their questions, if you feel satisfied that they are ready, you may ask, "Would you like to commit your life to Christ right now?" If they say no, then do not pressure them. In fact, it's important at this point to reassure them of your genuine care. You might ask them whether you could pray for their continued journey toward God, asking God to reveal his truth to them. This communicates that they may still open the door to faith at a later date and that their needing more time to consider has not negatively affected your relationship with them. But if they give you a green light, then you have the extraordinary privilege of leading that person to Christ.

At this point I usually give some direction as to how to proceed. I suggest that we pray out loud together and ask if they'd like me to start first. The answer is nearly always yes. (I find that eases the awkwardness and also models how to pray in ordinary, everyday language.) I suggest that after I pray they may talk to God just as if they were talking to their best friend. If they ask me for guidance about what to say, I tell them to simply say, "Lord Jesus, I am sorry for my sin of running my own life, and I turn from all my sins in repentance. I believe you died for me on the cross. I thank you for your love. Now I ask you, come into my life, Lord Jesus, and be my living

Lord. Strengthen me to serve you with my whole heart." Then we pray. After they have prayed, I then pray again, confirming God's work in their lives and thanking God for entering their lives.

We need to remember one last thing: the joyfulness of what is taking place! Simply believing that Jesus lived, died and resurrected for sinners does not make us a Christian. The devil believes the exact same thing! As one of my favorite preachers, Tim Keller, said in a sermon, "What makes the Christian different from the devil? The Christian receives these truths *in joy!*" Keller said that the literal translation for the "good news" is actually the "joy news"! Let us remember, then, that what we are sharing with seekers is God's amazing "joy news." As G. K. Chesterton once said, "Joy, which was the small publicity of the pagan—is the gigantic secret of the Christian!"[9]

One of the greatest thrills in life is leading a friend into a relationship with Christ. May God grant you the faith, the holy boldness and the experience of seeing the life of someone you know be transformed by him!

Reaping the Harvest by Displaying God's Love
Evangelism involves an appeal to the whole person: mind, heart and will. When we explain the truth of the message, we are appealing to the mind. There is content to the Christian faith, and we do not expect anyone to make a blind leap of faith. When we ask seekers to commit their lives to Christ, we are making an appeal to their will. We know that no one can come to the Father unless God calls them. At the same time we know that Jesus called people to make a decision. So we appeal to seekers to commit their lives to Christ not by pressure but by God-inspired persuasion.

But Christianity also appeals to the heart. We are inviting our friends into a love relationship with Jesus Christ. The Bible tells us, "How great is the love the Father has lavished on us, that we should be called children of God!" (1 Jn 3:1 NIV). We want seekers not only to understand the truth about God but to experience the love of God as well. How can God's love be expressed through us?

Life provides us with many opportunities to share our faith. Sometimes all that is required of us is short-term involvement. My experiences with Kay and Rick, whom I discussed in chapter twelve, illustrate a short-term involvement. We struck up conversations sitting next to each other in an airplane and a doctor's office. Perhaps one reason we developed quick rapport could be attributed to my outgoing nature. Yet I find many people are more likely to reveal themselves in short encounters with virtual strangers than they would to their next-door neighbors. We should expect that it will take a little longer to develop trust with those with whom we live and work. That means we'll need to develop patience and take the time necessary to develop friendships in the places where we live.

In my experience becoming friends with seekers who live in our immediate world takes time, energy and commitment. It takes time to know people, time for them to trust us. They need to see us in a variety of situations in order to know that we are real.

Even though my experience with Rick and Kay were short-term and they were both remarkably open to the gospel, I don't want to leave the impression that everyone I meet turns to Christ on the spot. Far from it. I have many friends to whom I have witnessed and for whom I have prayed for years, and yet I'm still waiting for them to put their faith in Christ. But the wonderful news is that God continues to pursue us.

One of the most reassuring qualities of God is that he never gives up on us. He pursues us, and he will seek us until we draw our last breath. For it is God's deepest desire that no one perish. As in Francis Thompson's famous poem *The Hound of Heaven,* God relentlessly seeks to track us down. And when we finally turn to him, what we see are his eyes of love. This aspect of God's character that refuses to give up on people must be present in our character as well. This insight really came home to me recently.

About fifteen years ago I befriended Sue. We had many discussions about faith, we studied the Bible together and I prayed for her fervently. In the end she decided that Christianity wasn't for her. We had become good friends, and I was heartsick over her decision. She moved overseas, and though I had not seen her for years, I never stopped praying for her. Then, just in the past several months, she seemed to be continually on my mind, so I prayed for her with increased regularity.

Out of the blue I received a telephone call from a dear Christian friend. Nancy told me that Sue had just moved to the town where Nancy lives, and so the two of them had reconnected. She said that Sue was considering faith again. In the past several years some difficult things had happened to Sue, causing her to reopen the question of God and faith. She had recently discovered an unread copy of *Mere Christianity* that I had given her fifteen years earlier. This time she read it and wanted to discuss it with Nancy. Nancy told me that she soon hoped to start a Bible discussion with Sue.

One of my fears all those years ago was that Sue's refusal of faith might have been permanent. But during those fifteen years Sue had experiences in life that had caused her to reassess her life. But most importantly, God had never stopped pursuing her. Will Sue respond this time in faith to God? I don't know. What I do know is that God nudged me to pray for her when I had no way on earth of knowing why. We do not evangelize in isolation. God delights in using all of his children to reach one lost lamb, even if it takes fifteen years—or a lifetime!

Another quality that demonstrates Christ's love is when we are willing to sacrifice for a friend. Maybe it is through the time we invest in listening to their pain, or in practical ways like baby-sitting for their children or cleaning up the mess after our roommate has come home drunk.

I tell a story in my book *A Heart Like His* that reveals the sacrificial, persevering love that God longs to demonstrate to seekers through us.[10] As a college student, I went to L'Abri in Switzerland. It is a study center and community begun by the late Francis A. Schaeffer for people from all over the world and from all walks of life who are searching for truth and reality. I had read Schaeffer's books, and I was curious as to what sort of person he would be. I hadn't been there a week when I found out.

My new roommate told me that she had been sexually abused by her father and brothers, had been diagnosed as an alcoholic at sixteen, and had been continually involved in the use of drugs. The message she had heard all of her life was that she was trash. When you hear that long enough, you believe it. And what do you do with trash? You dispose of it. That was what she was trying to do with her own life—dispose of herself in one way or another.

One night she came in drunk, and another night she was high on drugs. By the third or fourth night, she had taken some lethal combination of pills, and she had to be rushed to a medical center.

Dr. Schaeffer had been out of the country lecturing. He returned that night, exhausted and jet-lagged after a long trip. But when he discovered what serious trouble this newcomer was in, he immediately went to her and stayed by her side for many hours through the night. When she finally returned to our room several days later, the look on her face was almost impossible to describe. She looked at me with eyes as wide as saucers, and she said, "Becky, he didn't get mad at me for breaking all the rules here. He held my hand. And he begged me to give God a chance. He had tears in his eyes when he heard all the junk that had happened to me. He cared so much for my pain. But he told me over and over, 'Please, just give God a chance. He loves you. He can help you. Don't lose hope.' I told him, 'I have no hope. It's been beaten out of me.' And he said, 'I understand. Then hang on to my hope. Lean on *my faith* till you have your own. Trust my hope for what God can do in your life. Just please, please give God a chance.' "

That woman stayed at L'Abri for a long time, and as she was slowly nursed back to physical and emotional health, her life was completely transformed. Her despair turned to hope not because she had the inner resources of her own at first, but because she was willing to open herself to God in whatever way she could, because she had seen God's hope and love through the eyes of someone else. She was able to give God a chance by leaning on the faith of someone else. Then one day her hope in Christ was truly her own.

What did Schaeffer offer her? He offered the sacrificial love of Christ. Not simply by talking with her and holding her hand through the wee hours of the morning even though he was exhausted, but by ministering to her for a whole year and a half until she was finally whole. It was a sacrifice for him and his staff of time, of money, of listening for hours and hours to her painful story until she was finally healed. But if Jesus, who was used to the company of God and angels, was willing to come to us and mingle with prostitutes and lepers, and subject himself to death—how can we ever talk about the cost of serving him? If he was willing to be sacrificially involved in our lives, how can we do any less for others?

What is the moral of these two stories? Never give up! Always keep on praying. Even when you see no fruit or spiritual response, the story is never over in a seeker's life until their last breath is drawn. Let us follow Jesus, who said, "We must work the works of him who sent me while it is day; night is coming when no one can work" (Jn 9:4).

14

Reaping
the Harvest
in God's Power

....

How do we work in sync with the Spirit of God in bringing a person to Christ? First, by recognizing that conversion is a profound mystery. For one thing, the Holy Spirit is sovereign. He works as he pleases in his renewal of the human heart. That's why Jesus said, "The wind blows wherever it pleases. You hear its sound, but you cannot tell where it comes from or where it is going. So it is with everyone born of the Spirit" (Jn 3:8 NIV). In other words, conversion is beyond our ability to control. Again, it's a mystery, and "mystery," writes Flannery O'Connor, "is a great embarrassment to the modern mind."[1] Ernest Becker concurs: "Moderns try to replace vital awe and wonder with a 'How to do it' manual."[2]

The mystery and the paradox of conversion is also seen in the fact that God does all, yet he chooses to save us in and through human decision and obedience. On the one hand, we cannot find God without God. It is God's grace that initiates our search and God's grace that completes our search. As Os Guinness writes in his book *The Call:* "The secret of seeking is not in our human ascent to God, but in God's descent to us. We start out searching but we end up being discovered. We think we are looking for something; we realize we are found by Someone."[3] On the other hand, the only way we can become a disciple of Jesus is through human decision.

So we approach this stage of calling seekers to make a decision knowing that by our own power and cleverness we cannot induce conversions. Jesus makes it clear: "Apart from me you can do nothing" (Jn 15:15). Yet he has chosen us to be his instruments in his work of making disciples. Therefore, how do we depend upon God's Spirit as we seek to lead others to Christ?

What we need most of all is boldness and faith. It takes faith *in* Jesus to lead a friend *to* Jesus. And faith is a gift from God that we are encouraged in the Bible to ask for.

When Peter and John were threatened by the Sanhedrin for evangelizing the Jews, they were understandably concerned. When they were released from prison after receiving stern warnings and threats not to speak or teach in the name of Jesus, the disciples turned to the Lord in prayer (Acts 4:24-31). They began praying by reciting God's characteristics and reminding God (and themselves!) of his nature and character. Then, after a lengthy preamble, they finally mentioned their problem: "Now, Lord, consider their threats." But it's what follows that is the surprise.

If you had been physically threatened and thrown in jail for preaching the gospel, wouldn't your prayer be more along the lines of "Here I am, Lord—send Aaron"? Instead, the disciples prayed, "Now, Lord, consider their threats and *enable your servants to speak your word with great boldness.* Stretch out your hand to heal and perform miraculous signs and wonders through the name of your holy servant Jesus" (vv. 29-30 NIV, emphasis mine). And God answered their prayer immediately by giving them supernatural power from on high that was evidenced by the boldness in their preaching the gospel and by God's power working through them to heal and lead others to faith in Christ.

To lead a person to Christ, we need to freely ask God to give us the boldness and faith that we need in order to reach the people that he has given us. It takes a special measure of faith to reach out to someone we have tried to win over a long period of time. It takes even more of God's strength when that person is a family member. I know because it happened to me.

My Father's Story

I didn't become a Christian until I was in high school. I tell most of my conversion story in my book *Hope Has Its Reasons*. One thing I don't mention in that book, however, is what happened to me the very first night I gave my life to Christ. That night began a story in my father's life that illustrates the joy of reaping that can be ours when we've faithfully cultivated and planted— and waited on the Spirit of God to act.

On my first night as a Christian, when I had gone to bed, in the dark I began to pray. All of a sudden I knew that God was speaking to me. The message was unmistakable: "I want you to tell your father what has happened to you. I want you to tell him that I love him and that I want him to give his life to me." I was horrified. My dad was, by his own admission, an atheist. He was also a highly successful businessman. He was the quintessential self-made man: self-reliant, justifiably proud of his accomplishments, feeling he needed no one's help but his own. Furthermore, I knew he didn't talk easily about anything of a personal nature. The thought of telling him about my newfound faith was simply terrifying. I tried every way I could think of to weasel out of it and convince God it wasn't a good idea. But there was a relentlessness on God's part that made me know that I had to do this.

A few days later I asked Dad if we could talk. I felt awkward, embarrassed and uncomfortable, but I knew God had given me no choice. I told Dad in a very simple way that I had been searching for quite some time for answers to life's meaning. (That must have sounded comical coming from a young teenager to a middle-aged man.) I told him that I had surrendered my life to Jesus and that I had never known such joy and peace.

"How long ago did you do this, Becky?" he asked. He was not mocking or unkind, though it was clear from his expression that he believed it was merely a phase of adolescence.

"A week ago."

When I told him that I hadn't wanted to share this but that God had pressed me to tell him, he was intrigued. "Why is that?" he asked.

"Because I feel God told me to tell you something: God loves you, Daddy. He wants you to put your trust in him."

He smiled at me sweetly and said, "Honey, it's kind of hard to teach an old dog new tricks. But I'll certainly think about what you've said."

"Dad, is that all you're going to say? Why can't you . . . well, why can't you *just believe?"* I asked with characteristic teenage subtlety.

"Becky, you see everything around you?" he said, gesturing with his hand toward our home. "Honey, everything I've ever had, every accomplishment, everything you see in this home—no one gave it to me. It wasn't a gift. It came from *me.* It's all a result of *my* hard work. I just don't understand why someone needs to depend on God when, with discipline, drive and a little luck, you can accomplish it all yourself. I'm sorry, honey, but it doesn't make sense to me."

As the years passed, my father recognized that my faith in Christ was permanent, that it wasn't a phase. He even admired my faith. And the Lord gave me other opportunities to share Christ with him. But Dad always perceived Christianity as being "my thing," not something he could ever believe in. Even in those times in his life when I thought he might be the most open to God, such as when he and my mother divorced, he made it clear that faith just wasn't for him.

Nor was I the only one to witness to my dad. Dr. John Alexander, the former president of InterVarsity Christian Fellowship, witnessed to my father once and prayed for my dad for years. My brother and my sister also came to faith and witnessed to Dad but to no avail.

My father heard me speak only three times in his life. All three times were when I addressed the Urbana Missionary Convention. (Champaign, Illinois, the sister city to Urbana, is my hometown.) Knowing that my father was coming to hear me speak, each time I asked the leaders on the platform to pray. I vividly remember the late Paul Little pouring out heartfelt prayers for my father to come to know the Lord. But there never was even an ounce of spiritual response on his part.

The last years of my father's life, however, became very difficult. Even though he was only in his sixties, he suffered a series of minor strokes that affected his short-term memory. Then he developed Alzheimer's. Tragically, his wife, Dorie, after valiantly taking care of him, had to place Dad in a nursing home in Florida, where they lived, when he was only sixty-nine years old. My once strong, witty, razor-sharp father, who was used to being able to control everything, was for the first time in his life dependent and afraid. It was so wrenching for all of us to see him in this condition that I begged God to bring something redemptive out of this tragedy.

As with many Alzheimer's patients, some days he would be coherent and able to follow and respond to what others were saying, and other days he seemed to be in a total fog. On one of his good days we were talking on the telephone, and he was terribly depressed. I tried to cheer him up, but finally I said in utter anguish, "Dad, it grieves me to see you so lonely and depressed. If I could be there every minute, you know that I would, but I can't. But God is always with us. Dad, I just wish you could turn to God for help."

To my utter astonishment, he replied, "I've started praying; I've been asking him for help." I honestly assumed that this had to be a sign of his further dementia. Evidently my speechlessness gave it away, for my dad started to laugh. "I know, it must be pretty bad for your dad to pray, right?" However, I knew it had to be true when my brother, Bob, phoned from Florida, where he also lives, and confirmed that Dad had told him the same thing.

Jesus, Yes!

Then one morning, many months later as I was praying, the Lord spoke to me. Clearly, unmistakably, I felt that God was telling me to go to my dad and appeal to him one last time to become a Christian. It was such a strong urge that I spoke to a close Christian friend and told her what had happened. I felt I needed to be sure if this was God's guidance. For one thing, what if I flew out there and he was having one of his bad days and didn't understand what I was saying? Or what if he responded positively (which I could not in my wildest dreams imagine), but I couldn't tell if his response was genuine or just the result of his confused mental state? And even after all these years, even with my dad's diminished condition, I still felt weak in my knees at the prospect of witnessing to him. So my friend and I prayed for God's guidance.

I poured out my heart to God and told him how much I needed an extra measure of faith to be sure it was the right thing to do. How can one describe how God speaks to the soul? As we prayed, we both had an overwhelming sense that this was exactly what I was to do. I felt so strengthened in faith and courage that I called the airlines immediately and booked a reservation.

But on my flight to see Dad all of my anxieties began to resurface. I began asking the Lord, "What if Dad isn't well enough? Or worse, what if he understands and says no? Or what if I blow it and don't explain things adequately?"

Then the Lord reminded me of what happened the night of my conversion. I had almost forgotten the experience, it had been so long ago. I felt the Lord quiet my fears and calm my anxieties by saying, "You may have forgotten that experience, Becky, but I didn't forget. I asked you to go to your father over thirty years ago and you did. Now I'm asking you to go to him again. Don't worry; I'm in charge of this. Just be at peace." With that I fell asleep for the rest of the flight.

The next day my dad's wife, my brother and I took him out to lunch. The nurses told me it was the best day he had had since they could remember. He was overjoyed to see me and called me by name. He laughed at our jokes during lunch; he participated in the conversation as best he could; he even remembered the name of a person the rest of us were trying to recall. It was a wonderful time. But it was only in the last ten minutes that I was actually alone with Dad in his room.

Somehow I always seem to end up in bathrooms in order to pray and build up my courage, and this time was no different! I went into my dad's bathroom and begged the Lord to continue to make his mind clear. I asked God to help him understand everything I was saying and to let his response be positive.

As I emerged from the bathroom, Dad was sitting in a chair smiling at me. I pulled up a chair next to him. It is difficult to express in writing what he said because by this time he had difficulty in forming complete sentences and words, but I want to try to express it in the way that he actually spoke it.

I said, "Dad, I have something important I want to talk about. It's about having faith in Jesus. Dad, you told my brother, Bob, and me that you pray now to God. Is that right?"

"Yes . . . do now," he answered.

"I'm so glad you pray. Dad, I don't know quite how to say this, but when

I die and go to heaven, I want to know that we will be there together."

"Me too," Dad replied.

"Dad, do you know how you can be *sure* you are going to heaven?"

"No."

"Do you believe that Jesus is God's Son?"

Dad looked out the window and I could tell it was taxing every ounce of his brain cells to think and then try to speak. "Before . . . I . . . before . . . I . . . did . . . before, *didn't* believe. But then . . . so much happ . . . So hard. . . . Now . . . yes, I believe."

As I listened to him struggling to speak, I couldn't help but be amazed. One of my Dad's defining characteristics was his personal honesty. He could not tolerate dishonesty. It's why he always made it so clear that I was the Christian, and he was not. He didn't make the clarification out of meanness but out of integrity. And now, even at this difficult stage of his life, with so many brain cells deadened by this horrible disease, it was important to him that he was being honest. What he was saying was absolutely true: before his suffering, he did not believe. But as the suffering intensified, it had caused him to pray and turn to God.

I think it was at that moment that I realized how God had answered my prayer when I asked for something redemptive to come out of all of Dad's misery. The gift of Alzheimer's was finally evident to me: it had broken his pride. He finally had experienced something that he couldn't control, and through that he had seen his need for God.

"Dad," I continued, "Jesus loves you very much. Do you know that?"

"I just . . . hope so," Dad answered.

"Do you know why you can be sure that Jesus loves you? Because he died on the cross for your sins. I have to ask you an important question now: Dad, have you ever made any mistakes?" I held my breath as I asked him this. For my father to acknowledge any weakness or culpability was truly repellent to him. Owning up to sin was always the biggest stumbling block for him in regard to faith.

Up until this point my father had made perfect sense, but what he began to say now I could not follow. My biggest fear was that the Alzheimer's was too advanced for him to understand what we were talking about. I had told the Lord that if he began speaking incoherently, I would stop the conversation cold.

"Never mind, Daddy. We can talk about this another time," I said as I started to stand up.

"No!" Dad replied so emphatically that it almost scared me. In fact, it was the only time he came close to using a complete sentence: "Please, Becky. Want to say this. Let me try."

"OK. Just take your time, Daddy." I sat back down.

"It's . . . there's . . . road . . . walk on it . . ." he said, gesturing with his hands in a forward motion. "But then road goes . . ." then he gestured with one hand turning right, "but I went . . ." and he gestured with his other hand going left. "Understand?" he asked me with pleading intensity.

"Yes, I understand. You are saying that life is like a road. You start off walking and everything seems fine. Then there's a fork in the road. You sometimes turned left when you should have turned right."

"Yes! Yes!" he said, overjoyed that I had grasped what he was saying.

"OK, Dad, then I need to ask you the question again. Have you ever made any mistakes?"

Dad looked out the window for several seconds and then replied in absolute earnestness, "Yes . . . made . . . one . . . no . . . two mistakes."

I looked at him tenderly. I love my father dearly, but I know that, like all of us, he has made many more mistakes than two. My brother and sister and I have all suffered over many of my father's mistakes. Yet what amazed me in that moment was how little it mattered in light of eternity. Does Jesus ask that we understand the depth of our sinfulness before he will save us? Does he require a pound of our flesh before he forgives us? No, Jesus gave his *own* flesh so that we wouldn't have to.

"Dad, Jesus died for your two mistakes. That's why you can be sure that he loves you. But because he died, you need to tell Jesus two things: tell him that you are sorry for your two mistakes and ask him to come into your life. Dad, that's called becoming a Christian. Would you like to become a Christian right now?"

Again he looked out his window, this time for an even longer period. In fact, I began to wonder if he had forgotten the question. So I started to repeat it. But he interrupted me by saying, "Didn't forget." Then he looked me right in the eyes and said, "Yes. Yes . . . want to."

I realized at that moment that I had no idea how to lead someone to Christ who had difficulty forming sentences, so I said, "Dad, I know it's hard for you to talk. If you want, I will pray on your behalf. I'll speak for you. If you agree with what I am saying, then nod your head in agreement. OK?"

"OK," he answered.

I took my father's hands in mine and for the first time in my life I prayed with my father. "Lord, I am praying for my dad, Bob Manley. I'm coming to you now on his behalf. You know what he feels in his heart, and you know what we have just been talking about. So receive this prayer as if it were my dad saying it: Lord Jesus, I have made two mistakes in my life." Dad nodded his head vigorously in agreement. "Thank you for dying on the cross for me. I am so sorry I made those mistakes. Please forgive me." Again he nodded his head. "I believe you are God's Son, and I put my trust in you." He nodded yes.

But then I stopped. I suddenly realized I had to. I turned to Dad, whose head was bowed, and I touched his arm as he opened his eyes and looked at me. "Dad, you don't remember this, but you were once a very successful businessman. Something you always used to tell me was, 'Honey, you've got to know how to close the deal.' Well, Dad, I just realized that I can't take you beyond this point. You've got to close this deal for yourself. Dad, Jesus is with us right now—he's right here in this room. Just tell Jesus what you have decided. But *you* will have to do it."

My father looked at me in complete understanding, and bowing his head, he said in a voice that was uncharacteristically loud for him: "Jesus, *yes!* . . . and Jesus, . . . I love you!"

In my entire Christian life I never believed I would hear my father say those words. I looked up at Dad and he was beaming. The presence of the Lord in that room was astonishing and palpable. I threw my arms around him and through tears of joy I said, "Daddy, you belong to Jesus! You belong to his kingdom forever. Nothing can ever change that. I don't know when God will take you home, but I promise you, you don't have to be afraid. Jesus is with you now, and he'll take you by the hand when it's time to go to heaven."

"Can . . . can we . . . go heaven together?" he asked.

"If you don't mind, Dad, I'd like to wait on that. But when we see each other in heaven, it will be like we were never apart. And Dad, just one last thing. I know sometimes you get frustrated and afraid. Try to remember just one word: Jesus. That's all you have to say. Just say the name of Jesus, and he will comfort you and help you. And even when you can't remember his name, don't worry because he'll come to comfort you anyway."

I felt like I hardly needed the help of an airplane to fly me home the next day. I called my dad's nurses several times after that experience. I didn't explain why, but I asked them if they saw any observable change in Dad. "Yes," a nurse responded, "your Dad used to get so agitated. But we've all noticed how peaceful and serene he seems."

There's Hope Till the End

I saw my father several times after that. It was clear that what had happened on that trip couldn't have happened at any other time, for each time I saw Dad his condition had deteriorated. Toward the end he could barely speak at all, and yet even then, when I asked him if he'd like me to pray, he would smile and say, "Yes, please," and bow his head.

My father died on February 27, 1998—less than two years after he accepted Christ. When I received the news, I turned to my daily devotional, *The Daily Light,* and read the passages for that day: "He who hears my word, and believes on him that sent me, has everlasting life, and shall not come into condemnation, but is passed from death into life"; "I give them eternal life; and they shall never perish, neither shall any man pluck them out of my hand." All I could do was thank the Lord through my tears for being so merciful and for his extravagant love that never stopped pursuing my father.

There is nothing I can attribute my father's conversion to other than the sheer grace of God. But then, isn't that true of every conversion? There is a chasm between God and humans that has to be bridged, and the amazing news of the gospel is that God is willing to bridge it. My testimony is not that I never doubted Dad would be saved. To be honest, I frequently anguished over whether he would ever trust in Christ. Nor would I have ever described my father as a true seeker. He always seemed amazingly impervious to prayers or the witness of others. I don't think that was entirely due to his being spiritually hardhearted; it was also due to some deep emotional wounding from his childhood. Regardless, God got his attention. God responded to the prayers of so many that had spanned thirty years.

This deeply personal story reveals so much of what God is like. It also reveals the critical importance of the will, how terribly important our decision of faith is, even when our mental faculties are diminished. But most of all, it's a story about a God who love us and who reaches out to us.

Perhaps some of you reading this are feeling grief because you think you are reading it too late. Someone you love has already died before you had the opportunity to witness to him or her. We are told in the Bible that "the Lord is patient with you, not wanting anyone to perish, but everyone to come to repentance" (2 Pet 3:9). God's desire is that no one be lost and die without salvation. Tragically, some will. But no one can know what takes place between God and the soul of a person in the last moments or hours before death. What we do have assurance of is that God will use every means possible to reach a person before it's too late. We can trust that if there was any way of saving a person without violating the person's will, God will do so. But my father's story also reveals how vitally important it is to witness when God gives us the opportunity.

Let us not hesitate, then, to share his glorious gospel. Yes, I grieved at my dad's funeral. But I grieved in the knowledge of hope, the hope that God, who had the first word, will have the last. Dad's conversion reminded me once again that all is of grace. "What brings us home is not our discovery of the way home but the call of the Father who has been waiting there for us all along, whose presence makes home *home*."[4]

15

Revealing Truth Through Reason

....

Let's say Stephen Hawking, the world-renowned physicist, had a conversion experience. Now, for Hawking, facts are everything. But what if he suddenly declared to the public, "I had this incredible experience last week while looking at my tulip patch. I'm now a believer. And I get up early every morning and worship the tulip bulbs"?

I bet many people would say, "Oh, wow, that's really beautiful, Stephen. I mean, as long as it works for you, then that's great." Only a few would say, "How do you know it's true? How do you know you're not creating your own little world and calling it reality?" We would check his facts in any other area but this one, because when it comes to faith, as long as we are sincere, then it is true enough. Or so we are told.

But something is wrong here. Hitler was sincere when he tried to exterminate the Jews and to subvert the German church for his own purposes. The people involved with the Heaven's Gate cult were sincere when they committed suicide because they believed they would be joining extraterrestrials traveling behind a comet. The cultists surrounding David Koresh were sincere when they met their fiery death in Waco, Texas, with their self-proclaimed messiah. Sincerity just cannot be an adequate basis for determining truth. Our concept of truth in general and faith in particular has been so drastically reduced that something is true if it makes us feel good or comes from sincere motives. But as the adage goes, we need more than sincerity because we can be so sincerely wrong!

What we need is a faith that corresponds to the reality around us, that makes sense out of our world, that is internally consistent and hangs together. As Christians we do not have absolute proof for our belief in Jesus. There is in fact no absolute proof for any ultimate proposition, whether Christian or Buddhist or atheist or whatever. But the God of the Bible does not call us to leap in the dark; he does not require faith without evidence, for that is mere superstition.

I used to feel frustrated as an agnostic asking truth questions of Christians when they always answered, "It's just this feeling in my heart." I would respond, "But I need something for my head too!" And to my delight I found God offered both. He gives us the subjective experience of knowing him and objective evidence to act upon. It is not evidence that overwhelms us or answers every question, but it is evidence that is sufficient.

Apologetics and Its Limitations

The Bible tells us that we must give reasons for our faith as well as proclaim it. We should be prepared to give reasons for our commitment to Christ rather than to the idols of our age. Furthermore, we should try to understand what others believe in and think out the implications of our faith, especially so we can give a compelling defense of why we believe the gospel to be true. Giving reasons for why we believe our faith to be true is what theologians call "apologetics."

When I look back to my early twenties, I think I almost believed that if I could just *convince* someone intellectually that Christianity was true, then that person would be converted. Both biblical revelation and life experience reveal such thinking to be wrong. We aren't saved by knowledge but by the grace of God, because the core of our problem isn't ignorance but sin. Even if we were able to intellectually persuade someone that Christianity is true, God would still need to awaken the seeker's will for the person to be converted.

Experience has taught me something else. Over the years I have been asked tough, honest questions from seekers whose motives sprang from a genuine desire for truth. But I have also spent countless hours discussing the evidence for the truthfulness of faith with seekers, only to later discover that truth was never their barrier to faith in the first place! For when I asked, "If you could know without any doubt that Christianity was true, would you commit your life to Christ?" I was astonished by how often I was told, "No, because even if it's true, I don't want to give up control," or, "No, because if I surrender to God now, I may miss out on some fun," or, "No, because even if it's true, I still have a bone to pick with God over how he mishandled something." In other words, I've learned through experience that the real battleground between the seeker and God isn't in the area of the intellect—it is in the realm of the will.

Does that mean we abandon our attempts to use apologetics as a tool? Absolutely not. I don't believe, as some do, that we must abandon traditional apologetics altogether just because we live in a more experience-oriented culture today. To do that is to capitulate to our culture's excesses. However, I do believe we need to expand our understanding of the various ways we communicate truth in order to meet the seeker who is affected by the changing forces that shape our present culture.

Apologetics has a place so long as we recognize what it can and cannot do. We engage in apologetics because we take the seekers' questions seriously—maybe even more seriously than they do. We offer a defense of the faith because we long to intensify the seeker's hunger for the truth of God. We witness to the truth of the gospel in the hope that the Spirit will move that person to seek salvation. Yet we do so remembering that no intellectual argument can ever induce conversion. We cannot prove that Christ is the way to God, though we can and should make a case for faith's validity when we are asked to do so. But only God can quicken the human will that has been deadened by sin; only God can make the scales of unbelief fall so the blind can see.

In short, apologetics has its place and can be very effective, especially when it is combined with an effective presentation of the gospel. But it should be regarded as Søren Kierkegaard suggests as "waving the carrot before the donkey."

When we consider how to defend the truth of faith, however, we realize what unique challenges we face in our times. Much has been written about the culture of recent years, which is in the process of shifting from what has been called a modern culture to a postmodern culture. Our modern culture was shaped by the Enlightenment, in which reason reigned supreme and explanation led to experience. In our present postmodern culture we have become disillusioned with reason and disillusioned with the belief that technology can save us. Instead, the postmodern culture is seeking more spiritual and experiential answers to find meaning for life. The New Age movement is an example of this phenomenon.

The very fact that we live in such an experience-oriented culture leads us to ask, Why and how do we defend the truth of our faith to people who often could not care less whether anything is true? What kind of apologetic do we use for someone who is put off by intellectual arguments and responds more to experience than explanation?

Of course, not everyone we speak to has this postmodern mindset. There are exceptions, but it has been my general experience that the older a person is, the more he or she appreciates an appeal to the mind when considering faith. The professor on the plane, who I mentioned in chapter nine, is an example of a person with more of a modern bent. He wanted to know what evidence there was to back up the Christian claims. He was drawn to and trusted intellectual proofs. He wanted to hear objective, rational evidence more then he wanted to hear my personal experience. He was also over forty. So what do we say to the person who wants well-reasoned answers and evidence that supports our claims that Christianity is true? Is faith based on something that one can examine, or is a person required to take a blind leap in the dark?

We will examine the first two areas of apologetics—philosophical and historical—in this chapter. These areas may be more effective with the cognitive, more modern seeker. In the following chapter we will examine the next two areas—sharing the biblical story and sharing our own story. These may be more useful for the postmodern type of person who is more receptive to hearing truth through experience before explanation. And then in chapter seventeen we will turn to the last area of apologetics—depending on the resources of the Spirit. This one is a way to convey truth with everyone we seek to win for Christ, but it is especially appropriate when we are speaking to someone involved in the New Age or other alternative forms of spirituality. Let us feel free to use all the approaches whenever it seems appropriate.

Revealing Truth Through Philosophical Evidence

One thing that is encouraging to know is that the questions seekers raise don't vary much. For example, the commonly asked questions include these: How could a good God allow evil or hell? What is a human being? Are people basically good but simply misinformed and able to improve with the proper controls? How can we talk of absolutes (that something is "good" or "unjust") when everything is relative and has come about merely by chance? These are philosophical questions that Christians need to know how to answer.

When talking to seekers, see if you can get to the core of their beliefs by asking a few basic questions. It is surprising how few basic answers there are to life's ultimate questions. Listen carefully and sympathetically as they articulate their beliefs. The details of systems may differ, but most ideas can be put into a few slots. Here are some examples:

1. *The basic nature of the world.* Do people's arguments begin from the premise that there is no God, that we started from nothing or from matter only? Or if they believe in God, what kind of God is it (personal or impersonal, finite or infinite, involved with human affairs or aloof)? This is especially relevant when we speak to those in New Age spirituality, who believe that God is in everything, that he is an impersonal energy that lies within each of us.

Discovering whether seekers begin from a naturalistic premise or a supernatural one will determine a great deal. For example, if they do not believe in God and maintain that the universe is closed, mechanistic and impersonal, it would be impossible for them to believe in biblical miracles. If they do not believe in the supernatural, then it is pointless to keep arguing about something that their system could never accommodate. We should point out to them, however, that it is utterly consistent for us to acknowledge the possibility of miracles because our system allows for the supernatural. So instead of banging away at the possibility of miracles, we might ask, since

202 / OUT OF THE SALTSHAKER

they deny the existence of God and the existence of absolute truths, are they able to live consistently with such beliefs?

2. *Morality.* Closely related to the question of whether God exists—and if so, what kind of God it/he is—is the issue of ultimate morality. If a God who is interested in matters of ethics does not exist, then there is be no basis outside ourselves for determining what is right and wrong. I know many people who think in exactly that way, and they claim to be able to live consistently with that notion.

They advocate "tolerance" in sexual matters, for example, saying that since there is no absolute standard of morality, sexual ethics is reduced to a question of taste and preference. Nonetheless—and this is the point—those same people are rigid moralists in opposing racial prejudice, child brutality, war and so forth. And why are they against such things? "Because they are wrong, categorically and universally!" they retort.

But we cannot have it both ways. We must play by the same rules on different issues. We can legitimately and forcefully challenge them, "If you say there is no such thing as morality in absolute terms, then you cannot say that child abuse is always evil; it just may not happen to be your thing. And if you find you are not able to practice your premises with much consistency, then you need to reexamine your premises."

Most people's response to evil is one of horror. When we read of the Holocaust or of Bosnia's ethnic cleansing or of the Oklahoma bombing, our immediate response is, "That is wrong! It is evil!" Or when we hear of abject poverty or senseless torture, we say, "That is unfair, unjust!" Or conversely, when we see a masterpiece, we say, "It is beautiful." In all this we are seeing people responding to the fact that they are made in the image of God—a good God, a God of beauty.

Our feelings of justice, of goodness, of beauty stem from the God who enshrines these very qualities and who made us like himself. As C. S. Lewis says, to call a line crooked still implies we know what a straight line is. Whenever people protest evil, it tells us they have a strong sense of what is right and they are angry to see it violated. So we must ask, Where do our feelings of right and wrong, evil and good, come from? What is the origin of these qualities? Where did our culture derive these strong beliefs? Is it perhaps that we are made in the image of a God whose character is good, or is it that we developed such notions under an impetus toward cultural and physical survival?

Challenging our non-Christian friends on whether they live consistently by their own self-acknowledged principles is an effective way of casting doubt on their present beliefs. Some writers who deal with this same approach are James Sire in his book *The Universe Next Door* and C. S. Lewis in *Mere Christianity* and *Miracles*. Giving a reasoned advocacy of faith is a good thing; however, we must be careful when we do so not to act pridefully superior. The main reason people find it hard to believe the Christian message is not because of ignorance but because of hardness of heart, which weakens their wills and makes their understanding foggy.

Therefore, let us humbly but enthusiastically reveal that the Christian worldview gives solid, intellectually profound answers to the very questions most people ask when they find their own answers are inadequate.

3. *Human nature.* Because we live in a world that has replaced belief in God for self, there is immense interest in the question of what it means to be human. So we will examine this at greater length. People want to know, as Sire writes in *The Universe Next Door,* "Are we a highly complex machine, a sleeping god, a person made in the image of God, a 'naked ape' "?[1]

To use apologetics in this area requires that we explain the Christian view of the nature of reality as it pertains to the human condition, addressing the problem of sin, where we find meaning and fulfillment, and so on. Our hope is that if seekers understand the biblical description of reality, they may come to see why their lives lack meaning. For example, why are people today unfulfilled in spite of having so much of a material nature? Why do they still lack peace and meaning when we live in an age in which self is king? The task in apologetics is to help seekers understand that our misery comes *precisely* from placing ourselves at the center of the universe. The biblical understanding of what it means to be human is that we exist for God, and when we fail to put him first, our hearts will always be restless.

An excellent illustration of how to apply apologetics in this realm comes from Stewart Ruch, the senior minister at the church where we attend in the Chicago area. Recently he went to be in the wedding of an old high-school chum. He asked for prayer that he might have an opportunity to witness to the people attending, especially those in the wedding party. The only person he knew was the groom. But he knew the groomsmen would be just like the groom: in their midthirties, Ivy League educated, by nature very driven and all extremely successful. He left for Boston hoping for at least one opportunity to witness. He came back astonished by the fact that he never was able to initiate a single penetrating question. That is because once the groomsmen discovered he was a minister, *they* initiated every question! He feared they might be standoffish because he was a minister. On the contrary, at the reception several men took him aside, saying, "Listen, I hope you don't mind talking 'shop talk,' but I'd really like to ask you some questions."

Stewart said their questions initially ranged from "Who wrote the books of the Bible, and can you trust their reliability?" to "What do we really know about the person of Jesus?" In other words, they were asking for answers from the area of historical apologetics. But what they wanted to talk about more than anything else was the diagnosis of the human condition. What explanation does the Bible give for why the planet is such a mess? What are the roots to human behavior that would explain why people can't find happiness and peace, and why do we do such destructive things? What is the explanation for evil? These are questions demanding answers from philosophical apologetics, especially as it relates to a Christian understanding of human nature.

Stewart said they were astonished to hear that the biblical explanation of the human crisis was spiritual in nature, not psychological or an issue of addiction. Not one of the men he spoke to had ever heard before the idea of sin being a rebellious insistence on running the show rather than allowing God to be at the center.

"But taking complete charge of my life is considered a *virtue* in my world, not a sin! What a revolutionary thought," exclaimed one man.

Another man told Stewart, "In these last ten years since college I have worked very hard and played hard. I've met all the goals I set for myself in my twenties, but I've discovered two things in the process. I'm not superman like I thought. And even with the success I've attained, it's just not enough. What is it about knowing Christ that brings you such fulfillment?"

Another man asked, "I'm in a business where I work with people with enormous egos. They don't believe in God because they think they are God. I see their deception and pride. But how do you conquer self-deception from a Christian perspective?"

Stewart talked to him about the resources we have that guard against deception. For example, he told him that we surrender to and check our opinions against the revealed truth in the Bible. "Furthermore, we believe in a God who exists outside of us, who is transcendent and other and yet who speaks a personal word to his children through his Spirit. We learn how to listen to God. In fact, our church offers seminars on 'listening prayer.'"

"OK," this guy responded, "but how do you know that what you are hearing is really God and not what you ate for breakfast? What protects you from *spiritual* self-deception?"

"Excellent question! Man, I wish I could take you to my church! Church is where we seek God, we worship him, we gather to be taught by his word, and we come together to listen to God in prayer. If I am struggling to understand something, then I go to one of the prayer ministers during the service and they pray for me, or I go to my prayer partners and we ask God for guidance."

"Wait a minute, you have people at your church who pray for anyone who needs it—right while the church service is going on?" the man asked incredulously.

"Absolutely! It doesn't mean we always get it right. But the church is one of God's marvelous resources against deception!"

The last thing the man said to Stewart as they were leaving the wedding party was, "Listen, guys like you have to go and find guys like me so you can tell us these things. Otherwise, how will we ever know?"

Stewart astutely commented afterward, "I'm so glad I didn't meet these men when they were in their twenties. Their openness and curiosity came out of the fact they had lived enough life to know they didn't have all of the answers."

What fascinated me as I listened to Stewart was that almost every question he was asked dealt with the issue of what it means to be human. What is striking about modern people is how few truly cry out for solutions to metaphysical problems. We don't often encounter a person who says, "Tell me what the true nature of God is." What we *do* hear is humanity's cry to be saved from the reality and consequences of sin.

When we hear people asking, "Why am I not happy even though I'm successful?" or, "How could our political leaders do such morally reckless things?" or, "What possesses a person to bomb someone they disagree with?" or even, "Why am I still confused, lonely and miserable even after years of therapy and recovery groups?" they are seeking to understand what is wrong with human nature. They are trying to make meaning out of the central ambiguity and contradiction of human nature. Why is it, they ask, that the same person can be capable of greatness and horror?

Apologetics is helping seekers grasp that the answer to their questions lies in the biblical understanding of the nature of reality. Evangelism, the sharing of the gospel, is the answer to their piercing cry and need.

Stewart's friends were asking questions about the human condition. These men understood that—whatever it means to be human—somehow we matter; we are significant. But sometimes we meet people who think a human being is only a set of chemicals, a piece of protoplasm. That is a valid philosophical position. But we may ask, Can they live that way?

I had a biology professor who stated the first day of class, "Man is merely a fortuitous concourse of atoms, a meaningless piece of protoplasm in an absurd world." We were taught that having deep regard for random products of the universe where chance is king was inconsistent.

Sometime later, however, that same professor told our class in despair that his thirteen-year-old daughter had run away to live with an older man. "She will be deeply wounded. She will scar, and I can't do anything to help. I must sit back and watch a tragedy," he said grimly.

I raised my hand and said quietly that according to his system protoplasm could not scar.

His answer was devastating. "Touché. I could never regard my daughter as a set of chemicals, never. I can't take my beliefs that far. Class dismissed."

No matter how hard we try, we can never escape the fact that we have been made in the image of God. Sooner or later our God-image will be revealed. When the point comes when people are not able to live according to their presuppositions, we must lovingly challenge them to quit escaping reality and live as they were created to be—children of God.

4. *The fundamental problem in the world and how we deal with it.* Everyone from physicists to poets agree that something is wrong with the world. Philosophies, ideologies or explanations of the life process usually place the blame either on external circumstances or on individual decisions and actions. If they see the source as external, then they usually say the system needs changing. For example, an individual is not bad or selfish, he has just developed poor habits; she is a victim of an externally imposed evil. Whether the evil culprit is the capitalistic economic superstructure, as Marx suggested, or the environment, as behavioral determinist B. F. Skinner theorized, the focus of blame is outward, not inward. The other alternative sees the problem as derived from some kind of internal chaos. Christianity says evil has permeated both levels, and we must fight evil at both levels. But the source of evil is internal (Mk 7:14-22).

When we meet people, such as those involved with New Age, who believe humans are basically good, we must agree first. One pillar of our understanding of humanity is that God declared his creation good (Gen 1). Our ability to respond with compassion, to be moved by the beauty of a da Vinci painting or the soaring Austrian Alps stems from the fact that we were created with wondrously good qualities. But where do seekers with an optimistic view of human nature usually struggle? They have great difficulty understanding the problem of suffering. That is where the Christian explanation of reality is so satisfying because we are not naive about the other aspect of our humanness—our sinfulness.

The Bible deals utterly realistically with both sides of us. We are not intrinsically cruel; God did not make us evil. But he made us free, and we rebelled. We are not now what we were created to be. By our own decision, we became abnormal when we chose not to be in relationship to God (Gen 3).

So when seekers say that people are basically good, we must ask them, "How do you account for two world wars? For rampant bigotry that still exists in our age of enlightenment? How do we write off the atrocities of the Nazi or the Bosnian experience?" We must not be naive about the reality of evil.

Nor can we afford to fail putting tough questions to those who say, "All we need is a bit more education." No one should know or understand better the heights to which humans can climb or the depths to which we can succumb than a Christian. Therefore, we must force the world to take both human goodness and human evil with the utmost seriousness. And when their analysis of our dilemma is shallow or their solution is merely a Band-Aid approach, we must help them see that.

To help people take a look at their view of what is the fundamental problem in the world is based in the recognition that everyone has a worldview—a conceptual framework in which they place people and events. We can capitalize on this because surprisingly few people recognize their own worldview or can articulate why they know their beliefs are true. Mostly their thinking is a smattering of ideas from a favorite professor, a large residue from family background, a bit of opinion from *Time* magazine or their favorite television commentator, and so on. Our job is to help people develop their point of view more clearly, to recognize their beliefs and then push them to the point of conviction.

When we help people clarify their ideas, they will often be surprised to find out how unsupported they are by any hard evidence or how haphazard and inconsistent they now appear even to themselves. It is at this point that we can help people push their ideas to their logical conclusions and help them see why their positions are inadequate.

We need to raise questions that deal with the source of authority. In other words, we ask *why* they believe what they do. Is something true for them because it subjectively "feels" right or because of a tradition they were taught or because they believe it is scientifically sound?

For example, a person may be at the point of questioning the goodness of human nature. Perhaps our seeking friend used to believe the best about human nature; now he is not so sure that we are essentially good and that with a bit more education we will conquer our foibles and flaws. We need to start where he is, explore his ideas about human nature, raise questions and suggest the Christian view about these various issues. Maybe that is all the further we are supposed to go in the first conversation or several conversations. But we have accomplished a great deal if we have been able to help him see, for example, that we as people can create beauty, appreciate love, even respond heroically at times. Yet at the same time we cannot deny that we are deeply in crisis, that we struggle with greed and selfishness and hurt those we love, and that all the education and technology we have acquired cannot seem to curb this. Maybe we will be able to tell him God's solution to this dilemma in the first talk, or perhaps it will come later. But we must deal with each person's actual questions. And if he does not have any questions with his present position, we need to raise some for him.

Once I taught an eight-week course in evangelism to a Methodist church. One of the requirements of the course was to say to an unchurched friend, "I'm taking a class on the Christian faith. We are examining what we believe and how to communicate our faith more effectively. Would you be willing to answer the questions the teacher gives us every week?" I made it clear that the questions were not to be used for manipulative purposes but to genuinely discover what their friends believe and to provide a basis for discussion. Every time I've taught this course, by the way, the results are the same. The seekers are *delighted* to be asked questions; it's the believers who are initially nervous about the assignment!

One week we were studying the Christian view of human nature. A person taking the course, Tom, asked his seeker friend that week: "What do you think is the biggest problem in the world today?"

His friend answered, "Universal greed and selfishness."

"So what is the solution?" Tom asked.

"More education," the student responded.

Now at that point Tom could have said, "No, you idiot. Everyone knows education will not root out evil. The only one who can do that is Jesus!" But Tom was astute. He knew he had to bring his friend to the point of realizing that his idea was faulty. So Tom said, "You say all people, everywhere, are selfish? And the solution is education? Well, if all people are selfish, then who is going to teach the class?"

His friend looked at him, smiled and said, "You're right. It won't work. We must stamp out selfishness, but how? OK, so what does Christianity say can solve the problem of flawed human nature?"

Tom then clarified that the core of the problem is sin and that sin can't be "educated out" of us. Only God can change our hearts and our natures from the inside out. The man was ready to listen. Soon he came to an investigative Bible discussion, and eventually he gave his life to Christ. God, as it turned out, had been drawing him all along. But what helped accelerate the process was the fact that Tom had listened to him carefully, explained the truth of the Christian position, and in doing so was able to show him the flaws in his own understanding.

We still need to remember that helping people see the inadequacies of their thinking system will not convert anyone. Because, as we've said before, the power to spiritually transform a life does not rest in us; it rests with God. Furthermore, a lot of people are content having conflicting beliefs floating around in their head. But for some people, the realization that their beliefs are inconsistent or inadequate will make them willing to consider Christianity for the first time. That is why it is important to pay attention to the kind of person we are talking to. If this is a person who will not consider Christianity unless she knows that it is based in reasonable evidence, then that's where we start. The challenge is to communicate the whole gospel to the whole person: mind, emotions and will. But where we begin will depend in large part upon where the seeker's point of interest and need is.

So ask seekers questions about their position and help them see the holes in their own thinking. Then they may be ready to hear what the Christian perspective is. We may be led to communicate only one aspect of the gospel, or we may be led to share much more of it. That will depend upon the receptivity of the non-Christian and our sensitivity to the Holy Spirit.

Revealing Truth Through Historical Evidence

Have you ever encountered someone who discovers you are a believer and says, "I think it's beautiful what your faith does for you. It's really your thing. I mean, it's not my thing, but it's so nice for you"?

To which we may say, "But do you think it's true?"

People often respond with, "No, I don't believe it's true, but what difference does that make?" Then we can continue the conversation in a number of ways.

One way is to say, "How can a lie be beautiful? Either I am right or else I am hopelessly deceived. If I am wrong, then I have staked my entire life on falsehood. If I'm deceived, then it's ugly, not beautiful."

Another way is to say, "Despite your thoughtfulness in saying my faith is valid for me because it gives me such a warm feeling, all of the most tender feelings in the world cannot make a man rise from the dead. Either Jesus did or did not rise from the dead, quite apart from my feelings on the subject. And one of the best-attested facts in history is that his tomb was empty. The government was forced to issue a flimsy cover story because they couldn't find the corpse. Either Jesus was resurrected or there must be an explanation of what happened to his body. But neither conclusion depends on my warm glow to make it true. Jesus isn't true just because he makes me feel good."

This moves us into the arena of historical evidences. And in this arena we face questions such as these: How do you know the Bible is historically trustworthy? Weren't some of the worst wars in history fought by Christians, such as the Crusades? Wasn't Jesus merely a good teacher? How do you know he was resurrected? Did Jesus even exist? Why Christianity and not other religions? What makes Jesus so unique? Hasn't Christianity suppressed women? Haven't missionaries destroyed native cultures? These questions all require evidence—evidence that necessitates some knowledge of history.

The questions skeptics ask are remarkably similar. It would be helpful to have index cards with the problem stated at the top—"Evidence for the Resurrection"—and the basic arguments listed below. Also there are excellent books that address all of these questions, and I have listed some of them in the back. Any of these books would be a good place to start learning how the common questions may best be answered. But first find out if your seeker friend really is interested in these questions. They are fair questions and there are good answers. Even if the seeker isn't interested yet, he probably will be once he is converted. I often find this type of apologetic is even more meaningful to the new convert than to the undecided seeker.

But in some cases seekers don't have any interest at all in historical or philosophical evidences for our belief. These are people imbued with the postmodern spirit that is abroad in the world today. Facts and arguments won't work with them, but something else will—something we're all fond of—storytelling.

16

Revealing Truth Through Stories

....

A woman in her midtwenties recently said to me, "I'm not remotely interested in whether what you're saying is true—I want to know if it is *real*."

"What do you mean by 'real'?" I asked.

"'Real' means that you have actually *experienced* this truth in your life. It's not some dry dogma that exists only in your mind but has never touched your heart. I want to hear about what you have experienced, what makes life work for you, far more than I want to hear some didactic truth."

Here is a typical postmodern perspective. How do we speak to a person who values experience over explanation? The issue here isn't how we can speak to postmodern people without using any categories of truth. Rather, it's how we convey truth by using forms they are more apt to understand and respond to.

One effective way of communicating God's truth (especially to postmodern folk but to others as well) is through the vehicle of storytelling—by telling God's story from the biblical narrative, and by sharing our story as well. In stories we explore how we and others have been affected by God's action in our lives. When people hear of our experience, they can often gain a better idea of the reality of the gospel. Let's deal with telling God's story first.

Revealing Truth Through Telling God's Story

How do we go about sharing God's story in the Bible? Do we just dive in with a stranger and begin reciting Bible stories?

First, we need to pay attention to the story of the seeker. We won't be able to make God's story relevant unless we understand his or her story first. It's always important to be sensitive to the needs and hurts of people. But in a postmodern, experience-oriented culture like ours, being able to discern a person's needs is a vital skill if we are to help them see their need for Christ. Of course, what we know from the outset is that people are hungry for far more than they realize. Their dissatisfaction with life points to their hunger for God. Our ultimate aim is to help seekers understand that their problems in life, whatever they may be, cannot be solved unless they first resolve their bigger problem: getting their relationship with God right. But if we don't first listen carefully to their story, it will be difficult to draw their attention toward hearing God's story. As Ronald Johnson writes, "Learning to listen as a part of our telling the gospel is a challenge because we are people who have been trained almost exclusively in the act of monological presentation."[1]

I had an experience that illustrates this principle. As a birthday gift my family gave me a "Day at the Spa." Once there I was introduced to Jill, the manicurist. After talking for a few minutes, I said, "Tell me what is it that you most enjoy about your life right now? What really gives you joy?"

She excitedly told me that she had just become a first time homeowner, and she shared all the joys and frustrations of that experience.

"Have you had an open house yet so your friends and family can celebrate with you?" I asked.

"Well, yes, though my mother didn't come. She never celebrates anything good that happens to me," Jill answered with some bitterness.

This is a classic example of what happens in the course of a conversation. I had no agenda in asking her that question. I've never been the type of person who has five stock questions I always ask a person. I don't have a problem with people who do, but for me I find it impedes authentic interaction. I simply wanted to get to know her. The question popped into my head, so I asked it. Yet it led almost immediately to a revelation of deep pain in her life. Now what should I do? I decided to gently ask about her mother, and if she clammed up, then we'd move on to other topics. Only now I was praying for her as we spoke.

"I'm really sorry to hear that your mom isn't more supportive. That has to be painful. Has she behaved that way for long?" I asked.

"Yeah, like try for most of my life. My mom's a real piece of work," she sighed.

"I wonder what her problem is?" I asked tentatively.

"You know, I've spent half my life trying to figure that out. She is one of the angriest, most self-pitying people I've ever met. It's like, if anything good happens to anyone—even her own daughter—somehow it's always at her expense. She can't celebrate anything good that happens to me. She's always looking over her shoulder to see if I got more or better."

"Wow, it sounds like a pretty deep case of narcissism and envy. It's amazing how destructive envy is. We don't hear much about it these days, but it really destroys the person who has it and hurts everyone around them as well."

"I can't believe you're saying that, because that's just what I told my roommate yesterday. It seems crazy, but I think my mom *is* jealous of me. Sounds like you've done some thinking about envy. What do you know about it?"

"Well, I did a project recently that involved researching the subject of envy, among other things. What helped me understand the nature of envy was reading the story of David in the Bible."

"You mean the same guy that fought Goliath? That's all I know about him, but did he have a problem with envy?"

"No, but King Saul sure did. As you've been describing your mother, I've been struck by how much she has a personality profile just like Saul. He was profoundly envious of David, and Saul was always looking over his shoulder to see if David got more praise or attention. He could never celebrate anything good that happened to David for fear it was taking something away from him. In the end envy finally destroyed Saul."

"That absolutely blows my mind. There is somebody in the Bible who is like *my mother?* Man, wait till I tell my brothers. OK, tell me more about the story."

For the next several minutes I told her the story of David and Saul. She listened to every word of how ferociously Saul pursed David, how Saul was eaten up with envy, hatred and eventually madness. What she wanted to know after listening to the story was this: how had David coped with being the target of someone's envy and hatred?

"Don't you wish David had written a journal during all those years he fled from Saul? Wouldn't you love to know what he was feeling and how he coped with it all emotionally? Now *that* would be a page turner!" Jill said.

"Oh, but he did! We have the psalms, and many of them were written by David. When you read the books of Samuel, you get a fascinating historical account of what happened. But when you read the psalms, it's like reading David's personal prayer diary to God!"

"Well, what did he say? Wasn't he furious with Saul? Didn't he hate Saul? And wasn't David a little ticked with God for not knocking Saul off so David could have some peace?"

"It's amazing to read, Jill. You find nearly every human emotion in David's prayers. Often he starts off very depressed and discouraged. Other times he begins with fury and anger. And you can't blame him. What Saul did to David was an outrage. David had looked to Saul as a father figure, and Saul turned on him viciously."

"That's exactly where I am. Sometimes my mom makes me furious, and I feel nothing but hate. Other times I feel so depressed and alone. But I can't seem to climb out of it. How did David overcome his feelings of depression and anger? What did he do to pump himself up?" Then looking at me with utter seriousness, Jill said, "Golly, there were no self-help tapes in those days either."

"What I love about David is that he was so utterly human. When he felt pain, confusion, fear and anger, he acknowledged it. He didn't try to pretend. But David knew what to do with his humanity—he brought all of it right into the presence of God. He didn't blame God for his troubles; instead, he asked for God's help in his troubles. David didn't come to God in his Sunday best; he just poured out his pain and suffering right there in front of God."

"And God wasn't offended by his honesty?"

"God loved it! God wants to have a warm, open, trusting relationship with us. God even called David a 'man after my own heart.' "

"So was David helped by being that open with God?"

"You bet he was! David's prayers often began from the bottom of the emotional pit. But, somehow, just bringing his pain and naming it right in God's presence caused David's spirit to rise. It's amazing how often he begins in sorrow and concludes in hope and even praise."

"Did David ever forgive Saul?"

"Yes, I believe he did. David wasn't perfect; he made lots of mistakes. But slowly, over time, you see what happens to a person who gets to know God and chooses to obey him. David was deeply sinned against—just as you have been, Jill—but God helped David to forgive Saul and to not carry bitterness and anger in his heart. God helped David to let go of the injustices done to him and to wait for God to set things right."

"Well, there is no way I could forgive my mom, not after all she's done to me. I hate her. I'll never trust her again. Anyway, why should I?"

"It's clear she's hurt you terribly. But you know why I think God asks us to forgive those who have sinned against us? Because he doesn't want us to carry around the cancer of unforgiveness within us. Not to mention the fact that *we* need God's forgiveness too!"

"Well, maybe it was easier to forgive people in biblical times. I don't think that many people do it today."

"You know what? There was someone in my life that I had to forgive, and I desperately didn't want to. She was a person who caused enormous pain to people that I love deeply. I remember how shocked I was to discover one day that not only did I not want to forgive her, but I hated her. I didn't want to admit to the hate, but it was there, and it was deep."

"Would you mind telling me about it?" Jill asked.

I spent the next several minutes telling her about a personal story of my own battle with hate. I was honest with her about the circumstances, and I didn't try to present myself as being above temptation. I told her how deeply I struggled and how much I didn't want to forgive this person. In sharing this it naturally came out that I was a Christian. I told her that God requires his followers to forgive, just as David had to learn. Finally, through God's help and grace and my willingness to obey, I had been able to overcome hate and to forgive.

"Jill, I don't know where you are with God, but I know I needed God's help to be able to forgive. If you ever choose to forgive your mom, you'll need God's help too. I know from firsthand experience that we have to get our relationship with God in order before we can get the rest of our relationships straight. One thing I know, God cares deeply about your pain. He knows you've been sinned against and it's *not fair,* but he doesn't want to see you destroyed by being stuck in hatred like Saul was."

"Becky, I'm going to tell you something. I'm still flabbergasted that there is a story in the Bible that relates so much to my situation. I always thought of the Bible as a book of 'thee's and thou's.' I never dreamed there were people in there who acted like my mother! But if you hadn't told me your own story, I would have tried to blow off the story about David. But you've been through pain too. You didn't want to forgive any more than I do, but you did it anyway. OK, let's go back to David and tell me how he forgave Saul."

"Jill, I'd love to, but our time is up!"

"Man, I've never seen time fly by so fast. Becky, no joking, sometime you should think about writing a book about David," she said.

"Well, as a matter of fact, I did! That was the research project I mentioned earlier. I tell you what—I'll bring you a copy sometime."

I went home and my family said, "Wow, Mom, you look great!" But when I replied, "You guys, I *have* to go back. Honestly, it's for the sake of the gospel!" my children responded with rolled eyes and said, "Oh, yeah, right. Now there's a good excuse!"

I did return, and when Jill saw me, she said, "I'm so glad you came back. That day we talked I was up half the night telling my roommate about our conversation and that person in the Bible. What did you say the name was—Sammy? Sally? Susie?"

"It was Saul," I answered, trying to suppress my laughter.

"Oh, yeah. Well, I went out and bought a Bible so I can read that story, but I didn't know where to look. I even told my brothers that there was someone in the Bible with a personality profile like our mother. They couldn't believe it either!" Jill reported.

Each time I have returned we have spoken at deeper and deeper levels of what it means to forgive, how one goes about it, how we need God's help to do it. We are now discussing what it means to be a Christian. Jill is considering what it means to forgive her mother, but I believe, even more importantly, she is considering Christ. And I might add that my nails have never looked so good!

I have reflected on this experience a great deal, and I believe there are several levels of meaning. First, I was struck by how God's truth spoke to Jill, how it got through. But why? How?

For one thing, Jill heard something in the biblical story that she connected with. The story of David slipped past her defenses, caught her imagination, and she discovered she could identify with David. In other words, God's truth came across to her as personal and relational rather than didactic and distant. God's truth took on a human face and human frame through David. Through sharing the biblical narrative of David, Jill began to grasp that God cares about our problems, that God wants us to relate to him authentically and personally. In hearing about David's struggles, she began to consider why forgiving others is important. Most of all, she got a taste of what an authentic walk of faith looks like through the life of David.

Another interesting aspect of that experience is that, by conveying truth through the biblical narrative, it placed the weight of authority where it belonged—on God and not on me. For example, I was comfortable saying, "You know, David really taught me how important it is to forgive," or, "David showed me that first we must get our own relationship with God sorted out." Pointing to a third party for authority made it easier for both of us. I didn't sound like I was speaking *ex cathedra,* and if she disagreed with what I was saying, she could disagree with David and not me.

For example, at one point she got a bit heated over the idea of forgiving her mother and said, "Well, I don't think David would have forgiven my mother if he really knew her." She softened a bit later, but what I realized was that her responses were more authentic because she didn't have to worry about contradicting me—it was David she had the beef with. If I had said in a tone from on high, "Well, the *Bible* says . . . !" I would have lost her. But when I said, "You know, David really helped me understand something," it didn't seem like a cold, external code of beliefs being imposed but rather truth to be considered from what our, by now, mutual friend David had said. I sensed the weight of conviction and authority that comes through the Word of God, but she was able to hear the truth more readily because it came through a story about relationships.

Another reason why God's truth got through to her was because she saw that we *both* stood under the weight of truth's authority. In sharing my personal story it became clear that the truth of forgiveness had been just as hard for me to hear as it was for her. God's truth had placed demands on me too. It demanded my own conversion, my own willingness to humble myself and obey. I was not preaching truth from on high; I was sharing truth that I had followed with my life. My testimony was that the process of obeying had been difficult but worth it. Once she knew that I too had problems, that I too had struggled to obey God's command to forgive, it brought about an almost instant camaraderie. It built an authentic relationship between us because she saw that we were coparticipants, fellow learners on the human journey to obey God.

Parker Palmer writes that true learning always involves obedience to the truth for *all* the parties involved—for the teacher and the student, for the knower and the seeker. The problem, he says, is when "we want to avoid a knowledge that calls for our own conversion. We want to know in ways that allow us to convert the world—but we do not want to be known in ways that requires us to change as well."[2] I believe one of the most important aspects of my witness to Jill was allowing her to see my subjective struggles to learn how to obey the objective truth of God. But the entire experience was rooted in first listening to her pain.

Revealing Truth Through Telling Our Story

My illustration with Jill reveals how helpful it can be to share our own story as well as God's story. The world hungers—perhaps without even knowing it—for examples of evidence in people's lives. They want to know if God works. Has he brought us identity and meaning? Have we experienced his love in ways that fulfill and complete us? We can do this when we learn how to share our own Christian experience.

Sometimes God will lead us to share the biblical narrative and then our personal story. Other times we begin with a personal story that leads us into sharing some aspect of God's story. However God guides us, it is the combination of the two that helps seekers, like Jill, begin to pay attention to what God is saying.

Sharing a personal experience with a seeker does not mean that it needs to be deeply private. For example, I met a woman not too long ago who described herself as a "professional seeker." She told me of her constant search to find meaning, peace and identity. But then she said, "I think I'm on to something now, Becky. I've been listening to these tapes, and they are really helping me a lot!" I asked her to describe this new therapy.

"Well, every night before I go to sleep I play this tape that says, 'You are beautiful. You are extraordinary. You are kind. You are loving. You are wonderful. People look up to you. Your friends count it a privilege to be in your presence.'"

I asked, "How many times do you have to listen to these tapes for them to work?"

"A lot!" she answered.

"Excuse me if this sounds rude, but how can such affirmative statements mean anything when the person speaking on the tape has never laid eyes on you? It's like saying, 'Dear consumer, you sure are gorgeous.'"

"Oh, but for twenty-five bucks more you can get a personalized tape with your name on it," she answered.

"It sounds like you really want to improve your life."

"Oh, I really do."

What was she searching for? On the surface she wanted to improve herself, but I believe that behind her desire for self-improvement was a profound need for love. What one "heard" behind her words was the wistful hope that if she could just be good enough, then maybe someone would love her. She was trying to use self-help tapes to motivate herself into positive action that would fill the deep "hole in her soul" for love through constant affirmation.

The Christian answer to this is that our need for love and our capacity for positive change ironically lies in our willingness to face the negative: owning our sin and then coming into a relationship with Jesus as Lord of our lives. However, she had already told me that she'd had a negative church experience, so instead of starting with a Christian explanation of the solution, I said, "You know, the recovery movement says that the only way we bring about inner change is to first own our problem. What do you think of that as a change strategy?"

"Listen," she said, "I know what I'm listening to is a lie. It's just that these tapes kind of . . . oh, I dunno, they just help me get through the night."

Think of what she is actually saying. She is so lonely and so hungry for kindness and love that she is willing to pay money for a tape with a stranger's voice telling her lovely things that she knows have no basis in reality. I could have wept to hear it.

"What do you use, Becky, to get through life?" she asked.

"I have someone in my life, but he's no stranger. I don't have to pay him, because he already knows my name. He tells me the truth—that I am beloved and cherished. He also tells me where I'm in trouble and must change. But he never condemns me. Instead, he helps me overcome my weaknesses and enables me to become my true self, the self I am called to be."

"Where can you buy such a tape?" my new friend asked incredulously.

"It can't be bought. It's free," I answered. Then I shared with her the gospel and told her of the beauty of living in an intimate, loving relationship with God through Christ.

The point here is this: if I had tried to explain or defend the truth of the gospel by sharing the evidence for the resurrection, I would have lost her. She needed to hear that God longs to establish an intimate relationship with her, and that it is through Christ that she can experience wholeness and love. The way I communicated that truth was by sharing my own experience first, before I shared the gospel.

I have told many stories in this book—some of which have surprised me even more than the others involved. The changes God has worked in people always amaze me. But he has done good works in you too. Don't be afraid to tell people who you are and who you were before you met Christ.

True, some people only testify to themselves: "Once I was a louse. Now I'm great." God sometimes drops out of the testimony altogether. Or all of their witness is simply personal—what God has done for them. "I know he lives, because he lives within my heart." We must direct people's attention outward to God in Christ loving and reconciling the world to himself by the death of his Son on the cross. But the subjective dimension is equally real and, when balanced by the objective and historical, is a powerful witness to who God really is.

The subjective dimension is equally important in talking with that category of postmoderns involved in alternate forms of spirituality. But their beliefs create special issues and so I have chosen to devote an entire chapter to sharing one's faith with these people. God loves them and is calling them to himself through us.

17

Revealing Truth
Through the Power
of the Spirit

....

I t is astonishing to reflect on the rise of spirituality in recent years.
Twenty years ago we didn't even have names for spiritual categories
and practices that are commonplace today, or if we did, they were
considered so far out as to be inconsequential. Yet today these experiences
are considered almost mainstream: near-death experiences, out-of-body experiences, visualization, channeling—to name but a few. And what was called
the "new consciousness" is now known as the New Age.

The challenge in our present "spiritual" age is this: how do we define,
communicate and defend, in a winsome way, spirituality from a Christian
perspective—following Christ and making him Lord of all of life? That's a
challenge because what is perceived as spiritual can include doing crystal
therapy or life regression on Monday, finding our "inner child" on Tuesday,
meditating with zither music and Tibetan bells on Wednesday, having our
sessions for Quantum healing on Thursday, and swimming with dolphins and
getting aromatic massages on Friday!

This is an immense subject and far beyond the scope of this book to deal
with in any thorough way. However, there are books listed in appendix two that

I encourage you to read if you are in dialogue with people involved with alternative forms of spirituality. My intention is merely to examine some approaches we may take in defending the truth of our faith, especially in our dialogue with people in the New Age movement.

Revealing Truth Through the Spirit

It has taken me years to appreciate that God reveals his truth through the power and demonstration of his Spirit. When I did campus ministry years ago, if I saw a seeker slip into a "regular" Christian fellowship meeting, I'd get nervous. I was afraid it would be "too Christian" or "too spiritual" for them to appreciate. Who knows?—maybe back then it was true. Perhaps it's due to the rise of spiritual interest in our culture today, but I have seen seekers won to Christ because they saw the unmistakable power of God's presence during a worship service. There is no greater spiritual power than the power of the Holy Spirit, and God reveals his truth through the resources of his Spirit.

Let us be clear that the work of the Spirit operates in all of the apologetic approaches we have been discussing. We need the Spirit's help when we offer a historical defense of the faith just as we need his help when we share a biblical story with a seeker. What we are examining in this section is how to avail ourselves of the Spirit's power as we witness to those involved in alternative forms of spirituality.

We must not forget that one of the most powerful apologetics we have to offer the world is the Spirit's work in our own lives. It is important to take the time to reflect on how God's Spirit has been with us at every stage in our pilgrimage, whether in the times of suffering and crisis or the times of joy and victory. Such an exercise can only lead us to render thanks.

We also need to listen to God's Spirit as we meet people. Our attitude needs to be one of expectancy. We should assume that God's Spirit is at work in the lives of those people we meet, seeking to draw them to himself. As we witness, let us remember that the Spirit was no doubt at work in that person's life before we met him or her, and the Spirit will continue to work after we are long gone. Our task is to be sensitive to what the Spirit is doing in that moment and to participate with him in the process.

Above all, let us be careful to not quench the Spirit. One of the primary ways we block God's Spirit is through being judgmental and critical of others. Even the right message given in the wrong spirit makes it difficult for the Lord to use us effectively. Remember that we are called to "speak the truth in love" (see Eph 4:15). A great deal of our Christian message runs counter to where our culture is. So it is natural that there will at times be conflict in the seeker who hears it. But if seekers sense the welcoming and loving presence of God's Spirit in us, they will be far more likely to hear what we have to say. It's tragic enough that the world assumes that Christians are judgmental and critical. Let's not exacerbate the problem by proving them right by our behavior!

One of the ways we can facilitate the Spirit's work, and something I have emphasized in this book, is the need for us to listen. Effective evangelism requires it. It's not enough that we discover *our* style of communicating faith, as is popularly assumed, but we must also seek to understand the person we are speaking to. In other words, we need to understand the context of the seeker. As Alan Roxburgh writes in his excellent book *Reaching a New Generation,* "Our problem is not the inadequacy of the gospel but the fact that we have forgotten how to read the gospel through the realities of the context. Adequate listening demands that we hear the deep concerns shaping our time."[1] We listen carefully not so we may create a gospel that simply matches itself up to the current trends. Rather, understanding the seeker's context enables us to rediscover and proclaim the gospel with power and clarity as God's good news for all times, and in particular for "a time such as this."

Promotion to Godhood

What do we discover as we listen to those who are drawn to alternate forms of spirituality? A friend of mine who is a devotee of the New Age has taught me a great deal about why, for example, the New Age has such enormous appeal to people in our modern culture. She describes herself as someone raised in a mainline church but who has for years been trying, though unsuccessfully, to leave the Christian tradition. We have had several discussions about her beliefs, but it tended to be on a more surface and intellectual level. Then one day I got a phone call that changed all of that.

Anna called me on a day in which I was stricken with a virulent flu. I was vomiting every thirty minutes, and I had a pounding, violent headache. I was in bed, my children were at school and my husband was out of town when the telephone rang. I don't know why I answered the phone when it rang, but the minute I heard Anna's voice, I knew something was terribly wrong. Anna is a very strong, self-reliant person, so it was unnerving to hear her sound so frightened. "Becky, I'm in trouble. I've been having medical problems, and the doctor's office just called. It looks serious. I go in to the doctor's office tomorrow morning. They suspect it's cancer. Somehow I have to get through this night. I'm terrified, I don't want my children to see me so panicked, and I don't know what to do. Becky, would you please pray for me right now on the phone?"

Knowing there was no way I could minister to Anna in my present condition, I urgently offered a silent prayer: "Lord, I ask you in Jesus' name, please take away every symptom right now so I can pray for her." *Instantaneously* every symptom vanished. And though Anna and I were friends, we certainly didn't have an intimate friendship, so I also asked the Lord to guide me into truth as I prayed and to calm her spirit and give her peace.

As I began to pray for Anna, something remarkable happened. I not only felt the presence of the Lord in a special way, but I found myself praying things that revealed a far greater level of intimacy and knowledge about her than I actually had. I knew such knowledge had to be coming from God.

After I prayed, I asked Anna if she would call me back in fifteen minutes so I could give her Bible passages to read. When she called back, she said, "Becky, something extraordinary happened as you were praying. I felt as if God was speaking directly to me, letting me know that he knows me intimately. I could feel my anxiety just being lifted and taken away. It was almost a physical sensation. It was so powerful. I didn't tell you at first because I was sure by the time I called back for the verses I'd be a basket case again. But I have this *amazing* peace."

The minute we hung up, my own flu symptoms returned, though not at the same level of severity. I couldn't help but pray, "Uh, Lord, not to be impertinent, but just for the record, would it upset some great celestial plan here if I could be rid of this flu?" As it turned out, I was just sick enough to have to remain in bed for the next twenty-four hours, which gave me ample time to pray for Anna! So I decided my diminished flu symptoms were a mercy after all.

Two days later Anna came to my house. After running more tests the doctors discovered that she did not have cancer as they had thought, although she would still have to have surgery. However, for the first time she spoke candidly about what she believed. My praying for her had been both deeply meaningful as well as troubling, because now it forced her to reevaluate her beliefs. What she told me was remarkable.

As it turned out, when she received the upsetting doctor's call, she had not called me first. Instead, she had called a New Age hot line. It is a New Age service that provides prayer and counseling for people in distress.

"Becky," Anna said, "it was a horrible experience. I told the woman who answered that I was desperate, afraid and needed prayer. But her prayers weren't personal; in fact, they sounded vague. I came in crisis needing real help, but all she did was pray an 'I am the universe' and 'I am God' kind of chant. I didn't need to pray to myself or to the cosmos—I needed help from God! But even worse, I think she was cleaning up her address card file while she was praying for me. There wasn't an ounce of real love coming through. By the time we hung up, I was in worse shape than before the call. I knew I had to have someone pray for me who absolutely trusted in what she believed. So I called you. The difference between your prayers and the New Age prayers were like night and day."

"Anna," I replied, "part of me wants to say to you, what did you expect? Even though it's hard to pin down New Age beliefs, we're on pretty safe ground to say that one major tenet is their pantheistic belief that God is in everything. They don't believe there is a God outside his creation, that he exists outside of us as a personal being whom we address. They believe God is an impersonal energy, a creative force that runs through all of creation and lies within each of us. That woman was being faithful to New Age beliefs by praying what she prayed. But you inferred correctly how impotent such a belief is in light of genuine crisis.

"Anna," I continued, "though I'm sorry you didn't experience compassion when you called her, I'm not surprised. I think one of the great counterfeits in the New Age is the lack of love. I know they talk a great deal about love, but frankly, the movement is very self-centered. Their emphasis has always been on finding the God within, but it ends up promoting self-absorbed practices under a religious disguise. It's Christianity, not the New Age, that calls us to truly love our neighbor."

"Becky, there's something else. To be honest, I've experienced a power that operates through doing New Age spiritual practices. But when you began to pray, I experienced a power far greater than anything I've ever known through New Age. What underscored it was that I knew the power *had* to be from God, because you were too sick to have been its source. I was sure I was going to be awake all that night after I got the doctor's call, but after you prayed, I slept like a baby. I had this sense that God was right there holding me."

"Anna, may I ask you something? You say you experienced the power of God and his love reaching out to you through the prayers of a Christian far more than you have ever experienced through the New Age. So what is it that still draws you to New Age?"

"I like their emphasis on the positive. I'm turned off by how Christians talk about sin. It's so negative. New Age encourages us to turn from anything that is negative. It's freed me to realize that there is no bad in me, only good. Because I am God and God is me."

"But Anna, if God is simply you and the God-force intertwined, then *what kind of God gets cancer?* Not any God I would want to depend on. Didn't your cancer scare show you that you need a God who is outside of yourself and larger than your own psyche? How can you live in reality and not acknowledge that there is evil and sin? Don't things like cancer show us that we can't pretend everything in life is positive? What I love about Christianity is that it is rooted in reality. It acknowledges the problem of pain and evil; it tells us how we got into this mess in the first place and tells us what to do about it."

"You know what really bothers me, Becky, is that I realized for the first time that I don't have a philosophy that teaches me how to make meaning out of suffering."

"Oh, Anna, you've hit the nail on the head. Moderns are hopelessly inadequate when it comes to suffering because we think the purpose of life is for God to make us *feel* good. But what if God's purpose is to make us *be* good, to become godly people? Then suffering takes on a whole new meaning because God can use our difficulties to deepen our faith, strengthen our character and walk with us as we go through hard times.

"Anna," I added, "I forgot to ask you something. What did you think about the Bible passages you read?"

"I found them deeply moving, even strengthening. I just had to close my eyes when I hit words I couldn't handle. You know, like references to God being King and Lord."

"What's wrong with that?" I asked, puzzled.

"It's the language of dominance and control that is so rooted in Western thinking."

"Well, the Bible originated in the East, not the West. But what other language did you find offensive?"

"The language that suggested surrender and submission. I have a lot of trouble with that because it feels like the language of abuse. It grates on the ears of someone like me who believes in rights, choice and equality."

I must confess that at that moment I was stunned. Here we were, two women who had been raised in the same part of the country, who were about the same age and who had many other things in common. Yet language that I find deeply moving and liberating she found abusive and offensive. I realized as never before the challenge before us of communicating the gospel to today's ears.

All I could say to Anna was this: "Maybe the language of surrender and submission only makes sense once you've seen the greatness, goodness and glory of God. Just to be in his presence, to experience even for a fleeting moment his majesty and holiness and goodness makes the language of rights and choice seem laughable. Maybe what's needed is a new vision of who God really is."

"Well, where do you go to find that? And don't tell me the answer is church. I've never found anything that seemed spiritually vital when I used to go to church. It felt stale, rigid and doctrinaire."

"Oh, Anna, then come with me to my church! At our church the worship alone nearly punctures the ceiling!"

"Well, I quit going to church because I have a real bone to pick with God. I begged him to heal the daughter of a close friend, and she died anyway. Then I asked him to help someone whom I deeply love, and her life is still a mess."

"Listen, I'm sympathetic to your pain when your prayers aren't answered as you think they should be. I prayed for a person whom I felt had been a 'mismanaged case' by God too."

"What conclusion did you come to?"

"That I am not God. I can't see into a person's heart. I can't possibly see the big picture or what God will do in the future. But here's what I could say to God: I do not understand you in this situation, but I know your character is true and loving. Therefore, I can trust that *you* know what you are doing even though I don't."

"Well, I'm not willing to say that, at least not yet. I think God bungled the job, and that's when I knew I needed to start taking more control."

"Whoa! So what you're saying is that when God didn't do what you wanted, you found a religion that deifies self so that you can have more control? But your cancer scare made you realize that your God is too small. You know what your problem is, Anna? You're in a power struggle with God. And as your friend, I have to tell you this—you're not on the winning side. Life's great lesson is that God is God and we are not."

It was fascinating to see, as we peeled the layers away, that what was really at the heart of her struggle was rebellion. That is perhaps not much of a revelation because all of us struggle with rebellion against God. It's just that one doesn't often see it so clearly.

I owe a great deal to Anna. Besides the fact that I love her and enjoy our friendship, she has helped me to understand today's struggles and longings. She is still wrestling with what to do. She told me recently that she feels she can't give up on traditional Christianity, but neither does she want to give up the New Age approach. But God has his hand on her life. He dramatically reached out to her once, and I'm sure in his great mercy he will continue to reveal his love to her.

Exposing Spiritual Deception

How, then, do we reach someone in the New Age movement, or someone involved in other alternative forms of spirituality? The fact that they are searching for spiritual realities is a marvelous opportunity for us to share the gospel. How do we go about it?

First, we need to educate ourselves at least minimally about what they believe. Even though I am light-years away from being an expert on New Age beliefs, what I did know helped me enormously in my conversation with Anna. There are books listed in the appendix that will help us understand the basic tenets of the New Age movement. Then we need to understand how their beliefs differ from biblical truth. For example, the New Age belief that God is an impersonal force is radically different from the biblical understanding of God being a transcendent personal Creator who speaks to us and to whom we can speak. There are vast differences in what we believe, and we need to know what they are. Then we can explore ways to answer their questions as well as defend our own position.

Second, in the New Age movement we see a search for spiritual power, spiritual experience and transformed lives. Yet we know that there is no greater power than the power of the Holy Spirit. How, then, do we point seekers to the reality of God's Spirit?

I believe part of the answer lies in what we will examine in the next chapter, namely, by allowing outsiders to see the spiritual vitality of our own Christian communities. Seekers need to see the life, love, joy and peace the Holy Spirit brings to Christians' lives. When seekers truly see people set free and healed by the power of the Holy Spirit, their curiosity is aroused. What better apologetic can we offer true spiritual seekers than that of a vibrant, worshiping church?

It was experiencing the Holy Spirit's power that arrested the attention of Anna. What fascinated me about that experience was that I could have never engineered this "contest" between power centers. Nor could I have imagined that my being sick could be used by God to prove that it was his power and not my own. That experience reminded me once again that God truly is glorified in our weakness! So let us ask God to reveal the power of his Holy Spirit through our lives and communities. We must be careful not to tempt

God by capriciously seeking for signs, nor is it a guarantee that it will lead people to repentance and faith, but it is a valid avenue that we need to pursue.

Third, and most difficult, how do we reach people whose problem is not that their self is divine and king (as they believe) but that it is actually a prisoner? In other words, how do we deal with people who are spiritually deceived? Most of the alternative spiritualities seek to transcend Christianity by offering a superior, "deeper" spirituality. How do we respond? We start by understanding what it is that draws people to these other avenues in the first place.

One reason, for example, they say, is that they long to transcend the separateness they feel from the universe, from each other and from God. That is why there is so much discussion in New Age literature about being "connected" to the cosmic whole. Let us freely affirm their desire for a restored, unified creation. Indeed, the purpose of Christ's death and resurrection is to restore this broken earth with its marred people. Let us also agree with their notion that they feel separated. They are. We celebrate their desire for unity, their longing to overcome separateness, but we need to find ways of expressing how true unity with God is achieved.

The belief that our separateness can be *humanly* overcome is a spiritual deception from the biblical point of view. Sin indeed separates us from God. Sin brings disunity from the Spirit. True restoration cannot come from within the system. The only thing that brings us into unity with God's Spirit is confession of sin, repentance and trust in Jesus as Lord.

Another sobering aspect of spiritual deception in the New Age is their reliance on "spirit guides" through whom they seek guidance from the spirit world. This is a practice that is clearly forbidden in the Bible (Deut 18:11). Why aren't we encouraged in Scripture to contact higher spirits, employ them as guides and harness their wisdom or power for our human needs? Because God alone is to be our source of power, of wisdom and of knowledge.

This call to seek "higher guidance" isn't new. The Gnostics of the second century taught that God was too exalted, too far away, just "too busy" to be bothered with personal human affairs. They taught that other beings exist who are higher than humans but lower than God, whom we can contact for help.

But the biblical warning is stark: we are not to toy with the realm of spirits. There is only one God: there is no other. To seek guidance from anyone else—be it spirit guides, mediums, diviners—is blasphemy. God is our refuge, and it is to him and him alone we are to turn for help, guidance and wisdom. We do otherwise at our peril.

Besides spiritual deception, there is also the problem of self-deception in the New Age because the basis for evaluating truth is totally subjective. Evidence is not offered because it is not required in such a system. The only "proof" required is subjective certainty. "Because of its absolute subjectivity, the I-am-God or I-am-the-universe position remains beyond any criticism external to the subject."[2]

So we return to our question: how do we break into self-deception and spiritual deception? Speaking rationally into deception rarely works because the origin of the problem is spiritual in nature and not intellectual. Spiritual deception requires a different strategy. Our primary strategy needs to be prayer. We must ask God himself to find a way to break through the spiritual deception and self-deception, to help those involved in counterfeit spiritualities to see their rebellion and to repent. We must ask God to break any experience of false fruit, such as feelings of unity and peace that are self-deceived. But what we *don't* say is, "Boy, you sure are deceived and rebellious!" It is not something that we *say*; it is something that we *pray!*

Whether we begin by asking God to reveal his truth through the power of the Holy Spirit or begin by offering evidence or telling stories (as in the previous two chapters), let us remember that what motivates our apologetics is our desire to direct attention to Jesus. We want seekers to examine Jesus and his claims by what they see in our lives. Let us therefore offer the world models of head-and-heart-and-Spirit-filled Christianity.

Such models, however, do not spring solely from individual, personal witness. And that is why we must next turn to the witness to Christ that can flow from his body, the church, when it works as a coordinated whole.

18

The Witness
of Community

....

We were not born to be alone. God created us for relationships. So we have been born first into the human family and then, as Christians, born again into the family of God. All of us, therefore, are members of some kind of community—our own family, school, friends, fraternity, sorority or other social groups. As John Donne has said, "No man is an island."

Still, we often feel like islands. Our professional commitments frequently lead us not only into geographical isolation but into emotional isolation as well. And so loneliness—the very opposite of community, the most crushing of all emotions— descends on us. There is an important reason for this. It is by design and not caprice that we find loneliness crushing. Only in community can we become fully alive, fully human, finding rest and completeness in the context of others. It is not enough for one individual to imitate the ways of God, for God is not alone; he is the Trinity. Therefore, it is the community of God's people who will represent him more fully and completely.

Furthermore, it is in community—in seeing ourselves juxtaposed with others—that we learn who we are. In community we can exercise the gifts

God has given us. In all likelihood these gifts are gifts of ministry. For Christians especially, community is glorious, for it is in community that we can worship together, be nurtured and bear one another's burdens.

What then is the role of Christian community in evangelism? Some Christians feel that their community (be it a church, a Bible study, a small group or a friendship relationship) can prepare people to be launched out for witness to others. Certainly we need to be fed and nurtured and built up and trained. But we must remember, too, that our local Christian community itself can be a powerful witness to our non-Christian friends. Communities of Christians who practice what they preach arouse and stimulate curiosity in Jesus. When the teaching of Jesus is heard and demonstrated, there will be an impact.

No Lone Rangers

We are not called to be "Lone Ranger" Christians. We are called to love one another. Indeed, an understandable basis for rejection of belief in God, according to Jesus, is lack of love among Christians (Jn 17:20-24).

Unlike the American cowboy, out there dodging the arrows and bullets alone, we are called to be a close family that welcomes others into our midst. We invite people to come and share our love and our gifts. We are free to admit that we have not arrived and are far from perfect. But because we believe Jesus is the living center of our group, we invite our seeker friends anu acquaintances to hang around us and observe him.

I used to feel uncomfortable about the presence of skeptics in Christian groups. Would they feel weird listening to us pray and watching us read the Bible? As I said in a previous chapter, when I gave a talk to a group, I used to ask the leaders if there were any nonbelievers present. Upon reflection, I realized that even if there were, I would not change my message at all. The world is not as fragile as we think. Non-Christians can handle us in our natural habitat far more than we realize. All they need is to feel welcome and to be invited to come and see. In fact, people long to be a part of a community that will care for them (whether it is a Bible study group or a church).

Although that truth is ageless, it has never been more timely than today. For a variety of reasons, people are drawn in more often by the warmth of relationship than the brilliance of apologetics. In fact, people are almost too vulnerable to community; if they feel loved, they will tend to believe anything. This situation is exploited to the fullest by a number of the fringe religious groups.

As Christians true to Christ we do care about emotional needs, but we must be careful not to manipulate people through it. It is fine that unbelievers are drawn into our midst because they feel welcomed and cared for, but we must be as concerned for their minds as for their souls. We must offer not only love but excellent biblical teaching as well. There has to be solid truth taught in our warm communities or else our houses of faith will be built on shifting sand. The world needs to both feel God's love and hear God's truth in us.

Communities, then, can be powerful tools to communicate the reality of Jesus. Let us take a closer look at some of the forms these communities take.

Christian Small Groups

Our witness as a community can be especially demonstrated through a small group Bible study. The group should think of activities to which they could invite their friends. Bruce Erickson, a former InterVarsity staff member in Oregon, said that his small group learned of a man on welfare whose house needed reroofing. Bruce suggested that each member bring a non-Christian friend and make it a "roofing party." Someone would have to be pretty desperate to go to a party like this, but a group spent the day together, working hard, caring for the man and just having fun.

Some of them eventually became Christians. Without realizing it these Christians had been witnessing all day by the way they cared for each other, by their concern for the man, by their ability to have fun. We need to invite people along to see us as we live. Things we take for granted (that we pray for each other, that we sincerely try to love each other, and so forth) can make a deep impression.

Another way we can make a lasting impression on the world is in our attitude toward possessions. Jesus talks about few things as much as our possessions. He tells us that no person can serve two masters (Mt 6:24). To serve God as our first love means there can be no competing loyalties. We can stimulate a curiosity in the gospel when we demonstrate that we believe our money is God's, and we desire to use it to please him.

Lois (who I mentioned in chapter three) had her interest in the gospel stimulated when she came to a fellowship meeting and heard a Christian student say he had no money for a ticket home. Immediately three fellow Christians reached into their pockets and gave him what they had. Later, when Lois wanted to go to a Christian student conference but had no funds, another Christian told her he would sell his camping tent. He loved camping, but he felt that her getting nurture for her young faith was more important. When we demonstrate a biblical attitude toward money and material possessions, the world stands up to take notice.

Or take another example. Once a woman told me her small group wanted to reach out to their seeker friends, but they could not think of what to do. Then she said quickly that she had to dash to pick up tickets for her group to see Richard III, a play she was in. When I told her that would be a great thing for them to take their friends to, she asked, "What does *Richard III* have to do with God?"

"For starters, this play deals with the problem of evil. Is Richard responsible for his cruelty, or can he blame it on his 'genes' and his crippled body? Any discussion of the nature of evil leads one to discussing ultimate issues," I said.

So here we have an example not only of what to do but also of the importance of integrating our faith into our world. If we think God is relevant only in Bible studies, our witness will have little impact.

That means we need to be conscious of current political and cultural events. It is not necessary to see or read everything, but we do need to be aware of what our culture is listening to. Then we must develop our analytical skills in evaluating our culture from a Christian perspective. We need a "Christian mind," as Harry Blamires has suggested. I know a woman who does not go to many films, but she reads film reviews regularly to gain understanding and awareness of her culture, and it helps her in talking with others. Unfortunately her example is an exception.

When through our small groups we reach out to our skeptic friends in love and bring them into our midst, when we live as Jesus would have us live, regarding people as infinitely more important than material things, and when we demonstrate sensitivity and insight rather than ignorance toward our culture, the impact will be great. Our Christian group, then, will not become ingrown and isolated from the surrounding society. Rather, we will demonstrate that Christians are real people who care deeply for others. We study and love the Scripture because it, too, is passionately honest about life and is loyal to the truth about us. We meet together as Christians and we pray and study God's Word because we celebrate the call to live in the real world and are not trying to escape from it.

Nonetheless, perhaps we feel bringing our non-Christian friends to a Bible study full of Christians would be too overpowering at first. We may feel they need something less threatening to start with.

Investigative Bible Discussion

Sooner or later we must get our seeker friends reading the Bible. One effective way is to gather several skeptic friends with one or two Christians and discuss a passage that vitally confronts us with the person of Christ. This is a wonderful means of outreach to our neighborhoods. Our seeker friends need to see Jesus as he walks through Palestine—watch what he does, listen to what he says, observe how he relates to people. This was how his disciples slowly became convinced of who Jesus was. Our friends, too, need to hang around the Jesus in the Gospels.

Many people blindly accept Christ's deity as a child, and then blindly reject it as they grow up, without ever realizing that Jesus comes to us first as a person. Our aim is to allow Jesus to come alive to them in the Scriptures to give them a feel of what kind of person he is.

When you invite your friends, assure them that no previous Bible knowledge is necessary. They do not have to believe in God or the Bible. The point is for them to read firsthand what the Bible actually says. If they do not believe, then as my skeptic companion on the airplane said, for the sake of intellectual integrity they need to know what they are rejecting. We can assure them that it will not be churchy; we will not sing hymns. Rather, we will consider the passage as we would any historical document, arriving at conclusions that the text, not the teacher, demands.

This is an efficient way to present Jesus. Most people do not recognize their need for Jesus in a one-shot conversation. But when a Christian befriends them and eventually leads them into a study like this, they will grasp a much fuller picture of what it means to be a Christian. Even if we met only six times, we could look at (1) Jesus' sensitivity and compassion to people (Jn 4: the woman at the well), (2) his miraculous powers (Jn 11: Lazarus's resurrection), (3) who he claimed to be (Jn 14: "I am the way, and the truth, and the life"), (4) how to become a Christian (Jn 3:1-21: Nicodemus), (5) the death of Jesus (Jn 19), and (6) his resurrection (Jn 20).

Most importantly, to lead this kind of discussion it is not necessary to have lots of experience or training as a Bible discussion leader. The leader needs to draw out the members as to what the text says, not lecture for an hour.

If you would appreciate help in knowing how to ask the right questions and draw people out, it is not hard to find. I have mentioned some helpful guides in appendix two.

Evangelism Through the Local Church

As I have previously mentioned, I worked in the early days of my ministry with the parachurch organization called InterVarsity Christian Fellowship. One of the many things I appreciated about InterVarsity was their clear emphasis on the importance of the church. They continually emphasized to students that parachurch organizations will come and go but that the church, the agent of God's action in the world, is for the ages.

Moreover, the church can offer to the world a model that a college Christian group never can. It can offer to the world a model of unity amid great diversity—diversity of age, race, occupation, ability, interest and so forth. There are inevitable limits to a model of Christ that includes mostly people who range in age from their late teens to twenties.

If you are reading this as a student and you are not associated with a local church, let me say this to you: go immediately and find one where Christ is exalted and the Bible is trusted and acted on, and begin worshiping there. For only there will you find the full scope of what Christian community can mean.

Clearly, one of the most effective ways to do evangelism is through the local church. John Stott has described evangelism through the local church as "the most normal, natural and productive method of spreading the gospel today."[1] Michael Green, Advisor in Evangelism to the Archbishops of Canterbury and York, wrote in his book *Evangelism Through the Local Church,* "Whenever Christianity has been at its most healthy, evangelism has stemmed from the local church, and has had a noticeable impact on the surrounding area. . . . If local churches were engaging in loving, outgoing evangelism, within their neighborhood, many of our evangelistic campaigns, missions and crusades would be rendered much less necessary."[2]

The question is, then, how can churches become communities of faith reaching out and offering life to the world around them? I have often asked pastors how effective their congregations are in reaching out to their local area. Frequently they tell me they don't feel they are effective. Why is it, they ask, that when evangelism-training programs end, sometimes so do the evangelistic efforts? What makes people become inwardly motivated to share their faith?

E. M. Bounds wrote, "People are God's method. The Church is looking for better methods, God is looking for better people."[3] What can pastors do then to encourage their flock to evangelize?

First, as pastors, teach your congregation to nurture an intimate walk with God. Help them learn how to walk by faith, to pray boldly and to listen to the Spirit. That way your parishioners will be able to not only share the gospel but also the real difference that Christ makes in their lives.

Second, remind them that success breeds success. The more they dare to open their mouths and witness, the more they will see positive results. Encourage them to take risks, to exercise boldness, for only through obedience will they truly know that God is there.

Third, encourage them not only to build friendships with seekers but to introduce their seeker friends to fellow Christians. One pastor I know who wanted his church to be actively involved in evangelism began by building small-group neighborhood Bible studies. For the first time the members of his church began to trust each other, love each other and become involved in each other's lives. After they had met for six months, he then encouraged them to witness to their seeker friends. As they formed friendships with non-Christians in their neighborhood, they genuinely wanted them to meet their friends in the Bible discussion. Soon the Bible study members were bringing their seeker friends to their group and eventually to their church. The pastor told me that for the first time during his ministry there, real evangelism was going on in his church.

There is a reason for this. Using systems like going door-to-door or handing out tracts or giving a prepared speech can be initially helpful, but such methods have limits. Going door-to-door may help get a hearing, but once you are inside the door, your orientation can never be the same again. You only meet a stranger once. From that first meeting some kind of relationship will follow.

Asking a person a set of good, stimulating questions designed to draw out their interest in spiritual matters can be very effective. But once the questions have been asked, you can't use them again with the same person. The closer you become to an individual, the more awkward you feel using methods that are better suited for someone you don't know.

No matter how we initiate a spiritual conversation, what seekers ultimately need to see is the gospel fleshed out in a believer's life. Strangers, so long as they remain strangers, only hear a message and never see it lived out in human relationships. One of the greatest gifts (and evidence) that we give is the chance for others to see how Jesus lives his life through us. And the demonstration of his love, his holiness and his charity is especially powerful in a community of believers.

We live in a culture of people who feel like burned-over ground. They have heard it all. They have been assaulted by every experience imaginable. And when our style or initial approach reminds them of all the others, Jesus is reduced in their estimation to merely one option among many.

I am not saying there is no place for contact evangelism. But I am saying that by far the most effective, the most costly and even perhaps the most biblical kind of evangelism is found in the person or groups who look at the people around them, those with whom their own life naturally intersects, and then begin to cultivate friendships and to love them. When churches start to reach out to their neighborhoods through small groups, or whatever format works for them, the impact can be overwhelming.

How, then, is the church to become an evangelizing center? First, we have to believe there are people who are open to the gospel. In the Gospel of John we are told of an encounter Jesus had with a worldly, promiscuous woman. When the disciples saw that he was speaking to her, they were astonished. And Jesus' response to them was "Do you not say 'Four months more and then the harvest'? I tell you, open your eyes and look at the fields! They are ripe for harvest" (Jn 4:35 NIV). Do we believe that the fields are ripe for harvest?

Several months ago I called a good friend, Adele, and asked her if she knew of a hair salon that was near to my home. She suggested a place she had heard of. I went and a beautiful woman introducing herself as Meg told me she'd be the one cutting my hair that day. As we chatted, I asked Meg to tell me about her family. In doing so she casually mentioned that she had a brother who was a born-again Christian. Several minutes later she said he was also an avid reader. I didn't say anything then, but a few appointments later, having already told her I am a Christian, I mentioned that I had written a few things that perhaps he might have read. She said she'd be sure and ask him the next time they spoke long-distance.

When I came in for my next hair appointment, Meg said, "Wow, my brother was over the moon that I am doing your hair. He read *Out of the Saltshaker* ten years ago, and he said it really changed his life. Isn't that an amazing coincidence that he read something that you wrote?" she asked.

About one month later I was at the front desk paying Meg when one of the hairstylists nudged her, saying she should tell me something. I looked puzzled and Meg said, "Well, I didn't tell you this before because I was afraid it might make you feel uncomfortable. But remember when I told my brother that I was doing your hair? After I told him, there was this long pause of silence on the phone. Then he said that all those years ago after reading your book, what struck him was the feeling that someone with a personality like yours would be able to help me find God. So he knelt down and prayed and asked God to please send someone like Becky into my life. Then he said, 'Meg, ten years ago I asked God to send someone *like* Becky into your life. I didn't ask him to send Becky herself.' Then he kinda got choked up."

I stood there looking at Meg, whom I have come to genuinely love, and I could hardly hold back the tears myself. Then Meg said, "I didn't tell you because I didn't want you to feel funny. You know, talk about the *pressure* of having to help me find God!" Then we all burst into laughter.

But as I got into my car I couldn't help thinking, *How does God do this?* From the outside it all looked so casual and haphazard. I asked Adele if she knew of a hairdresser, and she casually mentioned a place. I didn't even ask for a specific name when I called. I just happened to get the person who was free at that time slot, who just happened to have been the recipient of her brother's prayer ten years ago. What a brother! What a God!

Right at the time I met Meg I was invited to do a conference for a large seeker-sensitive church in the area where I live. They had read my book *A Heart Like His,* and the pastor wanted me to do a conference training the leadership of the church in the area of deepening faith and developing character based on the life of David. Then on Sunday I was to preach to all the services, which comprised both believers and seekers with little or no church background. As I was speaking that Sunday, it dawned on me that this might be just the right church for Meg. The service was God-honoring and lively, the music and drama were great and there were lots of people around her age.

Meg and I have spoken freely and easily about faith, so the next time I saw her I intended to bring it up. But I never had the opportunity because the first thing Meg said to me was, "One of my clients goes to a church that she thinks I'd really like. She said you just spoke there. Do you think I would like it?" Of course, it was the very place I was going to mention. That's the thing about God—you can never beat him to the punch! Naturally I encouraged her to go.

Then about a month later Meg said, "Remember the church where you recently spoke and my client attends? Well, they are building a brand-new place because they've grown so large. And they're moving in soon."

"Yes, I knew that, but how on earth did you know that?" I asked.

"Because their new building is right across the street from my house!" she added.

Are the fields ripe for harvest? Two weeks ago I took a much-needed break from my writing schedule. My children arrive home from school at 3:15 in the afternoon, so I quickly dashed out to buy some pumpkins and gourds so

I could be back before they walked in the door. I felt a bit brain-dead from writing all day, but when I saw the vast array of beautiful pumpkins lined up in a row, and flowers and plants of every hue, the sheer beauty of this autumnal vision took my breath away! Feeling my own spirit revive, I quickly selected what I wanted and went up to the cash register to pay. I had noticed when walking in how life-weary the woman at the register appeared.

I was the only person at the register, so I showed her all of my items with great delight. She managed a weak smile and said, "You know, I forget to look at what I'm selling since I do it every day." We continued to chat as I got out my checkbook. Out of the blue she asked me what I did for a living. When I told her I was an author and speaker, she said, "Say, you aren't that famous romance novelist who lives in this area, are you?"

I laughed and told her that I wasn't but that I knew who she was talking about because she is my neighbor and a good friend.

Then she said, "Boy, maybe what I need right now is to buy a romance novel. Then I could see what it feels like to have a happily-ever-after ending for once."

"Oh, dear. Sounds like it's been a rather long autumn for you," I answered.

"Not long autumn. Try long life," she answered bleakly.

"Did you have a relationship that recently fell apart or something?"

"I've been divorced three times. And I'm involved with a guy right now, but I know he's not committed. He's always telling me that you can't force love; it happens if it's supposed to," she answered grimly.

"You're right, he definitely doesn't sound like a serious candidate. Why are you still continuing to see him?"

"Who knows? I guess it's because I'm lonely. Oh, I know, I've read all the self-help books that say you have to be able to live alone and like yourself before you're ready for a relationship. I know all about being my own best friend. I just wonder why none of it works," she said dejectedly.

"Well, I think you have to take seriously your need for a relationship. Your very hunger for one tells you that you've been made for intimacy. The trick is finding how to meet that need in satisfying and constructive ways rather than empty and hurtful ways."

"You got that right! Feel free to pass along any tips!" she said smiling.

"Well, I can tell you what's gotten me through the tough times," I answered.

"Fire away!"

By now we had picked up the pumpkins and were carrying them to my car. "First, it's developing a relationship with God. Once you turn to God, you find that he fills your need for love and intimacy in a way that enables you to develop much healthier relationships with others."

"Which means you're not putting all your marbles in a basket that was never meant to hold them all in the first place?"

"Exactly! The second thing may surprise you, but what has really helped me is going to church. You meet some great people there, you get reminded every week of what is real, and you form friendships that make you realize that you're not alone."

She looked at me in astonishment and said, "I can't believe you just said that. I've been so depressed lately, but yesterday I kinda hit the wall. Then all of a sudden this idea popped into my head: *Why don't you go to church?* I haven't been to church in twenty years, but yesterday I thought maybe I should start going. That blows my mind that you just said it!"

She told me that she'd already thought of a church where she wanted to attend, one that was in her neighborhood. I encouraged her to go right away and even if it didn't feel comfortable at first, to not give up on it. I told her that I'd come back again when it was time to buy some Christmas poinsettias and check to see how she liked church.

As I was pulling out of the parking lot, she asked me, "Do you think God knew that I was thinking about going back to church and he sent you here to confirm it?"

"God not only knew what you were thinking; it was God who put the thought in your head! And yes, I think God did want you to know that he loves you, that he cares about your problems, and he wants to meet you in church this Sunday!"

I walked in the back door of our home as my children were walking in the front. When I excitedly told them what had just happened, they shared my joy, but they also couldn't help but start laughing. One of our family jokes is how often I go somewhere to get some kind of service but return saying I absolutely must return there for the sake of the gospel. "Well, now we know where we'll be buying our plants for the rest of our lives!" my children joked.

The fields are indeed ripe and ready to be harvested. What God needs are laborers. The issue before us is not whether we must all become adept at sharing the gospel with those who sell pumpkins! I've said it before, but I will say it again: God made us different. Some of us are able to connect to people and get into serious conversations quickly, while others of us need time and trust to be established before we feel comfortable sharing the gospel. The point is not that we imitate someone else's style but that we find our own style and then get on with the business of sharing the gospel.

The question that concerns us, however, is this: what kind of church experience will these women have if they decide to go? Will they find the church welcoming and warm? Will it feel like a safe place to them? I don't even know the name of the woman who sold me pumpkins, but I know enough about her story to know that if no one reaches out to her, if she feels judged or is made to feel she isn't good enough to be "one of them," she'll never be back.

Even more important than our church evangelism training programs is whether the people in our congregations demonstrate the love of Jesus to those who walk through our doors. Is our church warm and welcoming? Do we practice hospitality and see it as a holy ministry? People today are desperate to connect in some meaningful way to others, yet modern life makes a deep sense of connection and personal integration terribly difficult. Before tracts and techniques, before programs and pamphlets, we need to open our arms wide and let seekers know that they bless us just by being in our midst.

19

Without a Vision
the People
Will Perish

....

How does the church reach out to seekers and become the evangelizing center it was meant to be? Before we think of programs or techniques, we need to be renewed in our vision of who Christ is and what God's purposes are for our world. Author Alan Roxburgh is right when he says, "We have lost the vision of a cosmic, transforming Christ who addresses all of life."[1]

We saw in chapter three that to call Jesus the Lord of life is to live under God's rule, which extends to all of life. To say we believe that Christ is Lord is to recognize that the purpose of Christ is the transformation of every aspect of our being and our world. How, then, do we live out this vision of a transformational reality in our churches? How do we translate our belief in the transforming lordship of Christ to those who are hungry and poor, to the homosexual, to the unwed mother, to the marginalized ones who slip between the cracks in our cities, to the institutional structures that oppress, to the political structures that may cause good or harm, or to concerns for our planet and its resources? What is our responsibility as Christ's agents to participate with Christ as he seeks to restore all things into wholeness in himself?

Recovering Our Vision

Let us begin by renewing our vision of what it means to live as radical disciples of Jesus in this broken world. Let us seek to connect and submit every area of life to the authority and transforming intention of Christ, for by our doing so seekers cannot help but be drawn to us. For example, if Christ's transforming power is concerned with every aspect of what it means to be human, then what do we do with a seeker who is suffering from cancer? Jesus didn't offer healing only for those who believed in him; he healed people whether they believed in him or not. Yes, it's imperative that we share the gospel with seekers, but isn't part of our witness to pray for their physical healing as well as their spiritual?

Are there individuals in your church whom God has gifted in the area of prayer and healing? Then let them go to suffering people, be they Christians or not, and offer prayers to God for their healing. It is a powerful testimony to the nature of Christ's love for all humanity.

Or what about those who suffer from sexual dysfunction, be it heterosexual or homosexual? My home church has a powerful healing ministry to those seeking sexual wholeness. Mario Bergner, the author of *Setting Love in Order,* leads a ministry at our church called "Redeemed Lives." Many have received profound ministry and have been restored to sexual wholeness in the loving and welcoming context of our church community.

Or what about the poor and the isolated in our cities? What can we in the church do to reach those who feel isolated and alone?

We need a renewed vision of who Christ is and what he has come to do: to heal, restore and transform his creation! As we translate Christ's vision into practical realities, evangelism cannot help but happen.

Reading the Signs of the Culture

To be an evangelizing church also means we need to read the signs of the times in our modern culture in order to know how to reach people effectively for the gospel. We read these signs not so we can water down the gospel to fit current trends. Rather, we listen to the modern cries for meaning while we plumb the depths of Scripture to see what the Bible says in regards to these issues. What we will discover is that we have far more to offer the seeker than we even realized.

The Church and the Hunger for Community

For example, one of the cries we hear in our modern culture is the search for family, for a community, especially with the isolating, fragmentary nature of modern life. The longing for community arises out of a search for connectedness with God, with others and even with nature. The modern sense of being disconnected due to isolation, loneliness, broken relationships or simply the frenetic pace of modern life creates a profound longing for integration and a longing for a sense of place.

Alan Roxburgh asks the penetrating question "Where are the resources for building communities of Christian witness in a culture where life is profoundly alienating?"[2] He answers this in part by examining the work of historian E. R. Dodds, who addresses the fascinating subject of why Christianity, a small movement among a plethora of Eastern mystery cults, should come to triumph. Dodd believed it was due to the fact that Christian congregations were bound together by a common life. The early church was a "context of hope, care and inclusion for widows, orphans, broken and destitute people in Roman society."[3]

The need for community hasn't changed. In an interview in *Leadership Journal* Pastor Mark Lauterback describes many touching and positive experiences he has had as a pastor seeking to be a witness to his community. However, he tells of one experience he and his wife had with a woman who had come to do housework. She came from a terribly dysfunctional family and was studying different religions to see what she would believe. Mark had long discussions with her about the gospel, and she talked at length to Mark's wife. But in the end, much to their distress, she chose to become a Mormon.

As Mark probed to understand why, it became evident that she didn't understand much of Mormon theology. What drew her to Mormonism was their sense of family. She was lonely and searching for community, and she felt they loved her. Lauterback astutely points out, "Our approach of assaulting her with truth was wrong. We should have taken her into our home."[4]

As an evangelizing church, we need to ask ourselves: Who are the poor and destitute, the widows and the orphans in our midst? How do we offer them the love and hope of Christ as a Christian community?

A divorced woman who was a single parent told me that she decided to return to the church after her divorce. She felt alone, afraid and desperately needing a support system to help her raise her three active boys. Most of all, she was seeking spiritual answers and needed to know if God was really there. She was initially afraid the people in the church might be judgmental. But when the pastor made his first pastoral visit, he simply said, "What can we do to help? The Bible tells us to care for the widow and the orphans, and we truly want to do that. But you'll have to guide us in the practical ways we can show you the love of Christ."

As they talked, the pastor began to see how the church could help. Some men in the church began to shovel the snow off her driveway and worked on her car, families with sons offered to take her boys on camping trips, and there were women who just listened to her when she felt overwhelmed. The church not only saw her through a difficult time but, because it behaved like a true community of Christ, she was led to make a commitment to Christ herself.

We also need to rediscover the sacred call of hospitality. My husband, Dick, told me a story that moved him deeply. Several years ago he was in a meeting that involved working on a large building plan. They had hired a very successful architect from another city. Dick had never met the architect, but as they began talking, he casually mentioned to Dick that he and his wife went to church. That opened the door to discussing their mutual faith. Dick then said, "What caused you to become interested in faith?"

"Many years ago we lived in Chicago," began the architect. "I had absolutely no interest in faith, but my wife decided she wanted to attend church. I told her that I'd go with her the first time but not to expect me to make a return visit. Church and church people held no interest for me whatsoever.

"To my surprise the sermon was pretty good. But afterward a very distinguished, elegant older man came over to greet me. He asked me questions about my work and our move. He seemed genuinely interested in me. Then he asked me if my wife and I had any plans for lunch. When I said we didn't, he then asked us to come to his home for lunch. I couldn't believe that a stranger was warmly inviting me to his own home. We had a marvelous lunch. It was clear to me that he was a very successful businessman—you could just tell by his quiet authority. But what struck me was the tremendous vitality of his love for Jesus. Just experiencing his kindness and seeing his faith made me know that I had to go back to church. We ended up joining, and I went every Sunday for the rest of the time we lived in Chicago. The man's name was Dick Evenhouse."

Dick looked at him in astonishment. "What, do you know him?" asked the architect.

"Yes, I certainly do. I was named after him. That man is my grandfather."

The architect answered, "Well, your grandfather had a profound spiritual impact on my life."

"He had an even deeper impact on mine," answered Dick.

And to think it all started with a simple offering of lunch. What a marvelous example of how to make the church a welcoming place. What an encouragement to all of us to pay attention to the newcomers and to greet them with the gift of hospitality.

What we have to offer a world that is lonely and searching for satisfying relationships is the community of Christ. Nicky Gumbel, the author of *Telling Others* and cofounder of the evangelism training program Alpha, told a fascinating story in a lecture I heard him give. A man who had recently become a Christian told Nicky, "I came from a very conservative Christian background, but I threw it all overboard because the unspoken message was that first I had to *behave,* then I had to *believe,* and then, if I was real lucky, they might let me *belong.*"

Nicky then challenged us Christians to model the exact opposite to seekers. First, give seekers a sense that they belong, that we are delighted to be their friends. Then pray they will come to believe. Then model and teach them how to behave. What a powerful inversion of what it means to be Christ's community!

To be a community centered in Christ means more than merely getting our own needs met. As Roxburgh writes, "We need communities of God's people bound to one another because they have discovered the One in their midst who takes up their pain and gives it meaning in the larger call of a great journey toward a transformed and healed creation. . . . Community demands a pilgrim band who are on a journey, caught up in something fantastically bigger than themselves and their needs."[5]

Lesslie Newbigin reminds us in his book *Foolishness to the Greeks* that the church "is not meant to call men and women out of the world into a safe religious enclave but to call them out in order to send them back as agents of God's kingship."[6] The church is to be focused not on itself but on its neighborhood. We are called, Newbigin reminds us, not to remain isolated in fear from the world, nor to engage in ceaseless programs to keep the faithful busy. Our focus is to bring the glorious news of the One who said: "As the Father has sent me, so I send you" (Jn 20:21).

The Church and the Quest for Spirituality

Another prominent aspect of our modern culture is the search for spiritual meaning and spiritual experience. What do we have to offer people in their search for transcendence and mystical experience? What can we say to people who tell us they want to connect to a higher cosmic consciousness? What can the church offer such seekers?

First, as we invite seekers to come with us to church, what we hope they catch is a glimpse of the greatness and the glory of God. Our services should testify to the fact that God is far greater than we imagine. What comes across in a God-centered service is an indirect challenge to the self-absorption that permeates our age. We are there to bless God. All our attention is on him because he is the center of the universe, not us. In our church service we are made aware, without ever saying it, that God is more important than we are—and such knowledge is liberating!

What means do we have to convey the greatness of God? First, we accomplish this by a clear proclamation of biblical truth. Nothing centers us or keeps us from confusion more than the Word of God.

Powerful preaching from the Word is a vital evangelistic tool. When I lived in Jerusalem, I met a woman who is a messianic Jew, or a Jew who believes that Jesus is the true Messiah. As I got to know her and observe her in many different situations, I marveled at the strength of her faith and her knowledge of the Bible. She had a very strong character. I could always count on Hannah to see things clearly and tell things straight.

One day I asked Hannah how she came to faith in Christ. She said that part of her nursing training required her to study in London for one year. She described herself at that time as a typical Israeli Jew: a skeptic, with almost no knowledge of the Bible, but faithful to her Jewish traditions. She became close friends with some women in the nursing school who were Christians. They invited her to attend their church. She went once out of politeness, never intending to go back.

As she sat in the pew, however, she was astonished to find herself strangely riveted by the minister in the pulpit. "I'm a very tough cookie by nature," admitted Hannah, "and I went in that day feeling intellectually superior to everyone around me, especially those needing to depend on some crutch to get through life. But as the minister began to preach, the first thing I noticed was his tremendous mind. He was so logical and lucid. And he understood my questions and doubts, my secular mindset. But more than that, there was an authority, a power that was impossible to deny."

So she returned, Sunday after Sunday, for the entire year that she lived in London. "I could have managed to escape cleverness or services oriented to entertain me, but what I couldn't escape from was the truth. And that man preached the truth of God's Word—faithfully and relentlessly."

On Hannah's last Sunday before returning to Israel, the minister asked if there was anyone who hadn't made a commitment to Christ and who felt they were ready to come forward. "It took an entire year of listening to him preach the Word of God for me to be ready, but I knew I had no other choice but to go forward. I gave my life unreservedly to Christ."

That preacher happened to be the late Martyn Lloyd-Jones. And her Christian walk truly evidenced the blessing of having sat under such wonderful Bible teaching.

Let us never underestimate what a powerful evangelistic tool there is in the faithful preaching of the Word of God. Donald Bloesch makes the fascinating point that what brought thousands of people to faith in the eighteenth century were not the skilled apologists but the evangelical preachers who preached the gospel and reached the masses—preachers such as George Whitefield and John Wesley.[7] But that doesn't mean we don't take the time to read our culture. Rather, let us address the themes of our modern culture with the relevance of the gospel through the power of God's Word. Whenever I speak to denominational conferences for ministers, I always encourage them to take their preaching with the utmost seriousness. Excellent preaching not only builds up the saints but God uses it to convert the seekers as well.

The second aspect that speaks to the seekers in our midst is our Eucharist and worship. I agree wholeheartedly with Alan Roxburgh, who writes, "There is no more profound apologetic for the gospel than the vitality of a people at worship."[8] In our experiential age we may shy away from anything that suggests an appeal to our hearts. And of course we do need balance. But John Stott says, quoting Handley Moule, "Beware equally of an undevotional theology [that is, mind without heart] and of an untheological devotion [that is, heart without mind]."[9]

The truth is that Christianity is both deeply rational and deeply experiential. Our message does not simply require an assent of our minds to a series of truth propositions; it also calls people into a love relationship with Jesus. We come to church to learn about the nature and truth of who God is, but we also come to church to experience being in God's presence. Again John Stott writes, "There is a place for emotion in spiritual experience. The Holy Spirit's . . . ministry is not limited to illuminating our minds and teaching us about Christ. He also pours God's love into our hearts. Similarly, he bears witness with our spirit that we are God's children, for he causes us to say 'Abba, father' and to exclaim in gratitude 'How great is the love the father has lavished on us, that we should be called children of God.'"[10]

We need to have a worship life in our church that directs people to an experience of the transcendent God, who is present. It is God's desire to meet us in a deep and personal way. He does not want us to relate to him merely as the sum total of our rational theological beliefs but to connect with his being at a profound level of intimacy.

In our age, which hungers to be reconnected with God, we must realize that what we have to offer is the very presence of God in our midst! We celebrate the sacraments because we have the true bread of life to share. Roxburgh said, "If there were a greater experience of God's presence, an expectation of intimacy, of knowing ourselves corporately connected to God and hearing ourselves addressed by God in ways not limited to a sermon, then our worship could be a means of mission to a spiritually hungry and disconnected culture."[11]

Let us worship God with our minds, our hearts and our souls. And let us be sure that we invite seekers into the church where they will hear the Word of truth and experience God's Spirit. Where there is the spontaneous overflow of a community of praise and the radiance of a supernatural reality, there is transformational power!

Tailor-Made Evangelism

How can we find a way of doing evangelism that is right for our church? How do we go about finding a model that fits our us?

First, as we have already discussed, we need to pay attention to our culture at large. What does it mean to be a seeker in a secularized, pluralistic modern world? This is a subject worth pursuing and Lesslie Newbigin addresses this issue as well as anyone in his book *The Gospel in a Pluralistic Society*.

Second, we must pay attention to our own setting, to the seekers with whom we are in dialogue. We need to understand the place where we are ministering. What are the types of people that God has called us to minister to as a church? What kind of culture or cultures are involved? What are the cries of their hearts? In other words, we need to listen and understand as best we can, the context of those with whom we are sharing the gospel. George Hunter in his very helpful book *How to Reach Secular People* provides ten characteristics of secular people and strategies for how to reach them.[12]

The gospel is unchanging, but our context does affect the way we go about presenting the gospel. I have preached the gospel to inmates inside of prisons. I have also given evangelistic presentations at a country club in Greenwich, Connecticut. The gospel didn't change, but how I presented it did.

The subject of contextualization in evangelism is an important issue and far beyond the scope of this book. Alan Roxburgh's *Reaching a New Generation* gives a splendid analysis of this subject.

Third, we need to understand who we are as well. One of the things I have learned, having traveled widely and spoken to many different denominations, is that every church has its own culture—its own language, its own traditions, its own ethos. Once I spoke in the same month to Hollywood Presbyterian Church in California and to the Pennsylvania Mennonites. Needless to say, their church cultures were vastly different, and so were the people they were seeking to reach. So examine who you are as a group. Are you a large, diverse inner-city church or a small rural church? Is your church made up more of elderly people or Gen Xers? An evangelism program that works for one church may not work for another

Does your church at least attempt to reflect the vision of a transformational community committed to healing lives and the world in the way that Christ intends? Or would you describe your church as ingrown and a place where only those from your own particular group would feel comfortable? Church was never intended to be a comfortable club for elderly Baptists or a fashionable spot for beautiful twentysomethings or an exclusive spa for middle-aged Episcopalians. "Our culture does not need any more churches run like corporations; it needs local communities empowered by the gospel vision of a transforming Christ who addresses the needs of the context and changes the polis into a place of hope and wholeness."[13]

We all need to be stretched beyond our comfort zone as we reach outside the comfortable ghetto of the church to others. But arming ourselves with an understanding of who we are as a people will help us as we choose which evangelism strategy will work best.

Last, we must develop a clear mission statement as a church with concrete objectives as we set goals for evangelism. Does your church have a strategy for reaching unchurched people? Don't underestimate the need for training like I initially did. My experience was very similar to what Ken Chafin describes: "I watched women who had drive and ingenuity enough to make them excellent presidents of the PTA yet who were unable to tell the children in their class how to become Christians. I watched lawyers who were qualified to try cases before the Supreme Court who could not sit down in the living room of an interested friend and present a good 'brief' for Jesus Christ. . . . I've discovered that most of the best people in the church need some help in learning to communicate their faith."[14]

So how do we train people for witness? There are many ways to approach it

For example, I have seen some churches focus their evangelism strategy on a Billy Graham crusade. In the mid-1980s I was invited by several churches in France to give evangelism training to churches throughout that country in preparation for a Graham crusade. It was an electrifying time to be with the French churches as they geared up for what proved to be an enormously fruitful crusade. What made the training exciting was that there was a clear goal: all those who came to my evangelism seminars intended to invite their seeker friends to the Crusade. They wanted help in developing their content and communication skills in order to share Christ more effectively.

The challenge after an "event" of course is what does the church do next to continue its efforts? The goal is for people to share their faith as an integrated part of their everyday lives. But as part of your evangelism training, be sure to include an evangelistic event to which your church can bring seekers.

It may be that your church decides to bring in an evangelism program from the outside. For example, one highly successful effort is the *Alpha* course, a program of suppers, lectures and conversation that is now the largest evangelistic effort in Britain and has spread to the United States and elsewhere. The *Contagious Christian* program from Bill Hybels's Willow Creek Church is another good plan. The key is to decide which of these and other programs best fits your people and the seekers you want to reach.

Don't be afraid, however, to develop something that particularly fits your situation. In training churches in evangelism over the years, I have realized that there are well-defined categories. We need, as Gabriel Fackre once said, to *get the story straight* by learning how to give the content of God's story and ours. We need to *get the story out* by developing natural communication skills. We need to *take the story in* by learning to depend on the Spirit's power. And we need to learn how to *defend the story to others* by being prepared to answer the common questions people ask about the gospel.

Evaluate your church in light of these categories and see where the need is greatest so you will know where to begin. Then think through the format that would best serve your people. Should you kick off the evangelism training through a weekend conference or offer an eight-week course that meets one night a week? Should you study a book in many small groups or in larger Sunday-school classes?

What helps make evangelism successful is when the people of the church see evangelism as a way of life, not just a program. It is discouraging to see people adopt an evangelism program but then stop witnessing once the program is over. How do we prevent that from happening?

For one thing, the ministers need to model an evangelistic lifestyle. That is a great challenge when their professional lives are spent almost exclusively helping other Christians. But ministers who engage in personal evangelism give their church a tremendous boost.

One of the ministers in my church has been sharing his evangelistic encounters from the pulpit recently. Some of his experiences are hilarious, some are touching. But *everyone* is motivated to go out and do the same!

Evangelism succeeds better when the program or strategy is not the vision of the pastor alone. Effective evangelism always involves the congregation. The more it's a grassroots vision with many lay people involved, yet with enthusiastic clergy endorsement and participation, the more likely it will succeed.

Lastly, throughout this chapter and the last I have strongly encouraged the church to invite seekers to come and see what God is doing in their midst. I don't intend to change that stance, but I will add one word of clarification.

When we share the gospel, we need to be careful that we don't appear to be pushing people to go to our particular church. We don't want seekers to feel that all we're doing is canvassing for new members to sign up. If they don't have any church affiliation and they are interested, then by all means invite them to your church. But remember that the goal in evangelism is not to make people exactly like us. Our desire is for people to encounter God—not to become our clones.

Freedom to Fail

We can learn a great deal of information, be full of zeal, master conversational skills, walk closely with God, participate in his community on earth and still blow it. That is one reason God told us so many stories of individuals in the Bible. He knew we would need the encouragement!

Take Peter. He loved Christ, and yet he constantly made mistakes. His most grievous error came in the last hours of Jesus' life. Jesus had told Peter he would deny knowing him, but Peter staunchly rejected the idea. After Jesus was arrested, Peter denied three times ever knowing him. He even invoked a curse upon himself if he knew him. As the cock crowed, what Jesus said had come to pass—Peter had denied the Lord.

Imagine how desolate Peter felt after Jesus' death. The last contact Peter had with Jesus was the scene of his own betrayal. In Jesus' most difficult moment, when he needed support the most, Peter had turned against him. Then a few days later Peter was told that the Lord had risen. Jesus was alive; his friends had actually seen him.

How did Peter feel now? He probably had ambivalent feelings. On one level he would be ecstatic, but on another afraid and ashamed. Maybe the Lord had given up on him. Maybe Jesus would feel Peter had made one too many mistakes.

But God knew how Peter felt. He had a messenger tell the women who first came to the tomb, "Go, tell his disciples and Peter" that he had risen (Mk 16:7 NIV). "And Peter"—two of the most beautiful words in the Bible. So the disciples went and said, "Guess what? Jesus has risen! A messenger from God told us to go and tell you he's here. And, Peter, he said to tell you especially!" Only two words, but they brought a world of hope to a man.

And what did Jesus say to Peter when he saw him (Jn. 21:15-17)? He asked, "Peter, do you love me?"

And Peter said, "Yes, Lord, I do."

Jesus asked again, "Peter, do you love me?"

Peter perhaps hesitated a bit, and then said, "Yes, Lord, you know I love you."

And then Jesus asked the third time, reminding Peter only too well of his recent painful history of thrice rejecting Jesus.

"Peter was hurt" and he said, "Lord, you know all things; you know that I love you" (NIV).

Peter realized that Jesus knew who he was, his fallibility, his limits, his warts. And yet Peter loved Jesus. Jesus knew that too; he had known Peter's faults long before they ever dawned on Peter. And Jesus told him, "Feed my sheep."

Earlier Jesus had nicknamed Peter (Mt 16:18). Of all the names to choose, Jesus picked the least likely: he called him Rock. We might have selected another, like Shifty or Quivery or To-and-Fro. But Jesus chose Rock.

Jesus is telling us something through this. First of all, he knows us—me, you. He knows your limits, your broken promises, your failures. But he also knows that beneath all of that, you have a heart of love for him. He knows that you care. And Jesus also has a name for you, a name you would have never picked for yourself or dared to dream of. He sees what he is making you into; he knows what he has in store for you. And he gives you a name that suits what you are going to become. We are people of hope and not despair because we have a future that has been secured by God.

More important than our wobbly love for him is his absolute, unswerving love for us. When Peter told Jesus he would always remain faithful to him, Jesus knew his resolve would crumble. Nonetheless, he said, "Simon, Simon, listen! Satan has demanded to sift all of you like wheat, but I have prayed for you that your own faith may not fail." And he went on to say, "When once you have turned back, strengthen your brothers" (Lk 22:31-32). Our Lord would not let Peter go. His love is the absolute of the universe.

Jesus knows our warts, but he also knows we love him. He knows what we will look like someday—not a grain of sand, as we so often feel, but a beautiful rock—and he loves us, eternally and mightily. And so he turns to us, as he did to Peter, and says, "Feed my sheep." It is that simple. Whatever gifts you have been given, whatever likes or talents, use them, give them, spend yourself on God's world as Jesus spent himself on you. Comfort his people.

Paul prayed as he wrote to the church in Corinth, "Blessed be the God . . . of all consolation, who consoles us in all our affliction, so that we may be able to console those who are in any affliction with the consolation with which we ourselves are consoled by God" (2 Cor 1:3-4). Earl Palmer says that the word "console" in this passage is most accurately described like this: a person is walking down a road alone, and he is then joined by another who walks alongside so he does not have to walk the rest of the road alone. And so we might retranslate the text this way: "Blessed be the God who has walked alongside of us, who walked alongside of us in our affliction, so that we may be able to walk alongside of others in their affliction with all of the 'walking-alongsidedness' that we have experienced."

That is what God is like—he is the One who walks alongside. And that is what he calls his children to do. Regardless of age, temperament, fears, inhibitions, he bids us to feed his sheep.

What will we look like? We will look like a man I have only heard about. When I first came to Portland, Oregon, I met a student on one of the campuses where I worked. He was brilliant and looked like he was always pondering the esoteric. His hair was always mussy, and in the entire time I knew him, I never once saw him wear a pair of shoes. Rain, sleet or snow, Bill was always barefoot. While he was attending college, he had become a Christian.

At this time a well-dressed, middle-class church across the street from the campus wanted to develop more of a ministry to the students. They were not sure how to go about it, but they tried to make them feel welcome. One day Bill decided to worship there. He walked into this church, wearing his blue jeans, T-shirt and of course no shoes. People looked a bit uncomfortable, but no one said anything. So Bill began walking down the aisle looking for a seat. The church was quite crowded that Sunday, so as he got down to the front pew and realized that there were no seats, he just squatted on the carpet—perfectly acceptable behavior at a college fellowship, but perhaps unnerving for a church congregation. The tension in the air became so thick one could slice it.

Suddenly an elderly man began walking down the aisle toward the boy. Was he going to scold Bill? My friends who saw him approaching said they thought, *You can't blame him. He'd never guess Bill is a Christian. And his world is too distant from Bill's to understand. You can't blame him for what he's going to do.*

As the man kept walking slowly down the aisle, the church became utterly silent, all eyes were focused on him, you could not hear anyone breathe. When the man reached Bill, with some difficulty he lowered himself and sat down next to him on the carpet. He and Bill worshiped together on the floor that Sunday. I was told there was not a dry eye in the congregation.

The irony is that probably the only one who failed to see how great the giving had been that Sunday was Bill. But grace is always that way. It gives without the receiver realizing how great the gift really is.

As this man walked alongside of his brother and loved him with all that he had received from Christ's love, so must we. This man was the good Samaritan. He made Bill feel welcome, feel as if he had a home. So he also knew the secret of the parable of the prodigal son: there finally is a homecoming, because we really have a home to come to.

Appendix 1
Gospel Outlines

·····················

THE PRINCIPLE THAT MUST GUIDE US AS WE SEEK TO SHAPE OR SHARE A gospel message for this generation is that we are faithful to the core of the gospel truth and communicate it faithfully and clearly. At the same time we need to remember that even the New Testament writers were unable to reduce the gospel to a single metaphor. No one paradigm seemed to be able to convey the full reality of God's deed in Jesus Christ.

Furthermore, because people and cultures vary there will be many forms for communicating the message of the gospel. In other words we don't need to use a one-size-fits-all approach. But it is also important to be able to explain the essence of the gospel.

The following are some examples of gospel presentations. There are many more than those listed here. I encourage you to examine as many as possible until you find one you are comfortable with.

1. New Life for All
One widely used and helpful gospel presentation is the credo of the "New Life for All" movement in Africa and Latin America.

1. God created all people for Life.
2. People, in their sin, have forfeited Life.
3. God came in Christ to offer people New Life.
4. People can receive this New Life by Turning
   ☐ from their sins
   ☐ to Christ in trust and obedience
   ☐ to the Community of New Life.
5. People knowing New Life are called to be faithful in all relationships.

Many denominations, traditions and movements use some version of this approach because, as George Hunter points out: "(a) It begins with creation—as the Bible does. (b) It includes the Church as part of God's saving provision. (c) It includes the Christian ethic and life-style as part of the message. (d) It begins with people's life concerns—a nearly universal point of contact. (e) Any Christian theological tradition can use it, and presumably in most any culture."[1]

2. The Bridge

Another gospel outline that is in wide use in one form or another is the Bridge. This was originally developed by the Navigators, but the version below has been adapted by Sonlife Ministries, an evangelism training center in Elburn, Illinois.[2]

It is possible to know God personally . . .

In fact, the very reason God created us is so that we might know Him personally.

But . . . to many people God seems very far away, distant, and impersonal.

Obviously there is a problem . . .

The Bible teaches that God loves you
"For God so loved the world . . . that He gave His one and only Son that whoever believes in Him will not perish but have eternal life" (John 3:16).[3]

And . . . God wants you to know Him personally
"Now this is eternal life, that men may know Him, the only true God, and Jesus Christ whom He has sent" (John 17:3).

But . . . we are separated from God and His love
"God is on one side and all the people on the other side." (1 Timothy 2:5). Why do you think we are separated from God?

Figure 1. The gap

The Bible says our sins have separated us from God...
"... your sins have made a separation between you and your God ..." (Isaiah 59:2).

"All have sinned, and fall short of the glory of God" (Romans 3:23).

God created us to know and love Him. But we chose to go our own way and that relationship with God was broken (Romans 1:19-21). This attitude and its results are what the Bible calls sin.

This separation caused by sin creates some severe problems.

Figure 2. Sin separating us from God

Sin causes us to:

☐ Miss God's very best for life. "Jesus said . . . I came that you might have life and have it to the full" (John 10:10).

☐ Face death and judgment. "For the wages of sin is death . . ." (Romans 6:23). "Those who do not know God . . . will pay the penalty of eternal destruction away from the presence of the Lord" (2 Thessalonians 1:8-9).

But . . . there is a solution.

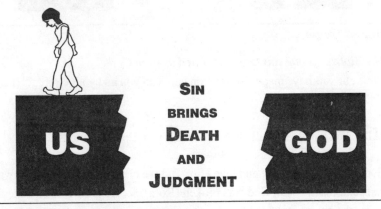

Figure 3. Sin bringing death and judgment

Jesus Christ died and conquered death for you.

We deserve death and judgment, but Jesus took upon Himself the punishment for our sins, so that we could have a personal relationship with God. "God is on one side and all the people on the other side, and Christ Jesus is between them to bring them together by giving His life for all mankind" (1 Timothy 2:5).

Jesus is the way to God.

"Jesus said, 'I am the way, the truth and the life. No one comes to God except through me' " (John 14:6).

Does this make sense to you? Still, it's not enough just to know this . . .

Figure 4. Jesus Christ the Bridge

Each of us by faith must receive Jesus Christ if we want to know God.

"To all who receive Him, He gives the right to become children of God" (John 1:12).

"For it is by grace you have been saved, through faith—and this is not from yourselves, it is the gift of God" (Ephesians 2:8).

The "A,B,C's" of faith involve:

Acknowledging your need—admitting you have sinned and desiring to turn from that sin (1 John 1:8-9).

Believing Jesus Christ died in your place and rose again to be your Savior—providing forgiveness for your sins (1 Corinthians 15:3-4, 17).

Choosing to invite Christ to direct your life.

You can evaluate your current relationship with God by asking. . .

Figure 5. Receiving Jesus Christ

Which life best represents your current relationship with God?

Figure 6. Self-centered life and God-centered life

Which life would you like to have?

Your desire to have a personal relationship with God, can be expressed through a simple prayer like this . . .

"Dear Lord, I want to know You personally, I am willing, with your help, to turn from my sins. Thank you for sending Jesus who died in my place and rose again to be my Savior. Come into my life and lead me. Amen."

Does this prayer express the desire of your heart? If it does, you can pray it right now and begin your relationship of knowing God personally. If you are unsure, what is keeping you from receiving Christ right now?

What happens when you receive Christ into your life?
The Bible promises:

☐ Christ comes into your life (Revelation 3:20).
☐ You become a child of God (John 1:12).
☐ Your sins are forgiven (Colossians 1:14).
☐ You have eternal life (1 John 5:11-13).
☐ You begin the adventure of knowing God personally (Philippians 3:8).

Am I to feel different?
It is important to remember that we rely upon God's Word, not our feelings, as proof of our having Christ "within us."

"If you confess with your mouth, 'Jesus is Lord,' and believe in your heart that God raised him from the dead, you will be saved" (Romans 10:9).

"To all who receive Him, He gives the right to become children of God" (John 1:12).

Regularly thank Christ for coming into your life . . . and be sure to tell someone else about what you have done.

"New Birth" Certificate
I believe that Jesus Christ is the Son of God, and that He died on the cross, was buried, and rose again that I might have forgiveness of my sins and know Him personally (1 Corinthians 15:3-4; John 17:3).

Today I have received Jesus Christ as my personal Savior and desire to obey Him as my Lord (John 1:12).

_____   _____

Date   Signature

How to grow in your relationship with God!
    1. Talk to God about everything!—This is *prayer* (Philippians 4:6-7).
    2. Listen to God by reading the Bible—This is *Bible study* (Hebrews 4:12).
    3. Spend time with others who know God personally—This is *fellowship* (Hebrews 10:25).
    4. Help others to know God personally—This is *disciple-making* (Matthew 28:19-20).
    5. Let God daily direct your life—This is *obedience* (John 14:15).

3. First Steps to God

The following is an outline of the Christian message that was developed for students and staff in InterVarsity Christian Fellowship. Many have found it a useful summary to keep in mind as they share their faith. You may wish to copy this on the flyleaf of your Bible or xerox this page and tape it on the inside cover.

God
☐ God loves you (John 3:16).
☐ God is holy and just. He punishes all evil and expels it from his presence (Romans 1:18).

People
☐ God, who created everything, made us for himself to find our purpose in fellowship with him (Colossians 1:16).
☐ But we rebelled and turned away from God (Isaiah 53:6). The result is separation from God (Isaiah 59:2). The penalty is eternal death (Romans 6:23).

Christ
☐ God became human in the person of Jesus Christ to restore the broken fellowship (Colossians 1:19-20a). Christ lived a perfect life (1 Peter 2:22).
☐ Christ died as a substitute for us by paying the death penalty for our rebellion (Romans 5:8). He arose (1 Corinthians 15:3-4) and is alive today to give us a new life of fellowship with God, now and forever (John 10:10).

Response

☐ I must *repent* for my rebellion (Matthew 4:17).

☐ I must *believe* Christ died to provide forgiveness and a new life of fellowship with God (John 1:12).

☐ I must *receive* Christ as my Savior and Lord with the intent to obey him. I do this in prayer by inviting him into my life (Revelation 3:20).

Cost

☐ There is no cost to you; your salvation comes to you freely (Ephesians 2:8-9).

☐ But it comes at a high cost to God (1 Peter 1:18-19).

☐ Ultimately your response is a life of discipleship (Luke 9:23-24).

Appendix 2
Books for Evangelism

....

IN EACH OF THE CATEGORIES BELOW, THE MORE GENERAL AND BASIC BOOKS are listed first, the more specific and complex books last. (All books listed are available from InterVarsity Press unless otherwise noted. You can get more information on IVP books by visiting IVP's website at www.ivpress.com or by writing for a free catalog.)

Booklets to Be Read and Given to Seeker Friends
(Most of the following booklets are 32 pages and retail for $1.00 each.)
Three Kinds of Love. Masumi Toyotome.
What Is Christianity? John W. Alexander.
Why I Believe in Christ. Charles W. Colson.
Have You Considered Him? Wilbur Smith.
My Heart—Christ's Home. Robert Boyd Munger.
Becoming a Christian. John Stott.
Can I Believe Christianity? Ken Taylor.
Christianity for the Openminded. Michael Cassidy.
Absolute Truth? Mark Ashton.
Are All Religions One? Douglas Groothuis.
The Authority of the Bible. John Stott.
The Evidence for the Resurrection. Norman Anderson.
Islam & Christianity. Donald S. Tingle.
Jehovah's Witnesses. Wesley P. Walters and M. Kurt Goedelman.
Jewishness and Jesus. Daniel C. Juster.
The New Age Movement. Douglas Groothuis.

The New Age Jesus. Douglas Groothuis.
One Catholic to Another. Peter Kreeft.
Safe Sex. Verne Becker.
Seven Lies About Sex. Alice Fryling.
Sexual Freedom. V. Mary Stewart.

Books to Be Read and Given to Seeker Friends
Basic Christianity. John Stott.
Mere Christianity. C. S. Lewis. (Touchstone)
Know Why You Believe. Paul E. Little.
Seven Myths About Christianity. Dale and Sandy Larsen.
Hope Has Its Reasons. Rebecca Manley Pippert. (Harper & Row)
Alone in the Universe? David Wilkinson.
Between Heaven & Hell. Peter Kreeft.
The Best Things in Life. Peter Kreeft.
Is the New Testament Reliable? Paul Barnett.
After Life. Douglas Connelly.
Miracles. Douglas Connelly.
Philosophers Who Believe. Edited by Kelly James Clark.
Professors Who Believe. Edited by Paul M. Anderson.
Black Man's Religion. Craig Keener.
The Universe Next Door. James W. Sire.
Why Should Anyone Believe Anything at All? James W. Sire.

Evangelistic Bible Study Guides
Introducing Jesus. Peter Scazerro.
Meeting Jesus. Leighton Ford.
Jesus the Reason. James W. Sire.

More Reading on Evangelism
How to Give Away Your Faith. Paul E. Little.
Speaking of Jesus. J. Mack Stiles.
Evangelism Made Slightly Less Difficult. Nick Pollard.
Tell the Truth. Will Metzger.

Master Plan of Evangelism. Robert Coleman. (Revell)
Evangelism & the Sovereignty of God. J. I. Packer.
Generating Hope. Jimmy Long.
Jesus for a New Generation. Kevin Graham Ford.

Books on Modern Apologetics
Know Why You Believe. Paul E. Little.
Give Me an Answer. Cliffe Knechtle.
Hope Has Its Reasons. Rebecca Manley Pippert. (Harper & Row)
In Defense of Miracles. Douglas Geivett and Gary Habermas.
The Historical Reliability of the Gospels. Craig Blomberg.
Confronting the New Age. Douglas Groothuis.
Darwin on Trial. Phillip E. Johnson.
The God Who Is There. Francis Schaeffer.

Books on Postmodernism
A Primer on Postmodernism. Stanley J. Grenz. (Eerdmans)
Postmodern Times. Gene Edward Veith. (Crossway)
Seven Myths About Christianity. Dale and Sandy Larsen.
Truth Is Stranger Than It Used to Be. Richard Middleton and Brian Walsh.

Books on the New Age
The New Age Movement. Douglas Groothuis.
The New Age Jesus. Douglas Groothuis.
Unmasking the New Age. Douglas Groothuis.
After Life. Douglas Connelly.
Confronting the New Age. Douglas Groothuis.

Appendix 3
Study Guide for Individuals or Groups

....

Study 1. Sleepless in Spain *(Chapter 1)*

1. Ask someone in the group to read the first paragraph of chapter one. Then ask: Can you describe how you have felt the tension between the desire to be sensitive to people and the desire to "blast them with the gospel"?

2. Why was the author surprised when her friends said they were curious about her faith (p. 17)? How can we evangelize without presenting the total gospel message at one time?

3. The author found it difficult to predict what sort of person might be most interested in coming to an investigative Bible discussion (pp. 17-18). How would you recognize or describe someone who is spiritually open?

4. When Mary returned to Becky with questions and shared some of her own life, Becky was slow to see that Mary was "grappling with God" (p. 20). What are some signs that someone is "grappling with God"?

5. The author says that whatever we fear the most, we will serve (p. 25). In what ways does fear of people determine how we relate to (and serve) them?

6. The author says our uneasiness often does not stem from not knowing the gospel message well but from not knowing how to be ourselves (p. 26). Can you give an example of what she means?

7. What sorts of things have you shared easily with another person (skills, books, hobbies, information) and how have you done this? What can you learn from this in doing evangelism?

8. How does living out our lives honestly, so people recognize that we are far from perfect, actually speak positively to the non-Christians around us (p. 27)?

9. What are some ways we can turn evangelism from a project into a lifestyle (p. 28)?

10. Make a list of three non-Christian friends you expect to be with this coming week. How can you be more free with them?

Study 2. Jesus—the Most Human of Us All *(Chapter 2)*

1. What does the first paragraph of the chapter indicate is the essential point and purpose of this chapter?

2. How was Jesus a model of being open with people with people (pp. 29-31)?

3. Summarize the ways in which Jesus identified with people (pp. 32-35).

4. Think of the people you've been in contact with during the last 48 hours. What needs do they have and how might Jesus have identified with them to meet those needs?

5. What were some of the crises pointed out by Pippert (pp. 35-38) that Jesus produced wherever he went?

6. We usually create a crisis or cause a controversy when our ego is being threatened or our needs are not being met. How is this different from the kind of crisis Jesus produced?

7. The religious people of Jesus' day were offended with him (p. 38). In what ways might you be disturbed by Jesus if he were with you today, even though you love him?

8. Give an example of a time when, with no forethought but simply acting on Christian principles, you (1) treated someone with compassion, (2) forced someone into a moral decision, (3) were able to be just plain, good company to a non-Christian, or (4) exasperated someone you were with.

9. What are ways in the coming week that you could try to act like Jesus as described in this chapter?

Study 3. Jesus the Lord of Love *(Chapters 3 & 4)*

1. In chapter three the author argues that the lordship of Christ is central to evangelism. In what way does the story of Lois demonstrate this close relationship (pp. 40-43)?

2. What are the four basic theological reasons that Jesus is Lord (pp. 44-46)?

3. Using the story of Cathy as a starting point (pp. 47-49), what are some specific decisions that you have made because Christ is your Lord?

4. What does the author mean when she says to Jack, "Whatever controls us really is our god" (p. 52)? Explain why you agree or disagree with this.

5. In chapter four the author begins a set of three chapters on what Jesus valued most, beginning with his love for troubled people.

The author reminds us (pp. 58-59) in the parable of the Prodigal that the father saw in the son some attributes that the neighbor did not. Think of two people you love and enjoy. What do you think God likes best about them? Think of two people you can't stand to be around. What do you think God likes best about them?

6. After discussing the parable of the good Samaritan, Pippert writes, "Before any religious activity, our lives are to bear the stamp of profound love" (p. 62). List your religious activities in the past two weeks. List your acts of kindness within the same time period. What do these two lists reveal about who you are?

7. Why is it so easy to treat individuals as evangelistic projects instead of as people?

8. What did Jesus think about the Pharisees' notion of how to please God and what was his view (pp. 62-64)?

9. What is more important to you—getting to church on time or having a good relationship with others in your family on the way to church? Explain.

10. How does the story of Carla (pp. 65-70) illustrate how we can look beyond someone's exterior background or image and see into their hearts?

11. Use the questions in italic on page 65 to guide you in thoughtful prayer.

Study 4. Questions of Holiness & Obedience *(Chapters 5 & 6)*

1. What is so disturbing about Sonny in the movie *The Apostle* (pp. 71-73)?

2. Before reading this chapter, how would you have defined *holiness*? By this definition would you have considered yourself holy?

3. How did Jesus and the Pharisees differ on what it means to be holy?

4. Pippert writes, "I frequently hear that the call to be holy and the call to demonstrate love to sinners are mutually exclusive" (p. 78). Rather she suggests that what true holiness is all about is how we treat other people. Do you agree or disagree? Explain.

5. The author reminds us that being under the lordship of Christ means having our compassion shaped by his moral absolutes and that "sometimes it is the very love of God that demands that we speak painful truth to a friend" (p. 79). How should we communicate the wrongness of a friend's sin and our love and acceptance of that person at the same time?

6. In the story of Jake we see how honesty about our problems can actually be a part of holiness (p. 80). How have you seen that to be true?

7. Moving on to chapter six, what was the Pharisees' view of knowing God and what was Jesus' view (pp. 83-89)?

8. What does the author mean when she says that "knowledge must automatically translate into obedience" (p. 84)?

9. Look at the case of Sue and the desk (pp. 89-91)? What does this story indicate about the relationship between knowledge and obedience?

10. Is one of your friends interested in the gospel but not sure it's true? What would you think of making him or her the same challenge Becky offered Sue? Explain.

11. What is the importance of understanding obedience as Jesus did for our evangelism and the way we call people to Jesus?

Study 5. Christ & His Presence *(Chapters 7 & 8)*

1. Chapter seven considers three resources Christ offers us in evangelism. In the first subsection, the author points out in the story of Mary and Martha that it is better to allow Jesus to serve *us* first (p. 95). What exactly does that mean? How are we to allow Jesus to serve us?

2. The second resource is illustrated by how the disciples allowed themselves to be limited by their apparently meager resources and the story of Maggie and the ice cream party (pp. 97-98). List your resources in evangelism (on a chalkboard or pad), however limited you think they are. In what ways can you offer each of them to Jesus to use?

3. Explain or give an example of each of the three things the author mentions that are needed to learn to care for others (p. 99)?

4. What practical difference does it make that the people we meet are created in Christ's image (p. 99)?

5. How is this illustrated by Mother Teresa, C. S. Lewis and the young nurse?

6. In chapter eight, Pippert looks four ways we can practice the presence of Christ: seeing people as Jesus does, loving them as they are, loving them as we are, and being salt and light in the world.

To illustrate the first point, Pippert tells of meeting a woman at the airport who wanted a drink (pp. 102-4). Give an example a time recently when you felt someone had interrupted your plans.

What would help you see such situations as divine interruptions?

7. How did Becky come to see beneath the crust of Betty (pp. 104-7)? Think of people you know who are closed or hostile to the gospel. How could you see beneath their crust?

8. Becky's relationship to Betty a success in ways and a failure in ways. Do you think their relationship was a waste of time? Explain.

9. On pages 109-13 the author discusses extroverts and introverts. In regard to evangelism, what are the advantages and dangers of each of these types?

10. What are some strategies for minimizing the dangers?

11. Find a prayer partner who is also concerned about evangelism and covenant with each other about practicing Christ's presence.

Study 6. Developing Conversational Skills *(Chapter 9)*

1. How did your roommate or spouse or sibling last let you know that you had done something he or she did not like? What does your answer illustrate about the importance of conversational skills?

2. How can our attitudes help in our presentation of the gospel or hinder it (p. 119)?

3. Pippert mentions a role-play exercise about telling a Christian what you are learning about evangelism and telling a non-Christian. If you are studying this book in a class, try it now. If you are studying on your own, find

278 / OUT OF THE SALTSHAKER

someone this week to do the role-play with. How did you feel about the difference in the two conversations?

4. What questions are you afraid a non-Christian will ask you? Why do these concern you?

5. What practical difference does or should it make to you that the Holy Spirit is the one who convicts people of sin and the need to turn to Christ?

6. What's the difference between exposing and imposing our faith (p. 122). Give an example of each.

7. Pippert mentions terms that sound religious and have a special mean ing to Christians (p. 125) such as *sinner, grace, salvation, justification sanctification, regeneration, redemption* and *born again.* What other terms can you think of?

8. Now explain these terms in everyday speech.

9. Assume someone ridicules your involvement in a church or religious group. Make a list of good questions you could use to respond (pp. 126-28).

10. Sometime during the next week, initiate a conversation with a total stranger, with no motivation other than trying to get to know something about that person. If you are studying this book in a group, tell about your experience next time you meet. If you are studying on your own, write out what happened.

Study 7. Witnessing & Cultivating *(Chapters 10 & 11)*

1. At the end of the last study (question 10) it was suggested that you initiate a conversation with a total stranger with no motivation other than to get to know something about that person. How did it go?

2. Pippert offers a definition of evangelism from Michael Green (p. 133). Break down this definition into four or five parts and explain what each part means in your own words.

3. On pages 134-36 three ways of proclaiming the truth of the gospel are mentioned: declaring God's truth, displaying God's love and demonstrating God's power. Give a couple examples of each that you have observed or participated in.

4. Why is it important at some point and in some way to put all three of these ways together?

5. In chapter eleven the first conversational model discussed is "Investigate, Stimulate, Relate." What are some good questions you could ask at the "investigate" stage?

6. When we "stimulate" curiosity in unbelievers, we don't give them the whole gospel but only part of it to arouse their interest. Give some examples from the book or from your experience, or create some examples of how this might be done.

7. In the concentric circles model of conversations, give examples of questions that might be asked in each of the four layers.

8. How is the third layer, that of underlying issues, so crucial in conversations?

9. Conduct a role play that moves a conversation through the four layers. (In a group setting, either divide everyone into pairs to conduct the role play or have one pair role play for the whole group, and then discuss what you observed and how the person playing the role of the Christian might have engaged the other person more effectively. If you are working through the book on your own, find someone this week to role play with.)

10. How can it be helpful to raise the question of authority (as suggested in model C)?

11. Why is demonstrating God's love so important during the first stage of cultivating an interest in Jesus (pp. 149-53)?

12. Take time to pray for God's power to be evident in your relationships and conversations with unbelievers in the coming week.

Study 8. Planting the Seed *(Chapter 12)*

1. Pippert identified four main elements in the gospel message that she communicated to Kay (p. 162). Explain each element in a few sentences in your own words (without using God-talk).

2. Take time to write out in a page your story of how you came to Christ. Your story should at least cover the following three questions: What were the key events? What were the important truths you learned? How has it made a difference in your life? (If you are in a group, either break into pairs and share your story with your partner, or have several volunteer to tell their story to the whole group. If you are studying on your own, ask someone this week if you can tell him or her your story.)

3. Pippert asks how we can communicate sin in ways that won't alienate people from the gospel. "Christians have tended to deal with the subject of sin in one of two ways: either by being silent or by being judgmental" (p. 164). What is the answer to Pippert's question?

4. In her discussion with Rick, how did Pippert communicate about sin clearly without alienating him?

5. Pippert didn't define sin as being certain bad behaviors but rather a desire to control our own lives rather than be ruled by God. Do you think this is a helpful distinction to make with unbelievers? Why or why not?

6. Kay and Rick ultimately had different theological issues that were of most concern to them—Kay was concerned about evil and Rick was concerned about his own sin. How could some of the following issues be doorways for a non-Christian into theological issues and the gospel: 1) concern for the environment; 2) sensing a lack of community in one's life; 3) interest in equal rights for women?

7. The author suggests that God often uses the Bible powerfully with others when we share the stories of Jesus and passages of the Bible that have had a deep affect on us. What are the stories that have affected you most and why?

8. Take time to access God's power in prayer by bringing to him those you know who need to have their hearts and minds opened to the truth of the gospel.

Study 9. Reaping the Harvest *(Chapters 13 & 14)*

1. For some people there is nothing so terrifying as the first time we lead someone to Christ. Why might this be so?

2. How do you feel about the prospect of guiding someone to faith in Jesus?

3. The author says conversion is not so much gaining information as going through transformation (pp. 175-77). Explain.

4. Give a brief explanation of the three steps of conversion: repent, believe, receive (pp. 178-80).

5. How do these three steps, properly understood, emphasize that becoming a Christian is a serious business and not a step to be taken lightly?

6. On page 180 Pippert suggests that when we believe a person could be ready to become a Christian, we should ask, "Is there anything that would keep you from becoming a Christian right now?" What reasons might be given for not taking this step and how can we respond?

7. Pippert says, "I find many people are more likely to reveal themselves in short encounters with virtual strangers than they would to their next-door neighbors" (p. 183). Do you agree or disagree? Explain.

8. What can assure us and give us confidence about people (like Sue) who may not make a decision for Christ for many years?

9. How is it that calling someone to conversion is possible only through God's power and still involves us as messengers?

10. Chapter fourteen describes the conversion of the author's father. Why is it often most difficult to witness to our family members?

11. What can help us in these situations?

Before next study: Ask a non-Christian friend, "What is the biggest problem in the world today and what is the solution?" (The goal is not to convince the friend of the right answer but to simply find out what he or she thinks.)

Study 10. Revealing Truth Through Reason *(Chapter 15)*

1. What answer did you get to the assignment at the end of study nine?

2. What is the value of giving answers to questions people ask about Christianity and what are the limits of the answers we might give (pp. 198-99)?

3. What are some of the differences between modern thinking and postmodern thinking (p. 200)?

4. What are the most common questions you get about Christianity?

5. Which are the most difficult for you to respond to and why?

6. It is not uncommon to meet people who do not believe in absolute right and wrong. Pippert says we can respond by saying, "If you say there is no such thing as morality in absolute terms, then you cannot say that child abuse is always evil; it just may not happen to be your thing. And if you find you are not able to practice your premises with much consistency, then you need to reexamine your premises" (p. 202). Do you think this is an effective response? Why or why not?

7. If a non-Christian were to ask you probing questions concerning your worldview, how would you explain: (1) the basic nature of the world, (2) morality, (3) human nature, (4) the fundamental problem in the world and how we deal with it (pp. 201-10)?

8. How do questions about the nature of true success or fulfillment in life reveal what someone thinks about what it means to be human (p. 203)?

9. "We don't often encounter a person who says, 'Tell me what the true nature of God is.' What we *do* hear," says Pippert, "is humanity's cry to be saved from the reality and consequences of sin" (p. 206). How can such discussions about human nature lead to discussions of the gospel?

10. Now think back to the answer you got to the assignment at the end of study nine. How could you possibly move from that answer to a discussion of the gospel?

11. Why does the historical nature of Christianity matter?

12. What can you do to be better prepared to respond to questions about the historical reliability of Christianity?

Study 11. Revealing Truth Through Stories & the Power of the Spirit (*Chapters 16 & 17*)

1. At the beginning of chapter sixteen, a woman the author met makes a distinction between what is real and what is true. Describe the difference and how valid you think this is.

2. Why are stories so helpful in talking to people who make this distinction between what is real and what is true?

3. Why is it important to start with the story of the person we want to share the gospel with (p. 212)?

4. How does the author suggest we do this (p. 213)?

5. How did the story of David fit in with the story of Jill, the manicurist (pp. 213-18)?

6. Pippert says it is also important to tell our story. Why is it often so difficult for Christians to be honest about their problems and pains in life?

7. How can we overcome this?

8. In chapter seventeen we are reminded how common alternative religious practices are these days. Which have you encountered and how?

9. What is the difference between making accommodation to contemporary belief and understanding the context of non-Christians so we can more effectively explain the gospel to them (p. 223)?

10. Personal power is one of the main issues for people who follow New Age thinking. How does the story of Anna (pp. 224-29) show what the gospel has to say and offer about power?

11. How can we avail ourselves more of the power the Spirit offers?

12. On page 230 Pippert notes that sometimes people are deceived spiritually in very serious ways. Yet she also says on page 224, "It's tragic enough that the world assumes that Christians are judgmental and critical. Let's not exacerbate the problem by proving them right by our behavior!" How can we both reveal the deception to others along with God's love without being unnecessarily condemning?

Study 12. Community & Vision *(Chapters 18 & 19)*

1. How have you been affected and helped by being part of a Christian community?

2. If you are part of a small group, how could you reach out as a group to show love and care for or just to have fun with other people (pp. 235-37)?

3. What steps might you need to take to start up an investigative Bible discussion?

4. What could be done to help your church grow to be more of a place where non-Christians would be comfortable and welcomed?

5. Why is incorporating non-Christians and new Christians into a Christian community so important?

6. Nicky Gumbel (p. 250) mentions someone who thought the church expected people first to *behave*, next to *believe* and then they might *belong*. How would your church then be different if it followed the opposite pattern, as Gumbel suggests?

7. The author says that preaching and worship can be very effective ways the church can reach unbelievers (pp. 251-54). How can these be both nurturing to believers and attractive to unbelievers?

8. Pippert gives three suggestions for finding the right evangelistic style or program for your church (pp. 254-55). How would you respond to each of them?

(1) What are the types of people to whom God has called us to minister as a church? What kind of culture or cultures are involved?

(2) Who are we? Large? Small? Diverse? Uniform? City? Rural? Young? Old? Strengths? Weaknesses? Ingrown? Outgoing?

(3) How can we ask God for his guidance in the ways he wants us to change and reach out?

9. Do you feel like you have the freedom to fail? Why or why not?

10. How does Peter's example (pp. 257-59) give you encouragement about your weaknesses and flaws?

11. Share how someone has walked alongside you, as the author described the man who joined Bill on the floor of the church (p. 260). What can you do this week to walk alongside someone else?

12. What on next step do you think God wants you to take regarding your witness? Take time to pray about this and commit it to him.

Notes

Chapter 2: Jesus—the Most Human of Us All
[1]G. K. Chesterton, *Orthodoxy* (New York: Image, 1959), p. 146.

Chapter 3: Jesus—the Lord of All
[1]John Stott, "Must Christ Be Lord to Be Savior? Yes," *Eternity,* September 1951.
[2]D. Martyn Lloyd-Jones in a talk given to the General Committee of the International Fellowship of Evangelical Students in 1963.
[3]C. S. Lewis, *Mere Christianity* (New York: Macmillan, 1969), pp. 54-55.
[4]Thomas Oden provides an evaluation of modernity as representing four fundamental values: moral relativism, autonomous individualism, narcissistic hedonism and reductive naturalism. Thomas Oden, "Back to the Fathers: Interview with Thomas Oden," interview by Christopher Hall, *Christianity Today,* September 24, 1990, pp. 28-31.
[5]G. K. Chesterton, *Orthodoxy* (New York: Image, 1959).
[6]Oswald Chambers, *My Utmost for His Highest* (London: Marshall, Morgan & Scott, 1927), p. 265.

Chapter 4: A Question of Love
[1]Parker Palmer, *To Know As We Are Known* (San Francisco: Harper & Row, 1983), p. xiv.
[2]E. P. Sanders, *Jesus and Judaism* (Philadelphia: Fortress, 1985); E. P. Sanders, *Jewish Laws from Jesus to the Mishnah* (Philadelphia: Trinity Press International, 1990); J. D. G. Dunn, *Jesus, Paul and the Law* (Louisville, Ky.: Westminister John Knox, 1990), pp. 61-88.
[3]S Westerholm, "Pharisees," in *Dictionary of Jesus and the Gospels,* ed. Joel B. Green, Scot McKnight and I. Howard Marshall (Downers Grove, Ill.: InterVarsity Press, 1992), p. 612.

Chapter 5: A Question of Holiness
[1]William J. Bennett, *The Death of Outrage* (New York: Free Press, 1998), p. 123.
[2]Gustave F. Oehler, *The Theology of the Old Testament* (Grand Rapids, Mich.: Zondervan, 1883), p. 18.
[3]H. Wheeler Robinson, *The Religious Ideas of the Old Testament* (London: Duckworth, 1913), p. 40.
[4]A. T. Robertson, *The Pharisees and the Jews* (London: Duckworth, 1920), p. 79.
[5]John R. W. Stott, *Christian Counter-Culture* (Downers Grove, Ill.: InterVarsity Press, 1978), pp. 24-25.

Chapter 6: A Question of Obedience
[1]Parker Palmer, *To Know As We Are Known* (San Francisco: Harper & Row, 1983), p. 43.
[2]H. Wheeler Robinson, *The Religious Ideas of the Old Testament* (London: Duckworth, 1913), pp. 73-74.
[3]Jim Wallis, "Conversion: What Does It Mean to Be Saved?" *Sojourners,* May 1978, p. 14.
[4]G. K. Chesterton, *Orthodoxy* (New York: Image, 1959), p. 154.

Chapter 7: Christ with Us
[1]Mother Teresa, "The Poor in Our Midst," *New Covenant Magazine,* January 1977, pp. 15-17.
[2]C. S. Lewis, *The Weight of Glory* (Grand Rapids, Mich.: Eerdmans, 1949), p. 15.
[3]Hope Warwick, "Lady in 415," *Campus Life,* May 1976, pp. 50-52.
[4]Mother Teresa, "The Poor," p. 17.

Chapter 8: Practicing the Presence of Christ
[1]There is a plethora of literature on this subject. Here are some books that deal with personality type and temperament theories from different angles: Paul D. Tieger and Barbara Barron, *Do What You Are* (Boston: Little Brown, 1992), pp. 12-32; Paul D. Tieger and Barbara Barron, *Nurture by Nature* (Boston: Little Brown, 1997); LaVonne Neff, *One of a Kind* (Portland, Ore.: Multnomah Press, 1988).

Chapter 9: Developing Conversational Skills
[1]Martin Luther, *Fastenpostille,* quoted in Donald Bloesch, *A Theology of Word & Spirit* (Downers Grove, Ill.: InterVarsity Press, 1992), p. 215.
[2]Karl Barth and Eduard Thurneysen, *Come, Holy Spirit,* trans. George W. Richards, Elmer G. Homrighausen and Karl J. Ernst (Grand Rapids, Mich.: Eerdmans, 1978), p. 219.
[3]Bloesch, *A Theology of Word & Spirit,* p. 244.
[4]Dietrich Bonhoeffer, *The Cost of Discipleship,* trans. R. H. Fuller (London: SCM Press, 1959), p. 165.

Chapter 10: Three Ways to Witness
[1]Michael Green, *Evangelism Through the Local Church* (Nashville: Oliver-Nelson, 1992), pp. 8-9, 11.

Chapter 11: Cultivating the Soil
[1]Sonlife Ministries, 526 N. Main, Elburn, IL 60019 or <www.sonlife.com>
[2]Mark Petterson, "Strategic Conversations," in *HIS Guide to Evangelism* (Downers Grove, Ill.: InterVarsity Press, 1977), p. 45.
[3]Ibid., p. 47.
[4]Donald G. Bloesch, *A Theology of Word & Spirit* (Downers Grove, Ill.: InterVarsity Press, 1992), p. 240.

Chapter 12: Planting the Seed
[1]Donald G. Bloesch, *A Theology of Word & Spirit* (Downers Grove, Ill.: InterVarsity Press, 1992), p. 13.
[2]Helmut Thielicke, *The Trouble with the Church,* ed. and trans. John W. Doberstein (New York: Harper & Row, 1965), p. 50.
[3]Kallistos Ware, *The Orthodox Way* (Crestwood, N.Y.: St. Vladimir's Seminary Press, 1986), p. 8.
[4]Bloesch, *A Theology of Word & Spirit,* p. 228.
[5]Rebecca Manley Pippert, *Hope Has Its Reasons* (San Francisco: Harper & Row, 1989), p. 106.
[6]There are various ways of understanding the doctrine of the atonement. What struck me on reflection was that Kay's and Rick's situations called for two different doctrines of the atonement. Kay was drawn to an understanding of the cross that emphasizes the risen Christ's victory over the powers of evil that ravage humankind. She found great comfort knowing that Christ had put down and destroyed evil by his death and resurrection, that God was in Christ

reconciling the world to himself, that Christ invites the saved to participate in his victory over evil by living under his rule and extending his victory in every area of life. This is an interpretation called the "Christus Victor" theory of the atonement. For further exploration, see Gustav Aulén, *Christus Victor* (New York: Macmillan, 1969). On the other hand, Rick was drawn to an interpretation of the cross that emphasizes the debt Christ paid. What deeply moved Rick was that God took our place and became our substitute when judgment had to fall. The sinless one stepped in for the sinful and accepted the penalty that we alone deserved. This is an interpretation of the atonement that is called "penal substitution." For further exploration, see John R. W. Stott, *The Cross of Christ* (Downers Grove, Ill.: InterVarsity Press, 1986).

[7]John Calvin, *Institutes of the Christian Religion,* trans. John Allen (Philadelphia: Presbyterian Board of Christian Education, 1936), p. 90.

[8]J. I. Packer, "Children of a Larger God," *Leadership,* summer 1998, p. 110.

Chapter 13: Reaping the Harvest in God's Truth & Love

[1]C. S. Lewis, *Mere Christianity* (New York: Macmillan, 1969), p. 182.

[2]Leanne Payne, *The Healing Presence* (Wheaton, Ill.: Crossway, 1989), p. 79.

[3]Blaise Pascal, *Pensées,* ed. and trans. A. J. Krailsheimer (Baltimore: Penguin, 1966), p. 138.

[4]H. Eddie Fox and George E. Moore, *Faith-Sharing* (Nashville: Discipleship Resources, 1998), p. 53.

[5]Jim Wallis, *Agenda for Biblical People* (New York: Harper, 1976), p. 23.

[6]The "lordship salvation" debate is well covered in Dallas Willard, *The Divine Conspiracy* (San Francisco: Harper, 1998), pp. 43-50.

[7]Mark Mittleberg, "Evangelism That Flows," *Leadership,* summer 1998, p. 29.

[8]Robert Webber, *Common Roots* (Grand Rapids, Mich.: Zondervan, 1978), p. 165.

[9]G. K. Chesterton, *Orthodoxy* (New York: Image, 1959), p. 160.

[10]Rebecca Manley Pippert, *A Heart Like His* (Wheaton, Ill.: Crossway, 1996), pp. 206-7.

Chapter 14: Reaping the Harvest in God's Power

[1]Flannery O'Connor, *Mystery and Manners* (New York: Farrar, Straus & Giroux, 1969).

[2]Ernest Becker, *The Denial of Death* (New York: Free Press, 1973), p. 164.

[3]Os Guinness, *The Call* (Nashville: Word, 1998), p. 14.

[4]Ibid.

Chapter 15: Revealing Truth Through Reason

[1]James W. Sire, *The Universe Next Door,* rev. ed. (Downers Grove, Ill.: InterVarsity Press, 1988), p. 18.

Chapter 16: Revealing Truth Through Stories

[1]Ronald Johnson, *How Will They Hear If We Don't Listen?* (Nashville: Broadman & Holman, 1994), p. x.

[2]Parker Palmer, *To Know As We Are Known* (San Francisco: Harper & Row, 1983), pp. 39-40.

Chapter 17: Revealing Truth Through the Power of the Spirit

[1]Alan J. Roxburgh, *Reaching a New Generation* (Downers Grove, Ill.: InterVarsity Press, 1993), p. 127.

[2]James W. Sire, *The Universe Next Door,* rev. ed. (Downers Grove, Ill.: InterVarsity Press, 1988), p. 170.

Chapter 18: The Witness of Community

[1]John R. W. Stott, *The Contemporary Christian* (Downers Grove, Ill.: InterVarsity Press, 1992), p. 241.

[2]Michael Green, *Evangelism Through the Local Church* (London: Hodder & Stoughton, 1990), p. ix.

[3]E. M. Bounds, *Preacher & Prayer* (Wheaton, Ill.: Institute of the Billy Graham Center & Worldwide Publications, 1993), p. 10.

Chapter 19: Without a Vision the People Will Perish

[1]Alan J. Roxburgh, *Reaching a New Generation* (Downers Grove, Ill.: InterVarsity Press, 1993), p. 127.

[2]Ibid., p. 55.

[3]Ibid., p. 56.

[4]Mark Lauterback, "Contact," *Leadership,* summer, 1998, p. 36.

[5]Roxburgh, *Reaching a New Generation,* p. 129.

[6]Lesslie Newbigin, *Foolishness to the Greeks* (Grand Rapids, Mich.: Eerdmans, 1986), p. 124.

[7]Donald G. Bloesch, *A Theology of Word & Spirit* (Downers Grove, Ill.: InterVarsity Press, 1992), p. 237.

[8]Roxburgh, *Reaching a New Generation,* p. 129.

[9]John R. W. Stott, *The Contemporary Christian* (Downers Grove, Ill.: InterVarsity Press, 1992), p. 121.

[10]Ibid., p. 127.

[11]Roxburgh, *Reaching a New Generation,* p. 119.

[12]George G. Hunter III, *How to Reach Secular People* (Nashville: Abingdon, 1992), pp. 44-72.

[13]Roxburgh, *Reaching a New Generation,* p. 105.

[14]Kenneth Chafin, *The Reluctant Witness* (Nashville: Broadman, 1974), p. 141.

Appendix 1. Gospel Outlines

[1]George G. Hunter III, *How to Reach Secular People* (Nashville: Abingdon, 1992), p. 87.

[2]Sonlife Ministries, *Knowing God Personally* (Elburn, Ill.: Sonlife Ministries, 1995).

[3]Scripture references in the outline are quoted from The New American Standard Bible, Living Bible and New International Version of the Bible.